ROOM for EXAMINATION

True Tales of a Disillusioned Dermatologist

❧

James Channing Shaw

Copyright © 2012 James Channing Shaw
All rights reserved.

ISBN: 1481262211
ISBN-13: 9781481262217

Dedication

This book is dedicated to my patients.

JCS

Table of Contents

Dedication	iii
Table of Contents	v
Preface	ix
Chapter 1 Commitments	**1**
Privilege	1
The Lightbulb	2
Preliminary Laps	4
Skin Is More Than Skin Deep	7
Make Up Your Mind	11
The First Match	12
Mister M.D.	15
Love Lost	18
Time to Get Serious	19
Residency Interviews	20
Chapter 2 Acceptances	**23**
Age Is Not the Issue	23
Mind Warp	26
Final Match	28

Chapter 3 The Rookie 35
    Early Stress 35
    Body Fluids 37
    My First Dermatology Family 38
    The Week Begins: Dr. White 39
    The 'VAH SPA' 41
    Life Goes On Tilt.. 44
    Dr. Wuepper 45
    I, The Patient 47
    Dr. Hanifin 47
    Morphology Rounds.. 49
    T.G.I.F. 51
    Back On The Wards.. 52
    The Thrill Of Diagnosis 53
    Dermatology Goes Surgical 57
    University Clinics 61
    Christopher Columbus's Gift...................................... 62
    It's True: Everything Changes..................................... 64

Chapter 4 Getting Up To Speed 67
    Under The Microscope... 67
    Brain Workup 68
    Dr. Storrs 69
    The Future 71
    The Chairman.. 73
    Highlight Of The Week 74
    What We Have Here Is A Failure To Communicate.................. 76
    Dr. A. Bernard Ackerman 77
    Taste Of Reality 79

Chapter 5 The Real World 83
    School's Out 83
    Downtown... 85
    The Disease Of The Century 87

Chapter 6 Getting Established 99
Bernie 99
Too Much Testosterone 101
Breakaway 105
It's All About The Patients 107
My Head 112
Ironies In Medicine 113

Chapter 7 Crawling Back To The Ivory Tower 115
Change Is Good 115
Great Case 116
Growing Pains 119
Speaking Of Which 120
Outlier 122

Chapter 8 Explorations 127
Corporate Medicine 127
Boston 129
A Look At Chicago 132
Taking The Leap 137
Prepare For Takeoff 139

Chapter 9 Chicago Beginnings 143
Drinking From A Fire Hose 143
The Starting Lineup 147
Opportunity Calls 150

Chapter 10 My New Family 155
The Plot Thickens 155
Ex Libris 159
Musical Therapy 161
The Plot Thickens More 162
Once In A Career Case 164
…And Thickens 165
Recruitments 'R' Us 168
…It Just Never Stops 170

Chapter 11 Chicago Endings 175
Pain Can Be A Good Thing 175
Ghost Billing.. 177
200 To One Odds Against.. 179
A New Colleague 181
Unprofessional 184
Skinned Alive 185
Writing On The Wall 187
The Search…Again 188
Unexpected Death..191
Choosing Toronto 194

Chapter 12 Toronto Beginnings 197
Canada *Is* A Different Country 197
Installed At The University Of Toronto 201
Reflections On My Father..204

Chapter 13 O, Canada 207
Whoa, Canada!...207
Sars..211
Organ Transplant Patients 214
Teaching Never Pays The Bills... 219

Chapter 14 My Tennis Game Is No Good 223
Patients Should Be Treated Like Family...........................223
Teledermatology 226
The Lure Of Beauty Care..227
This Writing Thing...232

Chapter 15 We Can Always Do Better 235
Whither Dermatology? 235
A Proud Woman...237

Afterword 245

Acknowledgments 249

Preface

WHETHER IT IS ABOUT SKIN DISEASE or skin health, people are more aware of their skin than ever before. One need only turn on the television to appreciate how much attention is given to skin by the advertising industry. And it is no wonder: There are fortunes to be made.

Our skin is our overture to the world. We wash it; we cream it; we pick at it; we scratch it; we caress and squeeze and kiss and love it; we hate it, we color it, cover it, pierce it and tattoo it; we envy others their skin. Most importantly, we could not survive without it.

Despite its importance, skin is underappreciated. The vast majority of people view dermatologists as doing little more than taking care of inconsequential health problems. Dermatologists are often viewed today as cosmetic pseudo-doctors. The truth, though, is that dermatologists are trained to recognize and treat an immense number of serious internal diseases that show up first on the skin. The list is impressive: AIDS, 'flesh-eating disease', toxic shock syndrome, graft-versus-host-disease, and many, many more. Patients die when a doctor misses the skin signs of a life-threatening disease. Sadly, that happens more often than it should.

The time and effort required for a doctor to acquire expertise in the diagnosis and treatment of skin disease is as extensive as for most internal specialties. And as with all fields of medicine, the science is expanding at an alarming rate, with new discoveries, genetics, new therapies, new drugs.

This is the story of a medical career from my perspective as dermatologist, student, patient, teacher, father, husband, researcher and administrator. It is about the training I received on my path to becoming an expert in skin diseases. It is also about doctors, the medical profession, and the academic institutions in which many of us have worked at some point in our careers.

Mostly, however, it is about the patients. Patients are at the mercy of doctors. All too often, outcomes or interactions are less than praiseworthy, for reasons as variable as the individuals themselves. This story explores some behaviors, mostly by doctors, some by patients, some by me, which I ultimately viewed as less than praiseworthy. We can always do better. That theme recurs throughout the book.

This being a true account of my career, I use real names. All names of doctors and those who taught me in one capacity or another are real with the exception of one or two, for reasons that will be apparent. When I mention friends and family, I use their real names. Patient names, on the other hand, with one exception, are all changed to protect their identity.

CHAPTER 1
Commitments

A happy childhood has spoiled many a productive life."
– Robertson Davies

■ PRIVILEGE

IF THERE IS one thing special about doctors, it is that society has granted us unique privileges. The license to probe the private lives and bodies of people is issued to no other group. If those privileges are not treated with the utmost respect, they can lead to tragic outcomes, prison sentences sometimes. I've known students who got accepted to medical school only to get expelled for cheating; I've known successful doctors who had their licenses suspended or revoked for alcohol or drug abuse, or for sexual abuse of patients. I've learned of elaborate cheating rings for the passage of specialty board examinations. I've watched doctors in leadership positions self-destruct because of their narcissistic exploitations of power. I've seen fraudulent behavior go unchecked. I've watched dermatologists lose malpractice suits because they went beyond their level of expertise, for financial gain.

I've observed the cruelty of doctors toward patients, nurses, women colleagues and men colleagues.

Sadly, a slow tide of disillusionment about my physician colleagues rose steadily during my career. I think that, based on the truths behind each occurrence, the disillusionment was justified. On the other hand, doctors are, by far, also the individuals I have respected most throughout my life, primarily for their intellectual brilliance but also for their dedication. The hard work, professionalism, and dedication often go unnoticed because that is what is expected of doctors. Medicine just happens to be a microcosm of intellectually high-achieving individuals with vicissitudes similar to every group of professionals, every union, government, family or tribe. And now, to my story.

■ THE LIGHTBULB

I ENTERED EXAMINATION room three, introduced myself and closed the door behind me. Thomas G., already in a gown, sat on the examination table, relaxed, impatient perhaps, right hand on his hip. I was running late.

"How can I help you?" I asked, and sat down. One nice thing about taking care of patients is that, once inside the examination room, all receptor sites focus on the patient. The rest of the world temporarily fades from view. It's why we run late.

"I have something on my penis," said Tom G. He was in his mid twenties, not much younger than I, and in good general health. He was matter-of-fact about the problem, not particularly worried or embarrassed. I asked more questions. The 'something' had been present for six months, growing slowly. He had no known illnesses, no family history of illnesses, took no medications. Yes, he was sexually active.

The next step was to examine him. In medicine, we learn objectivity very early on in our training. No part of the body is sacred. Any show of surprise, revulsion, or fascination is totally out of place. Patients generally don't appreciate hearing that they have the largest, or smallest, or worst case of anything.

I asked him to lie down. On the head of Tom G.'s penis (we call the head of the penis the glans penis, or just 'the glans'), was a two centimeter diameter disc-shaped growth, firm and painless, with a rough surface. Two centimeters is actually large when one considers that the glans itself, at rest, is usually not much wider than four centimeters. I had no clue what this 'growth' was, but suspected that it must be a specific disease with a name. A dermatologist would certainly know. It didn't look like the pictures of syphilis I'd seen. Nor did it resemble any other infection. The appearance most suggested cancer, and I knew that his being uncircumcised increased that risk. Not only was I uncertain of the diagnosis, I had no idea how to proceed. I had never biopsied someone's penis. I was fresh out of internship. A heart attack or pneumonia would have been a breeze, but this? Fortunately, I knew a dermatologist in the area, discussed the case, and referred Tom G. to him later the same day.

I never heard back from the dermatologist and, to this day, don't know what became of Tom G. I had been the middle man. Looking back, I suspect he probably had an unusual form of viral infection, the kind that can actually evolve into skin cancer. This was before the first reported cases of AIDS, before our medical training emphasized the importance of obtaining sexual histories on all patients. Odds were good that his sexual practices had put him at risk for contracting something. Of course nowadays, everyone understands that an accurate sexual history is crucial to good medical care. After hundreds of years of wrong diagnoses and poor treatment because of moralistic hear-no-evil ignorance, the taboo of discussing who is having sex with whom, is finally gone from medicine.

My career changed that day because Tom G., more than any other patient, helped me realize that I wanted to be a dermatologist, to diagnose diseases by their visual characteristics, not by how they sounded through a stethoscope or what the blood tests or X-rays showed. The irony was that patients like Tom G. influenced that decision to a much greater degree than the doctors who had taught me during medical school and internship.

Not all doctors enjoy the practice of medicine. No matter how enthusiastic a child, teen, or college kid claims to be about becoming a doctor, no one can ever know what it's really like until well into residency training or beyond, and once there, after all the years of school and debt accumulation, it becomes impractical for those who dislike medicine to quit. Many doctors slog through life hating one or more aspect of their careers. Getting rich becomes their goal, not doctoring. I felt lucky. I was thoroughly enjoying being a doctor, talking to patients, the treatments, the science. Even so, a wonderful thing happened to me that day when I finally decided what I was going to be when I grew up. At that moment, all prior career notions that had been swirling around my head, funneled into one finite, exhilarating ambition. On that snowy January day in 1980, I gained a friend. The commitment itself, so long in coming, would be my partner. We—the aspiration and I—would work as a team from that point on.

■ PRELIMINARY LAPS

MUCH HAD TO be accomplished before I could even consider specialties. Four years of college, four years of medical school and an internship were all necessary hurdles along the way. I had completed internship only six months earlier, in June, and carried in my wallet a medical license that allowed me to practice. I felt at home with much of the basics, but they merely formed a platform from which to take my learning to a higher level if I chose to make the effort. I knew from early on that I would specialize; I just didn't know what specialty it would be until that day.

It may be hard to believe that after four years of medical school and an internship, doctors understand only the very basics of diagnosis and treatment of disease. A full residency of two to six years beyond medical school is necessary even to get on the road to excellence. It was the thrill of expertise that allured me most into specializing. The credential—specialty board certification—would eventually materialize, but it was secondary. I already had tried on for size a few specialties. Internal medicine would be my fall-back position since I had completed one year of the three year residency.

When dermatology emerged as the choice, I was working twelve hour shifts in the emergency room at a Kaiser Permanente Hospital and at Urgency Care Clinics around Portland, Oregon. To stay in emergency medicine would have been fine, but I had learned to enjoy the relationships that developed over time with patients, relationships that would never happen while working in an emergency room. I would never be able to enjoy the satisfaction of being someone's regular doctor. Also, the shift work, each patient a stranger, at times unconscious or belligerent, concerned me. I had been spat on in the face at two o'clock in the morning by an alcoholic schizophrenic threatening to kill me. A lifetime of those types of interactions was not particularly appealing.

As for my other loves, I didn't mind placing them high up on the amateur shelf, out of reach for a while. I could return to them later. Jazz piano I could play solo at any time, and knew musicians in town if I wished to sit in with them. My photography interests I could apply to dermatology as a painter applies paint to canvas. There is an old joke in medicine: The generalist (GP, family doctor) knows less and less about more and more and the specialist knows more and more about less and less until finally the generalist knows nothing about everything and the specialist knows everything about nothing. The latter sounded better to me.

There were other reasons beyond patient Tom G, for my choosing dermatology. Not the least of those was my father, John M. Shaw, M.D., a dermatologist himself. He exposed me to the specialty in the first place. Though it meant little to me as a child in the 1950s and 60s, I grew up within a world of dermatologists. My father frequently spoke reverentially of his patients. He enjoyed his colleagues around the country, at least the ones in tweed, oxford button-down shirts and bowties. They were always drinking martinis and having a good time. Something positive must have rubbed off. My first pornography came from dermatology textbooks around the house. You can be sure I found them. And a prepubescent boy in the early 1960s with secret access to pictures of naked females carried considerable clout. Once in medical school, my father made sure I owned Walter Shelley's *Consultations in Dermatology*, inscribed to me by the author, for leisure reading.

But dermatology? It certainly was not the stuff of medical TV shows. No hero worship there. And back then, in the eighties, dermatology wasn't even plastic surgery 'light' the way it is today. Most doctors back then had no idea what dermatologists actually did, day to day. In the minds of many doctors, dermatology was primarily a source of jokes.

So, it took nearly eleven years beyond high school before I settled on a career choice. One thing for sure, the delay wasn't indecisiveness. Lack of direction, perhaps. Misguidedness, some may have said, but in reality I was enjoying life too much during those years to commit to a lifetime in one specialty. Picking a specialty was as profound as choosing a mate. Life would never be the same. Medical school had been highly demanding and I was busy frolicking in the playground of my twenties, with music, girls, nature, and sports. But now, a wedge of maturity slipped in. My long-standing respect for excellence had found a professional outlet. I was ready.

Long before all that, though, I first needed to become a doctor. It was during my second year of college in dreary Eugene, Oregon that I chose medicine. The time had come to start accruing A's in chemistry courses instead of partying directionless through French, music, and psychology just to fulfill curriculum requirements. After two years in that soggy university town where twenty year-old hippies came and never left, I transferred to Boston University and spent two nose-to-grindstone years in organic chemistry, biochemistry, and physics. It was quite the surprise to run into my intellectual brick wall during second semester physics. I had sailed through the spatial thinking of organic chemistry and Newtonian physics, but quantum physics was all advanced mathematics. Renowned physicist Neils Bohr once said, "A person who wasn't outraged on first hearing about quantum theory didn't understand what had been said." That statement fit me exactly. I didn't understand what had been said. From that point on I knew I could broaden my knowledge and skills, but would probably never be able to take my thinking to a higher plane (or quantum...).

Competition to get into medical school back in 1973 was considered fierce, about one chance in three. My first attempt failed after I foolishly applied only to my state school, the University of Washington, thinking that my chances were best and tuition was affordable. The interview was conducted more like a military tribunal: a semicircle of fourteen frowning men trying to undo me. "Why should we take you over the one hundred applicants who graduated from Washington state colleges and universities?" Good point, I thought. I did make it onto the waiting list, but someone would have to die for me to move up that list. My fortune cookie at lunch after that interview said "Your efforts today have been futile". It is the only negative fortune cookie I have ever seen.

I applied again the following year, this time to ten schools. When I received an invitation for an interview at Boston University, I moved back to Boston, worked in hospital laboratories and took advantage of the city from my apartment on Gainsborough Street in the era when dog owners never scooped up after their pets, and gun shots could be heard in the night.

Ultimately, blessedly, Boston University took a gamble on me. The acceptance letter arrived late in April, four months before classes were to start, just as I was seriously considering abandoning medicine altogether for a career in jazz piano. This probably would not have been a good idea since I might easily have ended up in mediocrity or dead from a heroin overdose. Better that, though, than dental school.

■ SKIN IS MORE THAN SKIN DEEP

FOR THE FIRST three years of medical school we worked on building the massive foundation of knowledge required for a basic understanding of human disease. By fourth year, I was intent on internal medicine which I viewed as the highest level of medical understanding. Coincidentally, my brother Josh was choosing internal medicine for his residency; he was finishing at UW where I had interviewed but made it only as far as the waiting list.

Fourth year of medical school was all electives. We could basically do whatever we wanted. I had arranged several months on the West Coast, the first being dermatology at Oregon Health Sciences University, so in September, 1977, I drove confidently into Portland in a brand new pumpkin-orange Ford Fiesta, the very first issue of a new model I had literally driven off the showroom floor. That hideous little orange car ran like a charm, handled like a European sports car, and for the first time, was all mine, including the debt and insurance.

I wended my way up the Southwest Hills of Portland to the medical school complex only to discover that the dormitory I reserved had no record of me and was completely booked for the month. Could I have overlooked confirming the reservation, just as I had stupidly forgotten to renew my student deferment back in 1970, and almost got drafted into the Army to go to Viet Nam? I suppose it was possible. The glitch, at first worrisome and annoying, resulted in my connecting very high-up within the leadership of dermatology. My father was, at the time, President of the American Academy of Dermatology. He and my mother had been fly-fishing the Deschutes River with their good friends Walter C. Lobitz, Jr., Chairman of the Department of Dermatology at Oregon, and his wife Betty. The four must have been into their second martini when I called to share the news of my embarrassing housing problem, because Wally and Betty Lobitz (Wally is what my parents called him) immediately offered me their home for a week. They wouldn't be returning for ten days. This was excellent. I got directions to the house on Council Crest, the hidden key, and was told to make myself at home in the basement guest bedroom. I did just that.

My week at the Lobitz home could not have been better. September can be remarkably rainy in Portland, but the weather behaved the entire month. I cranked Stevie Wonder's new *Songs in the Key of Life* album up to ten on their stereo, smoked Pall Mall straights from their silver cigarette box on the coffee table, and dream-gazed out at the panoramic views of Portland and Mt. St. Helens from their immense windows. I had the whole place to myself. I studied dermatology, ran on Council Crest Drive (it was called jogging back then), made new friends, and met an enchanting woman named Mimi, a fourth year medical student from St. Louis University who, like me, was visiting Oregon on elective. Mimi had a room in the dormitory where I was supposed to be staying. A small group of us medical students from that dorm became close friends. Mimi and I became more than close friends up there in the Lobitz's glass mansion high atop the hills of Portland.

By the time Dr. Lobitz returned, I had found a new place to live and was already one week into the dermatology rotation, assigned to senior resident Greg Raugi, a high energy bantamweight with a wry smile and evil little laugh. Under Greg's wing I enjoyed a brilliant month of first-time learning about skin disease.

My job was to interview and examine every hospitalized dermatology patient that came in. Dr. Raugi saw each patient after me, followed by our attending, Dr. Jon Hanifin, after which the three of us would discuss the cases. Most of the inpatients were admitted to our dermatology service, but surgery wards and obstetrics also needed our help periodically. Their approach was different. They had their jobs to do, surgeries to perform, babies to deliver. In their thinking, skin was someone else's problem. "Get a derm consult." Wipe your hands of it; that's how they handled the skin problems of their patients. Receiving the calls from other services taught me for the first time that non-dermatologists couldn't care less about dermatology, nor did they know anything about skin disease or how profoundly skin problems could affect patients.

One Friday, Mrs. Berenson, a woman in her late fifties, was hospitalized for severe psoriasis. Hers was much worse than most. I took a history and examined her. We ordered some standard treatments and I left for the weekend. Over the years she had become familiar with the hospitalization routine.

When I arrived Monday morning, Dr. Raugi broke the terrible news. Early Saturday morning Mrs. Berenson climbed out her tenth floor window without being noticed by nurses, and jumped to her death.

As soon as I could, I went alone to her room. It smelled of disinfectant. I closed the door, muffling the voices that came from the corridor. What had we missed? We must have missed something. This wasn't the psych ward; this was dermatology. I could hear a siren in the distance. I put my head against the glass to look down at the flat roof of the service entrance ten floors below. A shiver crossed my shoulders. Dermatology patients don't commit suicide. Had there been clues? Morning sun shimmered on the river and bridges below in the city. Admittedly, her diagnosis was a severe form of psoriasis, the pustular type of psoriasis, the von Zumbusch type that covers the entire body, and she had struggled with it for years. I pulled open the window, letting in traffic noise, and pushed it closed again. There had been prior hospitalizations. Maybe Mrs. Berenson had had enough of the repeated admissions and poor results. Did we make the mistake of directing all our attention to her skin disease while overlooking a profoundly depressed, suicidal woman? I looked around the room. Housekeeping had already made up her bed. More likely, we missed something much larger. We, Medicine, the profession of medicine, had failed her.

I recently wrote to Dr. Raugi at the University of Washington about the incident. He responded:

> "I remember the event. I think she was Jon Hanifin's patient. I was the inpatient derm resident. 1977 sounds about right. It was a Saturday morning. I remember that because it happened on the day that I had an oral interview in the afternoon for my Oregon license to practice. I remember thinking, Wow. If they only knew, they'd never give me the license. I don't remember her having pustular psoriasis, although that might have been the case. Just don't remember. I do remember the window. It wasn't an easy thing for her to do. The window was one of the kind that is hinged on the bottom and only opens a little way. She had to have stood on the window ledge and worked her way through that narrow awkward space. I do remember going to the post [mortem]. I'll never forget what a traumatic avulsion of the ascending aorta looks like."

One thing I did learn from Mrs. Berenson: Illness is about the whole patient. A bone breaks, the whole person suffers. One medical problem triggers a cascade of others, both physical and emotional. Sometimes the patient gets left behind; the interesting 'case' eclipses the person lying in the bed. All too often, patients themselves recognize that their disease is much more interesting to doctors than they are.

For months, I was beset by not knowing the reasons behind Mrs. Berenson's suicide. Now, after an entire career of observing (with some disillusionment) how doctors interact with patients, I am certain we can do better, but I don't know exactly how. All too frequently, though, the main goal in medicine is expediency, to complete the immediate task at hand. But it only takes seconds to ask about a patient's general wellbeing during a visit, and while a determinedly suicidal person may not reveal anything, the individual who could be helped might open up.

■ MAKE UP YOUR MIND

IT WAS NO surprise that I rejected surgery as a career. Standing over a patient for half a day in long surgeries during medical school had soured me to the specialty early on. But there was more. The arrogance of surgeons had repulsed me. I'll never forget my third year of medical school, at the foot of a hospital bed watching my sadistic surgery preceptor repeatedly plunge a large-bore needle into the upper chest of a young woman with newly diagnosed breast cancer, in search of her subclavian vein, all the while blaming her and her anatomy for his failure to find the vein! It was vicious. The patient endured the torture as tears ran down her face. I felt powerless to do anything.

I became incensed by the cruelty of surgery professors toward medical students. It was as if they thought that cruelty represented good teaching technique. Most medical students in my class at Boston were terrified by the surgeons. One exception to the rule was the silver-haired Dr. John J. Byrne, a masterful and caring teacher, a descendant from the old schools of Halstead and Osler. I never got the opportunity to scrub with him in the operating room, but the way he taught us in small groups was with encouragement and high expectations, not belittlement and humiliation, the way most of the other surgeons taught us back then.

Surprisingly, I don't recall being inspired by my dermatology professors in medical school either. During our one week of dermatology lectures, the lecturers, mostly part-timers from the community, ranged from not-that-good, to something worse. Their harsh Boston accents didn't help any. As one classmate said of his professors, "Some of them ahh smahht fellahs, the rest ahh fahht smellahs!"

One dermatology lecturer was flat-out offensive. His idea of a good lecture was a battery of anatomically explicit sexual jokes about women. This, in a classroom half-filled with women! "So you go to wewrk, a girl comes in with a vaginal dischaahge," he would say. "So what do you do? You get her up in stirrups!" as he projected the next close-up photo of her crotch. It got a few laughs, more out of nervousness than anything else. His knowledge was fine. His unprofessional style was hardly inspirational.

So, surgical specialties were out. Pediatrics had never spoken to me either, with its fragile, uncommunicative little patients, and where most of our time was spent counseling anxious parents. Obstetrics/gynecology was a contender for a while, but too much surgery and too limited in scope, I thought at the time. Neurology fascinated me but rarely could we help patients once we made the diagnosis. Pathology attracted me—I had always enjoyed working with microscopes—but I realized I enjoyed working with patients more. Psychiatry? Again, intellectually interesting but depressing if I were to do it all day every day. Basic science research? I wasn't smart enough. All the rest of the medical specialties such as cardiology and gastroenterology required training in internal medicine first anyway. Internal medicine it would be. If I could pull it off.

At the end of the dermatology rotation, Dr. Hanifin sat me down and asked if I was interested in a dermatology residency at Oregon. I didn't realize at the time the enormity of his offer. I ended up turning him down, and it would become the path not taken. I have thought about that conversation many times over the years. Back then, program directors could strike deals with students. Now it's all done in a highly confidential computerized 'match'. If I had accepted his offer, I would have bypassed much of the competition I experienced later. But at that time, my mind was made up, and although I ultimately circled back to do dermatology, I never regretted starting with internal medicine.

■ THE FIRST MATCH

I STAYED IN Portland another month to do a rotation with Dr. Fred Rabiner, Chairman of the Department of Medicine at Good Samaritan Hospital, down the hill from the university. Dr. Rabiner had come from Michael Reese Hospital in Chicago, and had brought to Portland a fresh leadership style, unfamiliar to many of the doctors, and essentially Jewish in flavor: Demanding but enthusiastic and caring, inspirational but somewhat rigid, funny but occasionally offensive, fast-talking and articulate, but annoying to those not familiar with the rapid fire style. He smoked cigars.

I loved this guy. His style was new to me as well. I had come from a nurturing home, from the WASPY stiff-upper-lip school of coping with life, somehow indoctrinated into thinking that happiness was an important goal by itself. Dr. Rabiner's interactions with his faculty and residents introduced me to the idea that showing emotion outwardly was okay, and that true happiness was overrated, that dissatisfaction in one's life often begot productivity in good ways. Once when I was drifting off to sleep during a small conference, Dr. Rabiner startled me with "Hah!!" and scary arm movements to reset my brain. No one had ever done that before. Another time, when I asked for four days off around Thanksgiving weekend to visit Mimi in St. Louis, he said, "St. Louis for a weekend? Jeeze, you must really be horny!" I had never heard an academic physician speak so honestly and directly.

In the middle of that month at Good Samaritan, I heard the sound of someone snapping fingers and looked up to meet Herb Kloss, an intern at the time. People don't just go around snapping their fingers, so I asked him, "You like jazz?"

"Yeah, man! You?"

"Yeah, man." (Jazz culture was a caricature of itself coming out of the 1950s and 1960s. It was about 'I'm hip' and 'Yeah, man.' Dave Frishberg's lyric said it all: "I even call my girlfriend 'Man'.").

"Do you play?"

"Yeah, you?

Herb played flute. I played piano. He was short like me, with sandy hair, a short reddish beard, and glasses. He looked the quintessential Jewish intellectual beatnik. Nurses in the hospital went nuts over Herb. We got together later that day and talked solid jazz. We had seen many of the same concerts and discovered many of the same inspirational players: Lenny White on drums with a Freddy Hubbard group; saxophonists Dave Leibman and Steve Grossman in Elvin Jones's group; Miles of course, Jeremy Steig on flute, Bill Evans on piano, and on and on. We found a piano where Herb was living, and played for hours. He became a soul mate like I had never before found in medicine. Herb did that to people. He was a soul mate to many. My relationship with Mimi had by that time become serious, but I think my new friendship with Herb may have been a threat to her.

After leaving Portland in December, instead of returning to Boston, I spent three months in Seattle and three in San Francisco, each

13

month at a different hospital in a different specialty. The first was infectious diseases in Seattle with the renowned William Kirby. A tall, distinguished man of little hair and much wisdom, Dr. Kirby had invented the internationally famous Kirby-Bauer technique of testing bacterial sensitivities to antibiotics. He taught me the art of the succinct consultation note. Short notes were the privilege of senior clinicians. Whereas my student notes traditionally documented everything, down to the date of a patient's first pubic hair, plus a long-winded discussion of all the diagnostic possibilities, Dr. Kirby's entire note might say "Absence of fever favors such-and-such infection. Wm. Kirby." And he was usually correct. I also loved his historical perspective. He told us stories from the 1950s when residents used to smoke cigarettes during ward rounds. "They would enter a patient's room with lit cigarettes hidden in the palms of their hands. It's hard to believe today."

Next was endocrinology and diabetes at Virginia Mason Hospital, the private hospital just up from downtown Seattle. My maternal uncle Jake had done his internship there (my family is infested with doctors: maternal grandfather, paternal great uncle, father, brother, and Jake). Uncle Jake's internship class photograph circa 1950 hung on the wall at Virginia Mason. Jake sat in the front row, one leg confidently crossed over the other, lit cigarette in his hand. Don't mess with me, it said. He became a surgeon.

I did ophthalmology at the Public Health Hospital in Seattle with a wiry athletic woman professor whose mountain climbing in the Himalayas, I must admit, interested me more than the spots on retinas and degeneration of optic nerves about which she was trying to teach. I probably wouldn't be choosing ophthalmology as a specialty.

In San Francisco, the intensive care unit at Pacific Medical Center gave me a preview of what internship would be: long hours, crises, life and death. I rode my bike three miles every morning from the Richmond district into Pacific Heights along Lake and Clay streets. At six o'clock in the morning it was a quiet ride through cool, moist air that exists only in San Francisco, past tastefully pruned trees and pastel stucco homes abutting their sidewalks. On clear days, at intersections, I caught glimpses of Alcatraz in the distance. San Francisco was the most beautiful city I had ever lived in. I extended my stay six weeks but would have been happy to never leave.

I effectively spent my entire fourth year in electives away from Boston University. The intention, apart from avoiding another Boston winter, was to sort out where to train in internal medicine. I knew it had to be the West Coast. I wasn't ready to settle on the East Coast. I determined that I preferred the less high-powered programs, i.e. the non-university based residencies. They were more like family. That probably meant, sad to say, I was not cut out for a career in academia which usually meant affiliating with a large university for residency. Community-based training would allow me to continue to dabble in piano, hiking, cycling. During the year, Mimi visited for a week in Seattle, and arranged a month rotation in San Francisco so we could be together. Though our relationship had become serious, it was rarely relaxed; she was still smoothing over rough edges of former boyfriends in St. Louis.

In March of 1978, I 'matched' with Dr. Rabiner in internal medicine at Good Samaritan Hospital in Portland. During orientation, Dr. Rabiner asked me, "How's Miss St. Louis?"

"We're getting married." Miss St. Louis had matched in New York. We would be engaged to be married while living three thousand miles apart. Some match!

▰ MISTER M.D.

INTERNSHIP IS SCARY at first. You are now the doctor, not just the medical student learning the ropes and doing all the scut work. You now are actually responsible for the lives of patients as well as doing all the scut work. There is no warm-up. It's like Carl Lewis out of the blocks in the hundred meter dash. Mine began in the Intensive Care Unit, where extremely sick patients tried to die and we tried our best to prevent them from doing so. Every third night I stayed up all night dialing ventilator settings and dopamine drips to keep hearts pumping and neurons transmitting. Rarely did interns sleep a wink the nights they were on-call.

Day one, I flipped through patient charts I had inherited from the previous intern, now a second year resident up on the wards. The sounds and smells of the ICU—they're the same everywhere—filled the room. Ventilators stood like sentries next to each bed, pushing oxygen into patient's lungs with a whoosh; pulse monitors beeped, each at different tempos; nurses scurried between beds, clanging side-rails up and down; patients moaned in semi-consciousness. All through the day and night, respiratory techs noisily cleaned lungs with loud suction tube devices. Patients mostly lay motionless in every bed. Coughing sometimes was the only indicator that patients were alive: they would cough, shaking their beds and triggering alarms. The place literally hummed. Scents of the ICU came in waves: alcohol, disinfectants, feces, liquid antibiotics, nurse's sweat, the rusty iron smell of blood.

This would be home for three months. I met the local cast of characters—unit secretaries, evening and night nurses, technicians. Nurses weren't always immediately available so it became important to know in emergencies where everything was stored: the drawer with central I.V. lines, blood tubes, linen closets, the kitchen, each serving important purposes. One important find was the Graham cracker supply, a lifesaver in its own right.

ICU nurses are a special breed. Interns have sauntered into ICUs over the years and tried to throw their weight around now that they have MDs after their names, only to be cold-cocked by ICU nurses. Legend had it that one of our veteran ICU surgery nurses, the tall one, about six feet, two hundred pounds, saved the life of a surgical patient by sticking her ungloved finger into a spurting ruptured artery in his chest. She held it all the way back to the operating room. No intern would have done that.

As interns, we felt responsible for keeping patients alive. If a patient kacked, it was our fault. That's how we felt. My good friend Rob one time had a patient die on him and he literally climbed up on the bed pleading, "No, you can't do this to me!"

Around midnight of that first night on call, a twenty year old man came in directly through the emergency room. He had fallen off a cliff near Mt. Hood, had crushed his chest, collapsed a lung, and was close to having a respiratory arrest. My ICU attending that night, together with the anesthesiologist, paralyzed the man with the curare-like drug used at the time, intubated him, inserted a large bore tube into his chest, and put him on a ventilator for a few days. Being young and healthy, he recovered rapidly. So this was modern medicine. No problem. The remarkable thing was that he hadn't hit his head during the fall. I didn't sleep at all that night, but overall, it was a relatively benign first night of being a real doctor.

George, another patient I took care of during that rotation, had not been so lucky. A motor vehicle accident had turned him instantaneously into a high-level quadriplegic. By the time I picked him up, he had stabilized medically but was not yet ready to be transferred to rehab. George, at the age of fiftyish, would be on a ventilator for the rest of his life. My senior resident Dr. Bernard and I managed George's slow recovery, first in the ICU, and then up on the wards. Nearly everything is a 'first' during internship. George was my first quadriplegic. A new quad is never easy, for patient, family, or doctor. For three months he was all about ventilators, pressure sores, movement impairment, infections, and despair. When Dr. Bernard and I first met George and introduced ourselves as the new team, George's wife laughed, pointing to us in succession, "George…Bernard…Shaw." It stuck. We enjoyed our daily visits with George and his wife. Despite George's terrible situation, both he and his wife shared with us a certain friendliness that seemed to go beyond the doctor patient interaction. The occasional inquiry into our personal lives, the occasional witty response. They helped me learn that it is always a dance, the professional and the personal, between patient and doctor. When the next team took over, it felt very strange to walk away from George and his wife forever.

Internship consumed most of my waking hours for an entire year. Time sprinted by in the Cardiac Care Unit, with its harem of nurses; the renal floor with kidney patients and late night back scratches from the head nurse; the general medicine wards with pneumonia patients, unexplained fevers or any of a hundred other serious ailments. I managed cancer patients, some receiving chemotherapy for the first time, some for the last.

I did, however, manage to carve out some music time. Herb had left the hospital after internship but still lived in town and we took up where we had left off, playing music whenever we could. He became well connected with the jazz community in Portland while working enough in medicine to stay afloat. We ended up renting a house together and I managed to import an upright piano from the basement of my parent's house in Tacoma. By word of mouth, musicians found us. The house became a hangout for jazz musicians, a terrifying thought in retrospect. A succession of players rented the third bedroom. Ted the bassist came first, then William the drummer, and finally Frank Griffith, a very good tenor saxophone player, along with various itinerant crashers. Music was on loudly all the time. Regular rehearsals took place, of Ted's groups, Frank's groups, Herb's groups. Girls came and went. The police, thankfully, never pounded on the door. Mimi visited from New York over the holidays, and after listening to Herb and me rehearse one time, she said, "Maybe you should marry Herb."

■ LOVE LOST

SIX MONTHS EARLIER, just before our residencies began in July, Mimi and I had become engaged to be married. During pillow dialogue, we foolishly agreed to take the plunge. We must have been out of our minds. Being engaged and living three thousand miles apart was an insane idea no matter how in love we thought we were. I also had committed to leave my residency at year end to join her in rural Washington State, doctoring the underserved as tuition debt payback to the government. But as the Billy Joel song goes, *"You Catholic girls start much too late"*. The engagement faltered at six months, and fell apart at eight. She met a surgeon. She had mentioned him once or twice. I learned of their relationship, however, on April fool's day in New York, having arrived the preceding night to spend a month in the emergency room (a.k.a. Knife and Gun Club) at Metropolitan Hospital in Manhattan.

I had suspected something. I had tried one night to call her when I knew she was not on-call in the hospital, but the phone rang and rang through the night. The truth came out gently, the morning after our first night in her 32nd Street studio apartment, with words to the effect of, "I slept with Richard." She said she wanted to go ahead with our marriage, but I knew I couldn't. Perhaps fidelity from a distance of three thousand miles was too much to expect, but there had been other signs: The residua of boyfriends, negative comments about the institution of marriage, the time I surprised her at St. Mary's Hospital in San Francisco with a kiss on the back of her neck and she thought at first the kiss had come from one of the doctors with whom she was working at the time, as if she was used to that sort of thing.

Although it hurt to the marrow, I recognized that it was better for this to have happened before we were husband and wife. The good parts would live on in my memory and the pain hopefully would fade over time. I sheepishly cancelled the rotation at Metropolitan and limped back to Portland. Come July, I would be reinventing my next year instead of going off to rural Washington State.

TIME TO GET SERIOUS

LICENSED DOCTORS CAN always find work. After internship, I worked emergency rooms and clinics around Portland. It paid the rent. Urgency Care clinics were popping up all over town. Population growth and itinerancy had created an opportunity for entrepreneurial doctors to create alternatives to family doctors and emergency rooms. These free-standing clinics, manned usually by one doctor per day, accommodated up to fifty or sixty patients daily if needed, had onsite X-ray equipment, mini-emergency rooms, and small laboratories. If anyone came in really sick, we called an ambulance and sent them to a local hospital emergency room. I practiced medicine days, played piano at night.

It was in those first few months that my interest in dermatology started to take hold. It began with curiosity and frustration. I had little diagnostic expertise in skin conditions other than what I had encountered as a fourth year student at Oregon. Diagnosing skin disease was not easy. It seemed to be more art than science. There was no method I could apply to all skin disease, and I couldn't start flipping through books and expect to stumble onto the correct diagnosis. Even the common conditions often had unusual variations that made them difficult to recognize. Skin complaints were much more common than I expected. At least two out of every ten patients who walked through the door had problems with their skin. While frustrated by lack of experience, I also became intrigued with skin and its maladies.

So, Tom G., the man with the growth on his penis, helped solidify my decision to become a dermatologist. The decision made, my future goal defined, now I had some serious work to do. I needed to find a dermatology residency program willing to have me.

▇ RESIDENCY INTERVIEWS

I HAVE A mental image of my first dermatology interview. A steel vice is bolted to the top of the interviewer's desk. I am called over to insert my genitals into the vice. The interviewer tightens until I no longer can stand the pain and beg for mercy, she releases me, makes a note in her file, and prepares for the next interviewee. What she did with women interviewees I don't know.

The image is obviously fiction, but the metaphor comes from a real interview conducted by none other than Dr. Frances Storrs, Professor of Dermatology at the Oregon Health Sciences University, for whom I have the utmost respect and admiration. After her interview, the rest of the day became somewhat of a blur.

Truth be told, Dr. Storrs's interview was entirely appropriate, if not entirely welcoming. She asked precisely the right questions. She knew me well enough to challenge my motives; I had played jazz piano occasionally with her step-son, an accomplished jazz drummer in Portland. She had no difficulty with him, per se, but how could I be trusted to follow through with a residency, work hard, become an excellent consultant, and enter into an academic career in dermatology if my main love in life was music? It was a legitimate question. She also knew my father, which probably didn't help any. He was a good old boy in dermatology circles. Dr. Storrs and good old boys got along like wet fingers in electric sockets.

Dr. Storrs was actually renowned for her interviews. She asked one applicant two years behind me, Joel Datloff, how he could stand out in her mind. He offered his foot instead of his hand for her to shake as his parting gesture. It worked. He got into the program and became an excellent dermatologist.

But I have jumped way ahead of myself with these interviews. We must go back a few months, to January, 1980, when I had just decided to become a dermatologist.

My timing to start applying could not have been worse. Residency programs began the first of July every year. Commitments by programs had already been made for the coming July, 1980, and dermatology programs had just completed interviews for the following year. The earliest I would be able to start was July, 1982, more than two years away.

I realize now with perfect clarity what I should have done. I should have taken that time to collaborate with a famous dermatology researcher for two years, do important science and publish important papers. The exposure would certainly have served me well. But such is the cruel wisdom of hindsight.

On the other hand, single again, I could easily have travelled the world for two years, unattached and unencumbered. If I survived, it might have had a nice maturing effect.

I did something in-between. I decided to go back to complete my internal medicine residency. More internal medicine would prepare me well for dermatology. Skin, after all, was the window into internal disease. Portland and Good Samaritan Hospital suited me well. My patients, colleagues and teachers had been excellent during internship. I would go there if they would have me back.

During the remainder of that musical year I worked mostly with Herb. He found the gigs. We played duos mostly, or trios with a bass player. We played with superb bassist Phil Baker who had backed Diana Ross and now plays with Pink Martini. We played with Jay Mabin, a Tacoma bassist who also was a fine blues harp player. We had an interesting two night gig with bassist Patrick O'Hearn, an innovative player who went on to create a successful solo career in electronic music. I blush when I recall one night at a noisy club in Portland with Herb and Phil Baker. Herb started into a tune, unannounced, by playing solo around some blues chord changes and Phil joined in on bass after a few bars. When I came in a few bars later, it was *in the wrong key*. I hadn't heard it correctly. Herb had started in B-flat and I joined in the closely related key of F, or the other way around. It was an extremely noisy club, I admit, but still, there was no excuse. I don't know if the audience picked up the mistake, but Herb and Phil certainly did, and I was mortified. Fortunately, that happened only once in my life.

The good thing about playing jazz that year was that I could let go of the concept of a music career. I could stop wondering what might have been. On the talent ladder, I knew my rung was somewhere in the middle. I would never be Keith Jarrett. It had been fun, a great learning experience, but I could now devote my energy to medicine.

CHAPTER 2

Acceptances

"At a cardiac arrest, the first procedure is to take your own pulse."
- Samuel Shem, from The House of God

■ AGE IS NOT THE ISSUE

On July 1, 1980, I returned to internal medicine training. It felt good to get back to academic pursuits, to reunite with colleagues and friends. Everyone was aware that I was planning to try for dermatology and I went along with their jokes. I carried around my trusty three-piece Canon FT with macro lens and ring flash, and began shooting Kodachromes of every patient I encountered with skin disease.

The increased responsibility of being an R2 (second year resident) that year suited me well. An R2, like a middle child, doesn't have the scut-work of a lowly intern. Instead, R2s take responsibility for interns not screwing up. But the R2 does not yet enjoy the senior statesman rank of a senior (R3) resident. I ran cardiac arrests that year, intubated patients, taught interns, and improved my diagnostic skills. I inserted chest tubes, kept ICU patients alive, even got comfortable with kidney dialysis.

Room For Examination

Each day something might happen that influenced how we would turn out as doctors. An interaction with a patient, a family, a doctor, could be life-altering. One patient stands out. She changed forever how I practiced medicine.

As the resident on-call for the night, I was responsible for two interns, new admissions to Medicine, and all cardiac arrests. We each carried a little red pager that went off with a sound like screeching tires when a "code" was called. There was no mistaking that sound.

At eleven o'clock the code beeper went off. I had been examining a man on 4-South whose kidneys had shut down. It had been a busy night and many patients were still waiting to be seen by the interns.

The number on the code beeper indicated Six-North. Surgery floor. Some medical screw-up by the surgeons, I thought at first. I ran down the long corridor to the north stairwell and up two flights.

A cardinal rule when running to a code is: Slow down and walk the final fifty yards, catch your breath, clear your head. The unit secretary pointed in the direction of the patient's room. I asked her the patient's code status — whether or not she had "DO NOT RESUSCITATE" instructions in the event of a cardiac arrest. None was listed.

Sprawled unconscious on the bed was a frail looking woman, a nurse squeezing an air bag over her mouth and an intern kneeling on the side of the bed performing external cardiac massage.

The head nurse rattled a 'crash-cart' into the room and started attaching EKG leads.

The other intern hustled in with the chart. "Mrs. Cheever. Eighty-nine years old, leg cellulitis (a skin infection), admitted two days ago, on I.V. antibiotics, laboratory tests okay except low hemoglobin. I don't see any underlying illnesses, but the entire admission note is basically two lines: Cellulitis; I.V. cefazolin (the antibiotic)."

A young nurse spoke up. She had just given Mrs. Cheever a sleeping pill when she fell back on the bed, unresponsive.

"That was some sleeping pill," I said.

"I thought she fainted at first, but then I couldn't get a pulse."

"She was lucky you were there," I said. "Or not, depending on how this goes."

We didn't know Mrs. Cheever. Without DNR status, we would be going the whole way—a full code. I hovered over the EKG machine.

"Do we have a rhythm?" asked the intern performing CPR.

"Looks like V-fib (ventricular fibrillation)," said the nurse — the patient's heart contractions were disordered and ineffectual.

"It is V-fib," I said, and began the protocol in place in 1981 for ventricular fibrillation that included several drugs. "Get the paddles ready." I asked the other intern if he would like to intubate the patient. The nurse handed him the laryngoscope—the curved metal blade to visualize the vocal cords before inserting the breathing tube.

"Stand back," the nurse said. The lifeless patient jumped grotesquely from the electrical jolt of the paddles.

No rhythm yet. The intern continued CPR.

The second intern was having trouble with the intubation. I heard the laryngoscope click against Mrs. Cheever's teeth. "I can't get her tongue out of the way."

I ordered a second dose of drugs. The nurses applied the paddles. The patient jumped.

"Still in V-fib," I said.

I put on gloves and went behind the head of the bed. The 89-year-old patient lay motionless: pale and dead except for the CPR on her chest. Blood on the laryngoscope attested to a difficult intubation.

This poor woman, I thought. This is the *last* thing I'd like to have done to me when I'm her age.

I leaned over her face, placed my right hand behind her neck to extend it, and with my left, inserted the scope into her mouth, pressing her tongue down flat, and then lifted the front of her throat with the tip of the blade. With my right hand, I slipped the tube past her vocal cords into the trachea. "We're in."

A nurse filled the balloon to secure the tube and gave three quick squeezes on the air bag.

"We have a rhythm," the head nurse said.

I looked at the EKG. "Looks like she had an M.I."(myocardial infarctrion). I ordered one last dose of drug cocktail and put a call in for transfer to the Cardiac Care Unit.

Mrs. Cheever stabilized; we transferred her and returned to our new patients. I hurried back to my kidney patient on Four-South, thinking that it had been a complete waste of time. Cracked ribs, broken teeth, electrical skin burns — a frail old lady at the end of her life. We kept her alive, but for what? Aren't we supposed to first do no harm? What we had done seemed more like assault and battery than treatment.

A few days later, I decided to check on her status. The operator said she was back on 6-North. Surprised that she had pulled through, I went to see her.

I entered her room. In the bed, propped up reading a hefty book was an attractive elderly woman. She looked up at me with a lilt. I informed her of my involvement in her case and asked how she was feeling. She said she would be going home soon, that her leg infection was better and that she was doing fine, except for pain in her ribs when she took a deep breath. No wonder.

She mentioned that she was looking forward to seeing her great-grandchildren, and proudly displayed the photograph of them she used as a bookmark.

I was flabbergasted. When I first encountered Mrs. Cheever she was near death, unconscious, gray skin, gray hair, gray eyes. I had considered it cruel to be resuscitating an eighty-nine year-old. Seeing her now, conversing and alert, with hopes for the future, was a lesson more powerful than any I could ever have found in a book or lecture.

From that point on, I no longer considered a patient's age as a determinant of the care they should receive. Instead, my newly-acquired reverence for elderly patients became a steady source of gratification for the rest of my career.

■ MIND WARP

TWO UNEXPECTED CHANGES took place that year of being a second year resident. I discovered I was losing the stamina to go thirty-six hours without sleep. During internship it had been a breeze. Maybe it was because I was two years younger; or because I was in love with Miss St. Louis, three thousand miles away. Whatever the reason, the stresses of internship had rolled off me like water off a rose petal. Now things had changed. My brain went on tilt if I didn't get enough sleep. I would grab a few minutes of sleep in the on-call rooms during the day. I became annoyed when my beeper went off. It got so bad I began to consider my commitment to the next two years.

The second development involved a woman. During the first two weeks in July, I attended a noon conference (every training program has its noon teaching conferences, usually with free food as a lure, paid for by drug companies). At the front of the room, sitting next to the speaker, was what looked like a cute high school girl. She had short, dark hair flipped in below her ears, dark eyes and a hint of olive color. I had been drawn to that look before. She was seated, so I couldn't tell how tall she was, but was immediately attracted to her and became more so as she occasionally made astute comments and nibbled on her fingernails. Who was this woman, acting smart and speaking like faculty but looking younger than any of us in the room? I left the conference early, thinking "this is not good at all!" The last thing in the world I wanted to do was to become infatuated with another doctor. It turned out that this high school-looking girl was a new addition to the faculty. In clinic that day, I asked my co-resident. "Who was that woman sitting at the front of the conference room?"

"That's Dr. Levinson. Wendy Levinson. The chairman just hired her."

"I think I'm in love," I said.

I kept wondering how this Dr. Levinson woman, this child, could be on faculty. I soon met her and over time learned that she was my age but had skipped a grade in elementary school and had gone to a three year medical school. She was at least three years ahead of me in career terms. The more I got to know her the more I liked her. She was serious though, and scary smart, not quantum physics smart, but capture-the-essence-of-a-discussion smart. She was also married.

She and I worked together at the Indian Health Center in the neighborhood of Good Samaritan Hospital. We often walked there after noon conference for the afternoon clinic. The center took care of Native Americans, of which there were a few thousand in Oregon. Hypertension and diabetes filled our plates, with some alcohol-related disease and tuberculosis occasionally. The staff brought in ethnic foods such as sacks of wild rice from reservations in Minnesota, and contraband fish. One patient named Clifford gill-netted large steelhead trout from Oregon rivers, a practice that was illegal for all but Native Americans, and sold them to us, a practice that was illegal, period. Our relationship with Clifford carried on long after my rotation at Indian Health. The nurses at Good Samaritan gave it the nickname Outpatient and Fish Clinic. When Clifford was not in jail, which, tragically, was less common than any of us would have liked, he would pull into the ER parking lot in his pick-up truck with an ice cooler in the back loaded with freshly caught twenty pound silver-colored steelhead. We learned to love the delectable taste of those beautiful fish. Pink meat, like salmon, but more delicate.

In the middle of the year I made the difficult decision to leave the residency at the end of the year, and not continue with the R3 year. My decreased mental stamina during those thirty-six hour marathons had forced it. I had discovered how crucial mental and physical endurance were to productivity, and how fragile both could be. I rationalized the decision. There were plenty of ways I could spend my time during the coming year. And besides, did I really need to be a certified internist if my plans were to switch to dermatology? But rationalizations they were. In the meantime, I had six more months of contract to finish.

In January, Wendy invited me to dinner at her house. It was a foursome: I and my girlfriend, she and her husband. The invitation was a follow-up gesture for my working with her at Indian Health. It seemed, however, that over the prior few weeks she had begun to notice me as more than just another resident. She had mentioned to me that she and her husband were having difficulties and were contemplating a separation. This could get awkward. Over the next weeks I fantasized madly about her. I even considered telling her my feelings, but never did. A month later, when she invited me to play squash with her one rainy February day, I knew there must be something brewing between us. She beat me handily at squash, but in a bar at a downtown restaurant following the squash game, we spilled the truth about our feelings for each other.

▪ FINAL MATCH

AS I WAS wrapping up my second year of internal medicine, I searched for a dermatology program. I shudder to think how difficult it is today to get into dermatology. I seriously doubt whether I would be successful. Most of my contemporaries say the same thing about themselves.

I applied to three programs and luckily received invitations for interviews at all three: Oregon, Michigan, and Iowa.

At Oregon, the interview with Dr. Storrs (vice bolted to the desk) had the biggest impression on me, but the rest of that day progressed without problems. The next step was to finish my interviews elsewhere, submit a rank list to the Match Program and wait until match day in October. Each program did the same: finish interviewing candidates, submit a rank list, and wait. The rules of the match program were that private negotiations between program directors and applicants were NOT allowed. Rank lists were to remain strictly confidential. I doubted whether program directors actually followed the rules.

After Oregon came Michigan. The University of Michigan had trained my father in dermatology during the early 1950s, and his uncle before him, in the 1920s. That's probably why I got the interview. It can be a mixed blessing to be the son or daughter of a well known player in any profession. During the interviews, many of the dermatologists mistakenly called me John, my father's name. Maybe John was easier to remember than Jim or James, but my insecurity bubbled to the surface every time they praised him. Some of the diplomas on their walls were signed by my father. I learned years later that residency programs always feel pressure when the child of a known dermatologist applies to their program.

I met with the residents, half being women, and most of the faculty, before a final wrap-up session with their imperious chairman, Dr. John Voorhees.

The interview I remember most clearly was with James Rasmussen, the boyish-looking pediatric dermatologist who had trained at Oregon. He played the role of bad cop. "I see from you C.V. that botany and trees are of interest to you," he said, thrusting pencil and paper at me. "Draw me a picture of a Ginkgo leaf."

Dr. Voorhees turned out to be the good cop. When I met with him at the end of the day, he said, "Don't pay any attention to Dr. Rasmussen. He does that with everybody." Dr. Voorhees exuded high I.Q. The thick glasses, mustache and frontal balding fit well with the scientist he was. He went on to ask whether I had any intention of remaining in Ann Arbor after training, because if I did, they were not interested in me. He might as well have said, "Hombre, Ann Arbor just ain't big enough for the two of us." I was not offended. In fact, I quite respected Dr. Voorhees during our meeting. I learned over the years to respect him even more as one of the leading researchers in dermatology. It took years to discover that more than a few academic dermatologists around the country disagreed with Dr. Voorhees on various issues, including his leadership and mentoring style.

Back home, personal life was becoming tense. Wendy had not yet separated from her husband. One evening, I picked up my girlfriend at the hospital where she worked as a physical therapist. "Well, I had an interesting day," she said with a look of strain on her face. She, like Wendy, was also short, with dark hair and dark eyes. Wendy's husband and my girlfriend happened to work at the same hospital, and that day he had called her into his office and broken the news about Wendy and me. I never discovered how he knew. There had been a leak. There are always leaks. The accelerated meltdown that evening of both couples was painful for us all, each in our individual and coupled ways.

University of Iowa came last. My day went smoothly with neither a faux-pas nor a knock-out punch. The chairman of the department at Iowa, Dr. John Strauss, had recently been recruited after twenty years at Boston University, to head dermatology at Iowa. He and his wife, in the tradition of long-standing denizens of Boston, had agonized over leaving their fair city. Over time they learned to accept Iowa City, and the position turned out to be a good one for him.

At Boston, John Strauss had collaborated in the earliest research on hormones and acne, an area in which I would years later take a keen interest. He might also have been instrumental in my acceptance to medical school, again because of the connection with my father. Bearded, bespectacled, and bald, Dr. Strauss exuded wisdom like King Solomon. I always held a fondness for John Strauss and would later have the privilege of working with him in the American Board of Dermatology.

Life's complexities at home demanded that I rank the three programs on the basis of personal circumstances as much as academic goals. The academic part was easy. I would have been honored to train at any of the three programs. The future of my relationship with Wendy, however, was far from certain. My girlfriend moved out, but it was more difficult for Wendy. She was still living with her husband.

One month before submitting my ranking order, I made a decision. I told Wendy that if we were going to continue together, the relationship would have to be overt and it couldn't happen with her still living in the same household as her husband. Covert relationships have a way of slowly asphyxiating both parties. I invited her to call me if she became available.

I distracted myself for a month in the summer. I fished the Beartooth Mountains of Montana with my father, a superb fly-fisherman. I photographed Portland trees and catalogued best specimens with hopes for future publication. I worked emergency rooms. Whether the upcoming year would include Wendy remained uncertain.

During that summer, the chairman at Michigan phoned to inform me that he was ranking me number one—a divulgence that went against the rules of the match program—and wanted to know which I preferred, the clinical or the research track. I enjoyed the praise, especially because when I finished interviewing at Michigan, I didn't know how I had fared. He said he was impressed by my undergraduate and medical school standings. I knew both had been solid but neither was stellar, and I suspected I was being given special treatment because of dear old dad. Regardless, the clinical track interested me most.

Wendy called at the end of the month. She and her husband had separated and had begun divorce proceedings. Her future would not be smooth but she had made a choice. Now we didn't have to hide. She also said that she had two front row tickets for Keith Jarrett at Portland's main concert hall in two weeks. It would be our first legitimate date. I accepted. For an encore to the solo concert, Jarrett played a version of the standard, 'All The Things You Are', which was the highlight of the concert for me. It led the way to his now famous trio work that he has maintained for almost thirty years.

Without discussing it with Wendy, I sent in my rank list: Oregon first, Michigan second, Iowa third. Both of our futures now lay in the innards of the Match Program mainframe computer somewhere in the Midwest. If I didn't match at Oregon, the odds of continuing any relationship with Wendy were exceedingly low. But this was love the second time around, and, as the song goes, I had *'both feet on the ground'*.

In mid-October Wendy and I spent a long weekend at the Oregon Coast. We reveled in uncharacteristically sunny skies at a private house surrounded by grassy dunes. I arrived home to discover an acceptance letter from Oregon! Totally elated, I immediately phoned Wendy and my parents to share the good news. My parents already knew. Word had travelled fast. I called the chairman of dermatology at Oregon, to thank him. He was the one who had called my father. Things were finally starting to come together. The rest of the year would be a breeze, knowing I'd start dermatology in July, eight months away.

My romance with Wendy survived the year, though not without some significant potholes in the road. Even the most amicable marriage separations have difficulties, and theirs was far from amicable. Her family and friends warned her that I probably was merely the 'interim' lover, to not count on our relationship lasting. In May, I went off alone to cycle in Italy. It would be good preparation for the upcoming three years in the trenches. The plan was for Wendy to join me after two weeks for some car touring in Tuscany. I settled into a *pensione* in Torino (Turin) near the train station and, first thing, went out to buy a bicycle. I walked into a high-end cycle shop, eyed a bike that looked right, paid full price and walked out with a brand new Benotto with no climbing gears, road gears only. My Italian, after three months of preparation, had actually been passable during the transaction. I discovered though, that, in my impulsiveness, I had ignored an important piece about the tires. At home I was used to 'clincher' tires. What I bought in Torino was a bike with 'tubular' tires—tires that sew together and are glued directly onto the rim. Most racers used them at the time. I had never fixed a flat tire in a sew-up. For two weeks I cycled hundreds of miles through the foothills of the Italian Alps, and luckily never once suffered a flat tire. In fact, I rode those tires for a decade after the trip and never had a flat. I still don't know how to patch a punctured tire in a sew-up.

The day before Wendy was scheduled to join me in Torino, all airlines in Italy went on strike, a common occurrence in Italy apparently.

With no warning, all air travel was paralyzed for two days. I telephoned her right away and suggested that she fly to New York and try for a flight to Europe from there.

Wendy ended up flying from JFK to Paris where she hoped to find a train to Torino. More surprises greeted her there. Paris was having a bank holiday. Everything was closed and the train from Paris to Torino was inexplicably cancelled. The only reasonable itinerary was a train to Lyon with a connection to Torino. She had no food, no French money or credit cards, and couldn't contact me about her change of plan. This was 1982, before ATMs or cell phones. She had only American dollars and travelers' checks for Italian lire, and banks were all closed. Fortunately, in the Paris airport, she met a middle aged business man named Ettore Stanghellini who was trying to get home to his wife and teenage children in Milano. He took pity on her, and brought her under his wing.

From the train depot in Paris, she finally made telephone contact with the *pensione* in Torino where I had stayed. *"Il partito, il partito!"* said the proprietress who spoke not a word of English. I had checked out of the *pensione* earlier that day and booked at a bona fide hotel in anticipation of Wendy's arrival. Fortunately Wendy gave her the number and time of the train from Lyon in case I called back, and later in the day, when at the train station I discovered the cancelled train from Paris, I returned to the *pensione* so see if, per chance, Wendy had called. They were so excited, in frantic Italian, to see me again and pass on the new information.

Torino's metropolitan train station was vintage World War II. I pictured Mussolini and soldiers getting on one set of trains, Jews getting on a different set. A typical high, arched ceiling covered the fifteen to twenty tracks. There were few written signs. We were not given the benefit of anything so advanced as track numbers, and I could barely understand the echoing Italian from the public address system. The ticket office was no help either. All I had was the time of arrival from Wendy's message. I positioned myself in view of as many incoming tracks as I could, and waited. Several unlabeled trains pulled into the station and slowly emptied as I scanned the crowds. No Wendy. It was getting close to thirty minutes past her arrival time. I eventually approached a man with an official looking blue hat and asked about the train from Lyon. "Il arrivato venti minuti fa." It had arrived twenty minutes ago! Holy shit. I hurried out to what I thought might be a reasonable place to intercept her. It was like Penn Station at rush hour. This could be difficult, I thought. But there, in the middle of a crowd of people, not knowing what to do like a lost child, stood Wendy, gaunt, her black hair matted, her dark eyes wet with tears. She looked totally, wonderfully pathetic.

The next day, after she had drunk enough water to prevent kidney failure, and slept a few hours, we picked up a rental car to drive to Milano. There were debts to settle, there was bread to break with new friends: Mr. Stanghellini had given Wendy two hundred dollars worth of Italian lire when he left her in Torino, and had invited us to dinner with his family whenever it worked out. During the drive, about midway between Torino and Milano, I asked Wendy if she would marry me. Perhaps I caught her at a vulnerable time, but she said yes. There was no ring. No kiss. With the exception of a brief intercalation of my fingers with hers, a quick glance and a smile, I had to keep my eyes on the road and both hands on the wheel. They drive fast in Italy. We've always cherished that moment.

CHAPTER 3
The Rookie

The education of the doctor which goes on after he has his degree is, after all, the most important part of his education.
-John Shaw Billings, MD, first director of the New York Public Library

■ EARLY STRESS

FOUR DAYS BEFORE starting my new career as a budding dermatologist, I went from happy bachelor to *status spousus*. My head throbbed all day as I shuttled furniture from our respective houses to our matrimonial rental house up on Aspen Street. I barely finished before rushing off to judge's chambers. Immediately following the pronouncement, our best friends Josh and Lisa—attorney and psychologist, respectively, and sole witnesses to our wedding—drove us to Reed College for an exclusive rehearsal of a Chamber Music Northwest string quartet (Josh was Chairman of the Board at the time), complete with Champagne, to toast our marriage in style. I felt a little like Eliza Doolittle in Pygmalion. After one night at the Benson Hotel, we hurried home to spend the remaining thirty-six hours of our honeymoon weekend rearranging furniture in our new house. Then it was *back to work.* Our marriage would become intimate with *back to work,* jealous mistress though she is. Wendy returned to academic medicine at Good Samaritan Hospital, and I set off on my new journey into diseases of the skin.

The first thing I noticed in residency was that the science of dermatology was more foreign than I had expected, the terms staggering, concepts complex. I couldn't build upon my two years of internal medicine, much of which no longer applied. The mere pronunciation of skin diseases required considerable practice: *Lupus miliaris disseminata faciei* or *Perifolliculitis capitis abscedens et suffodiens,* to name only two. Each was a big mouthful of Latin, and there were hundreds more to know intimately.

I had some familiarity with Latin. It definitely had not come from my two unfruitful years of high school Latin. I had picked up some from my botany interests. A Douglas fir tree, for example, had become *Pseudotsuga taxifolia.* But even before high school, my father had tried to infuse Latin into us. One of his long-time patients, a profoundly geriatric former Latin teacher, expressed great enthusiasm about the concept of coming out of fifteen years of retirement to teach us privately. My father jumped at the chance, and we three oldest siblings—sister Elisabeth, myself, and brother Josh, ages fourteen, thirteen, and twelve—went to her haunted tree-enshrouded house every week for at least a year or two. The only things I remember about those sessions were the geriatric odor and the green, scratched-up, six-ounce bottles of 7-up she opened for us and poured into glasses mid-way through each lesson. I eventually came to realize that Latin is really only useful when there is a use for it. In dermatology, it looked like there might be.

Six weeks into residency, on a hot August Saturday, I finished a long bicycle ride and came into the house to hang up the bike. After about two minutes, I was greeted with, "How long was it going to take before you asked about the pregnancy test?"

"Of course! Yes! I'm sorry." I said, knowing I had completely botched it.

"It was positive. I'm pregnant." Wendy should have been smiling, but wasn't.

"I guess we don't fuck around, do we?"

No laugh. Maybe she didn't get the joke.

"I can't believe your bike ride was more important than knowing if I'm pregnant. You're supposed to be the father." This was turning ugly.

The fact was that I did care. The thought of being a father was actually thrilling in a strange, anxiety-provoking, 'this-is-what-normal-people-do' sort of way.

So there I was. A new residency, a new marriage, a new house, a newly pregnant wife who thought I didn't care, plus—and this I haven't mentioned before—joint custody of Wendy's two year old daughter in a highly acrimonious settlement between Wendy and her ex-husband who was still very much incensed over many of the circumstances leading up to the divorce. If I allowed the combined stresses to sink in, I felt that characteristic knot I once felt in my solar plexus just before a car crash. Despite that, I distinctly remember also being explosively upbeat. My career decision of two years before had begun to take shape. I figured I would let my stresses and joys battle it out on their own. I had other things to do.

■ BODY FLUIDS

I'LL ALWAYS REMEMBER the words of Dr. Arthur Zbinden, one of my favorite teachers at Good Samaritan. He once told me, "You have to choose the body fluid you want to work with." He had chosen sputum—he was a pulmonologist, a lung specialist. I could never have been a pulmonologist. I gagged at the sight and sound of mucus and sputum. I also never developed a particular liking for urine, vomit, or feces. I didn't much care for amniotic fluid. I did once entertain the possibility of blood (hematology) for a while during medical school.

Dermatology had no fluid per se. Diseased skin certainly could be as foul-smelling and unsightly as body fluids, but skin didn't have its own unique fluid, or so I thought. I soon came to appreciate that skin did have at least two: sweat and oil. Neither was as glamorous or disgusting as something coughed up from the lungs, but oil and sweat were nevertheless hugely important in skin diseases. Acne, after all, happened expressly because of oil glands (called sebaceous glands).

And people who perspired excessively became social outcasts, their hands and feet dripping all day, while those who couldn't sweat at all risked death from hyperthermia in hot weather.

Dr. Zbinden also had a special place in his heart for a fluid of another kind. He introduced me to California wines I had never before tasted: 1974 Geyserville Zinfandel, 1974 Heitz Martha's Vineyard Cabernet, Chalone Chardonnays. I can't decide whether his lessons in medicine or wine had a more lasting effect, but I appreciated both.

I would eventually incorporate oil (sebum), sweat, and even saliva into my jurisdiction as a dermatologist. But luckily, dermatology was less about fluid analysis and more about visual observation and interpretation.

Good visual memory was the important asset. Nobody color blind should ever be allowed into a dermatology program. Unlike other specialties such as kidney disease with its ceaseless calculations of laboratory numbers that can be done in black and white, dermatology had color and pattern to see, texture to feel. It was painting and sculpture rolled into one. The visuals of dermatology fit well with my brain function, my tree identification hobby, my talent for pattern recognition. For two hundred years, the enjoyment of visual detail has influenced many a budding dermatologist. For those who do not take pleasure in those details, making an accurate diagnosis often becomes an onerous chore. And, sadly, there are color blind dermatologists out there. Testing of applicants is not permitted. It would be discriminatory. There could be law suits.

■ MY FIRST DERMATOLOGY FAMILY

I SPENT THE next three years on the fifth floor of the architecturally dreary outpatient clinic building at Oregon. The only charming part of that 1940s pale yellow brick structure when I started was a fifty foot high Spanish Fir tree, *Abies pinsapo* if you please, in front of the side door. It was a magnificent specimen, one of only two in Portland of that size, both on the medical school campus. Plump, dark green needles and grayish, lightly textured bark. Beautiful. But ornamental trees get taken down when they quit serving a purpose, and I can recall my sadness and dismay two years later when it lay on the ground one morning as I approached the door, sawdust all around, to make room for a new driveway. But, *back to work*. I had to let it go.

To erect a University hospital complex high on a hill was my idea of poor planning. Ambulances had to wind their way up a mile of tight steep curves to bring sick patients to the emergency room. But choice of building sites, for some universities, is a secondary priority. The hilly acreage at Oregon had been given to the state by a donor for the sole purpose of creating the medical school, so it was there to stay. And I admit that on the odd clear day, views of Mt. Hood were spectacular.

A bank of elevators opened directly onto a corridor that encircled our dermatology floor. Faculty offices and examination rooms faced out from the hallway, and filling the center were conference room, library, nurses station, and ultra-violet light-boxes. A few other small rooms served as resident closets and pathology room with its six-headed microscope. At the time, the entire department was a self-contained cadre of five full-time faculty members, nine residents, one or two research fellows, and at least ten secretaries, nurses, and other ancillary help, all women.

I soon realized how lucky I had been to get into the program when I did. My co-residents Larry Peterson and Susan Denman had already spent time in research at Oregon and had been hand-picked long before the match. The third position came down to a choice between me and one other applicant. One of us would get the clinical track; the other would do the four year research track. Either would have been fine, but I certainly was delighted to get started with clinical dermatology at the outset.

▇ THE WEEK BEGINS: DR. WHITE

EVERY WEEK KICKED off with dermatopathology, or 'derm-path', jargon for microscopic examination of skin, a crucial part of skin diagnosis. Dr. Clifton White selected six unknown slides for us to study during the week, and on Monday at eight o'clock, we staggered one by one, up to the front of the conference room, wiped the sleep from our eyes, and tried to point out abnormal findings from the microscopic images projected onto the screen. Clif White had studied at New York University with Dr. A. Bernard Ackerman, the most influential dermatopathologist the specialty has ever known. Dr. Ackerman revolutionized pathologic diagnosis of skin disease, and Clif White was one of his disciples. Clif's unflappable but inclusive demeanor put us at ease even as we went down in flames at the front of the room.

Many years later, after seeing how derm-path was taught at other institutions, I came to appreciate the value, the necessity, of Clif White's approach. He started with the basics: learn to recognize normal skin, normal cells under the microscope. Over three years he systematically introduced us to nearly every skin disease known at the time.

A poorly prepared resident could self-destruct up there in front of the screen. I loved preparing for Monday sessions, pouring over each unknown slide, the thrill of detecting an abnormality, flipping through piles of textbooks, building a case for a specific diagnosis, getting sidetracked to other fascinating diagnoses. My time for reviewing the slides was Sunday evenings when I had the microscope room completely to myself. I preferred making my own discoveries, having learned long before that knowledge through self-discovery lasted much longer. I saw what happened when residents reviewed slides as a group: the more experienced or talented residents found the critical features while the more passive ones got the answers spoon fed to them but totally missed the concepts.

Sunday night studying presented a bit of a problem, though. I'd leave home after dinner and usually got home late. Wendy was growing larger with child every passing month. She didn't particularly enjoy missing out on precious weekend time we would otherwise have spent together.

Every specialty has its jargon. Not just the thousands of unique words, but the way in which we couch a report. In derm-path we learned cell types and sub-types, patterns for benign versus malignant disease, features of young versus old skin. At the microscope we would start at the skin surface with low power and go to higher magnification only if needed. Pathology reports were written in a foreign language, familiar only to dermatologists and pathologists. A biopsy from a patient with 'hives' might read:

"This punch biopsy shows a normal epidermis overlying a dermis demonstrating scant perivascular lymphocytes and a few scattered eosinophils between collagen bundles. Diagnosis: consistent with urticaria (hives)."

It was succinct and specific. With practice, we learned to rapidly survey each pathology slide with similar language almost as second nature, and for that we had Clif White to thank.

▰ THE 'VAH SPA'

AFTER DERM-PATH CONFERENCE, I would catch the university shuttle over to the Veterans Administration Hospital where clinic started by about nine-thirty. Bob-the-bus-driver had driven that faded green shuttle with pride, it seemed, since before the Spanish-American War. On the surface, he was as gruff as a hydrophobic dog. Bellowing through his tobacco-coated vocal cords, he usually had us groaning from highly politically-incorrect jokes by the time we reached the VA. Deep down, he was a gentle soul.

I spent most of my time at the VA with second year resident Brooks Cofield, doctor of osteopathy and military man. He had a great laugh that either put people in a great mood, or annoyed them. Brooks taught me a lot, and had fun doing it. He also made a mean beer batter for deep-frying the smelts he caught on tributaries of the Columbia River.

Our third-year, senior-most resident at the VA, Eric Rasmussen, was a bit more serious than Brooks, but also an excellent teacher. He had spent a year in the research laboratory of Kirk Wuepper, one of our faculty members with a reputation for having a temper. Brooks and I guessed that maybe it had taken a toll on Eric's sense of humor.

And then there was Nora, our nurse and guardian angel. She mothered us in her quiet way, with an under-the-surface smile. Nora could also crack a whip if we got too far behind. She did the same with the VA patients. They loved her. We were extremely lucky to have Nora. Many of the VA clinics had no nurses at all. Through our barrages of insults, we made it clear to Nora that we couldn't live without her.

VA hospitals have a culture unto themselves. I had spent four months at the Boston VA during medical school, and knew well the cast of characters who received their care through VA hospitals. VAs had typical architecture, often situated on a hill, the green wall paint, the stench; it was all familiar to me and I felt right at home with the anxiety of the place. Patients could use any VA hospital in the country and itinerant vets moved around, not uncommonly by freight train, chasing clement weather. Nearly all men, most VA patients had fought in World War II or the Korean War, but by 1982 when I began, we were starting to see younger men who had survived Viet Nam in the sixties and seventies.

Agent Orange, the toxic chemical defoliant, was becoming a political hot potato when I started, and we evaluated many Viet Nam vets who had filed claims. Rarely, if ever, could we identify skin disease attributable to the chemical. I suspect that we did not have the knowledge or testing capabilities to confirm subtle associations. As a result, the U.S. government usually emerged as the winner, and the vets received little or nothing. Fortunately, most cases weren't serious.

Clinics at the VA always ran late, frustratingly so at times, but I rapidly learned to appreciate that late was better than not busy enough. In medicine, nothing is worse than sitting around with nothing to do. During residency, it's not about the finances since residents don't pay the rent; it's about intellectual stimulation, and we had plenty of that. Morning clinic could be a mad house. Things would start to slow down by twelve-thirty every day but we frequently didn't get out of there until two o'clock to arrive late to our afternoon clinics on the University side.

VA medicine in the 1980s was largely do-it-yourself. Residents were given considerable free rein in treating patients. Attending physicians traditionally kept their distance and medical decision making was often left to residents. Despite the highest of expectations by our senior attendings, learning by trial and error was common. At the Boston VA, I rarely saw the senior physician other than for weekly corridor rounds that were more about academic one-upmanship than patient care. It was the culture of the place. It was as if veterans were put on Earth so that medical students and residents could learn how to become good doctors. Collateral damage was an accepted part of the learning, just as it had been part of the soldiering.

The Portland VA was no different; we residents ran the show. We often called patients from the waiting room two or three at a time, put them into individual rooms, prepared surgical trays of instruments and cleaned up after ourselves. Nora couldn't handle everything. Dr. White would arrive toward the end of clinic to help us with difficult patients we had detained until the end of the morning. Clif was ultimately responsible, and unlike the real world of private medicine, where it would be unheard of to ask a patient to stick around two hours to see Mr. Pooh-Bah doctor, the veterans mostly obeyed, and we received superb teaching once Clif arrived.

My introduction to liquid nitrogen as something other than a high school physics experiment happened at the VA. Liquid nitrogen, as technologically primitive as it might seem by today's standards, is one of the most valuable modes of treatment in a dermatologist's practice. With a boiling point of minus 196 degrees Celsius, it freezes nicely many skin growths, especially small surface ones such as warts and 'keratoses'. Usually, we spray it on with a cryo-gun or apply modified cotton Q-tips to the skin after dipping them into the liquid that boils at room temperature. After close to thirty years of practice, liquid nitrogen remains a mainstay of dermatological treatment.

Liquid nitrogen could have other uses too. One day in September, an angry yellow-jacket found its way into our office and buzzed around tormenting Nora. Brooks Cofield, being the chivalrous military man that he was (and not wanting that yellow-jacket to sting his shiny head), grabbed the liquid nitrogen spray canister and chased the nasty wasp around the room until its wings froze from the frigid spray and it plummeted like a Messerschmitt to the counter top where he finished off the job, freezing it to a crispy white corpse. "Thank you, Dr. Cofield," said Nora. Brooks just laughed his high-pitched laugh and went off to see the next patient.

So, the VA was my first exposure to high-volume skin disease. Practice does make perfect, and we got very good at common skin conditions on the hairy heads, hairy faces, sweaty feet, and sweaty groins of our VA patients. We treated fungal infections, skin cancers and drug rashes, really bad dandruff (called seborrheic dermatitis), and more skin cancers. The rare and bizarre would occasionally walk through the door as well. Under Clif White's mentorship, more than a few published articles were borne of that clinic over the years. I absorbed huge amounts of dermatology knowledge during those first four months.

While vets were usually grateful for the care they received, some were notorious for their alcohol consumption. They could be belligerent or even inebriated during clinic visits. But one privilege that patients collectively bestow upon doctors is the license to explore their personal and private lives. They rightfully assume that doctors will use the information to help them. And when I would ask a patient how he lost his leg and he would perk up with all the details of a battle in France during World War II, he and I deepened our relationship, and my medical management suddenly became easier, my experience richer. Not everyone enjoyed that kind of exploration, the kind that strays from the immediate medical problem. I have witnessed many residents whose only goal was to be done with each patient, finish the clinic, the week, their residency. For some, taking more time with patients was an annoyance. I found the veterans' war stories one of the enrichments of working with those wonderful crusty guys.

■ LIFE GOES ON TILT

ONE MONTH INTO residency, my brain quit functioning normally. I started experiencing what I can only describe vaguely as 'head symptoms'. Every day about mid morning at the VA, I started floating sideways, weightless. I would almost miss a step walking. I wanted to lie down and close my eyes. The symptoms would occasionally settle down after two hours, only to return more severely in the afternoon. I never felt sick with nausea or fever, and never had spinning vertigo, but my nerves were sharpened, on edge. When I grasped a door handle it felt as if I had no flesh, just bone, and I might let go with a shiver from the eerie sensation.

There would be times when the symptoms were absent. Those were glorious days. But then they would return and I started to fear the worst. For the first time in my life, I began to think the way patients sometimes think. I went through all the unlikely possibilities that patients do to explain their ailments. My obvious first thought: It must be coffee. I was addicted to coffee. So I cut it out, but all I got was three days of splitting caffeine-withdrawal headaches and no help with the symptoms. I gave it a good month, but the feeling that my head was inside of a vacuum bell jar persisted, so I went back on coffee. Oh, what a pleasure to be back on my high-octane French Roast!

Then I cut out alcohol. I wasn't a heavy drinker but figured that abstaining for a month was worth a trial. It was no help either. I was back to square one, with the sense of floating and head pressure. But one carries on in life, so carry on I did.

On free afternoons, I would sneak over to the on-call rooms in the hospital for short naps whenever I could. My brain demanded it. Naps helped with alertness but didn't help the symptoms of fuzziness and the feeling of being suspended two feet off the ground. It was rapidly becoming clear that this was not a temporary illness like a virus. It was a chronic neurological problem and I would have to learn to cope. That is, if it didn't kill me. I would soon have to see a doctor. I told nobody but Wendy.

■ DR. WUEPPER

MY FIRST FACULTY clinic convened Monday afternoons with Dr. Kirk Wuepper (pronounced like 'pepper', or to be more dermatological, 'leper'). Each faculty member held one or two clinics every week to which residents were assigned on a rotational basis. Kirk Wuepper had a brilliant scientific mind with an impressive C.V. to show for it. He discovered the toxin that caused *toxic shock syndrome* but was famous around campus for having tested it on himself and his research fellow. They both ended up in the hospital and were lucky to have survived without permanent organ damage.

Dr. Wuepper would have been happy to do only basic science research and never leave his laboratory. But that's not the way it worked. Some clinic time was required of all faculty members. One had to see patients and teach, if only to maintain respectability as a clinical dermatologist. More often than not, few patients showed up for his clinic. I attributed the light load to his demeanor with patients, that of German scientist. That may be too harsh, but he lacked a sense of "I'm going to help you with this problem if I can." A few patients would trickle in during the afternoon, but many were no-shows, and for that, I felt sorry for him.

One time in clinic I helped Dr. Wuepper medically. He had his first heart attack at age thirty-nine. Strong family history. The smoking and being overweight didn't help. One day he said he was in atrial flutter or fibrillation. He could feel the jiggling sensation in his chest. It happened regularly despite his being on treatment. I had just finished two years of internal medicine training and a year of emergency medicine. I asked whether he had ever tried a Valsalva maneuver to break the fibrillation. Valsalva is when you hold your breath and bear down to produce increased internal pressure. He tried it, and to his surprise, converted to regular lub-dub, lub-dub heart rhythm. I was hero for the day. A few weeks later he reported that the maneuver consistently helped convert his rhythm back to normal. Whether deserved or not, I had gained his respect. He trusted my medical judgment from that point on. He also came to admire my dermatological and surgical skills, enough to become my patient, at first informally as a resident, and then officially when I started my practice.

Dr. Wuepper's research activities declined over the three years of my residency. He ultimately gave up his research and left academics altogether for private practice in the coastal town of Astoria, seventy miles west of Portland. After less than five years in private practice, he died suddenly from a heart attack. He was fifty-nine.

When news broke of his death, I was surprised by the lack of compassion from his peers. The majority of comments I heard from the dermatology community reminded me of Dickens's *The Christmas Carol*, with business men standing around on a snowy London street belittling Ebenezer Scrooge after his death. Kirk Wuepper had made larger scientific contributions to dermatology than most would ever make. His personality had rubbed some colleagues the wrong way, and for some, the negative carried more weight than the positive. Throughout my career I've heard similar sentiments about colleagues in all specialties, those who might have been irritable or impatient even though they had something valuable to offer. The bad traits obscured the good ones their whole careers. In the case of Kirk Wuepper, there was gold to be found; one just had to mine for it.

■ I, THE PATIENT

MY HEAD SYMPTOMS were no better and I decided to make an appointment with a neurologist. After an EEG and other tests, he was uncertain about what was happening. He recognized that the life of a resident who just got married could be stressful, and recommended a trial of beta-blockers, drugs used at the time to treat panic attacks. I suspect he thought my problems were 'supra-tentorial'—the anatomical euphemism for 'psychiatric'— and maybe this was his first step toward referring me to a psychiatrist. I knew the symptoms were not supra-tentorial. I tried the beta blockers. They made things worse and I stopped them after a few weeks. I monitored myself and noticed that if my adrenaline levels were sufficiently high, as during a speaking presentation or during a very busy clinic with patients or surgery, the symptoms were less noticeable. I could essentially override the spaced-out brain sensation, or at least not think about it. I also noticed that the head fullness was worse an hour or two after eating. Perhaps there was a connection there.

After beta blockers, the next approach was Dilantin, the anti-seizure drug. In a neurologist's black bag, Dilantin remained one of the most used and highly effective drugs. Its use went beyond the treatment of seizures.

Dilantin was fairly heavy artillery. I knew the drug for its life threatening skin rashes and the lymphoma-like illnesses it could cause. But I was getting to the point where big artillery was fine with me. Anything, if it would help. I started on a standard dose of three hundred milligrams per day.

It was magic. I don't know if it was placebo or real, but my fogged-up head pressure and brain-on-tilt symptoms lessened substantially. I didn't savor the idea of being reliant on Dilantin forever but would gladly have done it if I continued to get the relief I achieved at first. I stayed on one hundred to three hundred milligrams per day of Dilantin. The diagnosis, though, remained a mystery, and my neurologist followed me closely for new clues.

■ DR. HANIFIN

TUESDAYS I WORKED with Dr. Jon Hanifin, who, like Dr. Wuepper, was scientist first, clinician second. In medicine, anyone really smart and motivated ends up scientist first, clinician second. The very smartest of doctors rarely see patients at all. While there are special talents to being an expert clinician, taking care of patients is not pure intellect. More art, perhaps. The brightest find their way into scientific exploration and experimentation. I can say that because I am not one of them. From the start, I knew I was destined for clinical work.

Jon Hanifin had a reputation for being an 'Après animal' (a skiing term). He could stay out drinking and dancing late into the night at conferences and preside over a seven o'clock committee meeting the next morning. I always envied him that stamina. Jon, of good Irish stock, was also famous for his gift of the gab and for flirting with women in the department. No one seemed to mind. To my knowledge he never crossed ethical boundaries.

Dr. Hanifin was then, and still is, one of the fathers of research in eczema (medical term: Atopic Dermatitis). Eczema is the skin rash that runs in families along with asthma and hay fever. It is more an immune disease than a skin disease. Instead of a rash that itches, eczema is affectionately known as 'the itch that rashes' i.e., scratching the skin causes the rash, sometimes to the point of weeping. Patients with eczema were often strong-willed, hard-working individuals, almost stoic, and I'll always remember the words my co-resident Larry Peterson said concerning patients with eczema: "The skin weeps for those who can't."

Dr. Hanifin was the first to publish specific diagnostic criteria for eczema. In his lab, he researched errors in immunity that contributed to eczema. He also became an essential lead investigator in large eczema drug trials. The name Jon Hanifin needed to be on the study if they wanted to get respect from the FDA and from dermatologists who would be prescribing the new drug.

My strongest memory of clinics with Jon was a little piece of teaching that became invaluable in my own practice:

A woman in her early twenties came in with a wart on the tip of her finger. Warts, while extremely common, are often exasperatingly difficult to treat. They frustrate both patient and doctor. The time-honored method was cryotherapy with liquid nitrogen. The treatment was painful though, produced a blister in two days, and required a month of slow healing. After all that, the wart would often recur as it had in this patient. So Jon Hanifin taught me his method.

First, he anesthetized the patient's finger tip pad with an injection of lidocaine anesthetic. A needle in your finger sounds terrible, but it is worth the pain to prevent what comes next. After the finger tip was numb, he used a cautery needle to introduce an electric current into the deepest part of the wart. I watched electrical sparks splay out from beneath the wart. The patient felt nothing.

"There," he said to me. "Look at the spark separate the wart from the surrounding skin." Then he took a pair of small scissors, inserted and spread them under the wart. He grasped the electrocuted somewhat charred wart with a pair of forceps (tweezers), gently cut around the edges, and lifted it off. There was no bleeding. A dry crater remained. He touched the base with light cautery, put a bandage over it, and said, "Let me know if that doesn't take care of it. The wart should be gone, without a scar."

Dr. Hanifin's method, called electrofulguration, became essential to my practice over the years. Over time, newer treatments such as lasers were introduced, but I found electrofulguration to be the best treatment for recalcitrant solitary warts. The downside was that I could spend twenty minutes on a patient who was scheduled for ten. However, many grateful patients have thanked me for succeeding where others had failed, and I always think of Dr. Hanifin.

MORPHOLOGY ROUNDS

WEDNESDAY MORNING MEANT weekly patient 'rounds', a tradition that every dermatology department around the world conducts, where faculty and residents examine patients with unusual or difficult diagnoses, and residents get grilled on what they know. The sessions go by different names—Special Conference, Grand Rounds, Noon Rounds—but all run similarly. Ours was called Morphology rounds for reasons that will become clear. The reports from Europe were that patients paraded nude onto a stage for all to look at. We in the West tended to be more modest, used examination rooms and gave patients gowns to wear.

At Oregon, the focus of patient rounds was teaching. The goal, aside from trying to help the patient, was to hone our skills in *morphology*, i.e. the anatomy of skin disease: how it looks, how it feels, the colors, texture, distribution on the body. Patients invariably benefitted from these conferences, especially when the diagnosis was in question, but the main beneficiaries were residents and faculty who sharpened their diagnostic skills.

Each week, we would examine four to eight patients between eight and nine o'clock. We were not allowed to ask questions. It was strictly morphology. It must have been strange for patients to have three or four doctors at a time examining their skin in total silence. They were forewarned by the nurses, but the silent studiousness of residents and professors could create a disconcerting surrealism in those small examination rooms.

The discussions took place at nine o'clock in our modest conference room. A dermatologist from 'off the hill', i.e. not university faculty, moderated. He or she chose a resident to describe each patient and come up with a list of possible diagnoses, the so-called 'differential diagnosis'. Some moderators were more tolerant of incompetence by residents than others. Humiliation was always a risk. I still blush when I remember things I said from inexperience or misguided self-confidence, only to be shot down by the moderator.

We discussed dermatology at the highest, state-of-the-art level. In that one room sat faculty and resident alike, teacher and student, parent and child. The conference gave faculty a good measure of how well we residents were expanding our knowledge base in dermatology. My head symptoms usually didn't kick in until about ten o'clock, so I usually felt reasonably normal during the sessions, which was fortunate. Later in my career, moderating those weekly conferences became one of my most gratifying teaching activities.

Wednesday afternoons, for me, were unscheduled during much of my first year. When I compare my residency in the 1980s with training today, we had it easy. We were granted one or two afternoons every week where nothing was scheduled. We were expected to remain on campus but were free to use the time as we chose. First year, I poured over text books or carrousels filled with slides of skin diseases. The studying was slow going at first, but what a luxury it was to have the free time. Nowadays, I am amazed at the amount of material residents need to absorb while having little free time to study other than evenings and weekends.

Thursdays kicked off with Journal Club. We congregated, coffee and muffin in hand, in a private room just off the cafeteria dining room. Every specialty has its medical journals, and very few doctors outside each specialty are able to differentiate between the high and low quality journals of another specialty. Once an insider in a particular specialty, it quickly becomes obvious which are the highest level journals, which are less respectable, and which are 'throw-away' journals that serve as vehicles for advertising and padding of one's CV.

It would have been helpful if someone had taken the forty-five seconds to explain to me the hierarchy of our specialty's journals. Instead, I had to learn it the hard way. My assignment first year was a journal called *Cutis* (Latin for 'skin'). In my mind at first, this was serious science. I laugh now when I think what the senior residents and faculty must have been thinking during my ardent discussions of its articles. Within a month or two I realized that *Cutis* was essentially a throw-away, a journal of drug studies and light commentary. No academic promotions were made on the basis of publishing in *Cutis*.

Fortunately, interpreting medical literature has come a long way. Nowadays, there are on-line impact ratings for journals, and promotions committees know the breakdown of journals. Even so, the average doctor doesn't know the hierarchy within other specialties. Doctors are instead taught to use critical appraisal techniques to assess each article for its merit, but in my present experience at journal clubs, very few clinical doctors actually use the techniques. Misleading science can still take root in the average doctor's mind.

▪ T.G.I.F.

FRIDAYS WERE A mix of lectures, clinics, surgery and conferences. Dr. Frances Storrs, the inimitable, held a session that became one of my absolute favorites. It was known simply as 'Unknowns with Dr. Storrs'. She truly loved the specialty of dermatology, and although she had carved out an important niche in allergic skin reactions, she was an excellent diagnostician and had built up a world-class collection of slide transparencies from her own patients and from academic dermatologists around the world.

She sat at the carousel projector in the back of the conference room with a stack of slides carefully hand-picked during her lunch. The first photos were easy, the so-called 'warm-ups'. Then she would get into meatier stuff, more difficult diagnoses or treatments, and ultimately end the ninety minute session with rare diseases or rare presentations of common diseases, as a final challenge.

She would pick a resident to discuss each slide. Describe what you see. Come up with a list of possible diagnoses, the so-called 'differential diagnosis'. If you don't know the diagnosis, how would you work up the patient to figure out the answer? What additional history is important? Family history? Exposure history to environmental chemicals? Think on your feet! She made every resident perform. We learned dermatology, and Dr. Storrs learned how residents were progressing in their understanding of skin disease at the expert level. Later in my career, once I moved into full-time academic dermatology, I came to fully understand the importance of having residents perform like that and think on their feet. Without doing so, a resident can slip by an entire residency and still not know how to think appropriately about a medical case. I adopted Dr. Storrs's approach and used it extensively in my teaching of dermatology residents throughout the rest of my career.

■ BACK ON THE WARDS

THE FIRST FOUR months of residency came to a close. I wrapped things up at the VA, bid Nora adieu, and began my second tour of duty: University Hospital inpatient wards. These dermatology patients would be sick enough that they needed to be hospitalized. Now, after eight o'clock conferences every morning, instead of riding to the VA with Bob-the-bus-driver, I walked across the street to University Hospital to round on my inpatients and consults. I was the contact person for all inpatient dermatological problems throughout the University complex.

I felt right at home on the hospital wards: the comings and goings of sick patients, teams of doctors, nurses scurrying, overhead announcements and the symphony of various buzzes and squawks from electronic devices on the wards. Two years of internal medicine residency had somehow left a positive impression. It felt good to be back. This was real medicine.

Back then, we hospitalized psoriasis patients as well as medically ill patients with skin disease. Severe psoriasis cases came in for spa-like treatments: three to six weeks of whirlpool baths, ultraviolet light treatments, student nurses rubbing them down with ointments and creams. It may sound pleasant but it wasn't always a picnic: the smothering ointments usually contained black smelly tar. Nevertheless, the hospital stay was like a holiday for many patients and the reduced stress always helped psoriasis. They usually responded beautifully; their skin would return to normal and they would leave the hospital feeling great. The psoriasis always came back eventually, but these patients might get one or two good years after a spa admission. Insurance companies have long since quit paying for those treatments.

Early on in my hospital rotation, one such spa patient, a cantankerous middle-aged man, was left in the light box for over five minutes when the treatment should only have been less than two. According to the nurse, the timer didn't go off. Those ultraviolet light boxes emitted powerful rays. He suffered a terrible burn, almost as if he had been scalded with hot water. We were forced to treat him with oral prednisone, a drug we normally don't like to use in psoriasis. The University settled the lawsuit out of court. What we had done was indefensible. In the 1980s, burning a patient in the UV light box was the most common cause for a malpractice lawsuit against dermatologists (today, missing a cancer diagnosis gets that prize). Nowadays, safeguards are in place to reduce medical errors, but back then, each doctor or nurse took individual responsibility for avoiding mistakes, and because of that, mistakes were made.

THE THRILL OF DIAGNOSIS

"In the field of observation, chance favors the prepared mind."

–Louis Pasteur*

(* This quotation from Louis Pasteur was first introduced to me by the most emeritus of our faculty, Dr. Tom Saunders, age about eighty-three, who was mercifully allowed to lecture to us first year residents every Thursday afternoon. He was a wonderful person, but like so many doctors whose identities are permanently welded to their professions, he had outlived his usefulness as a teacher, preferring proverbs and humor to up-to-date instruction. The quote, though, I always remembered.)

I earned my first dermatology stripes during the hospital rotation. No matter how humble a doctor might be, one of the great pleasures of medicine is the gratification that comes from making a correct diagnosis, especially when no one else has made it. Each patient can be a challenge, a ninety mile-an-hour cliché curve ball. To make the correct diagnosis is to hit the cliché out of the park.

One such homerun diagnosis was Annie Pritchard, a sixty-three year old sent in from a small town in Oregon because her dermatologist wasn't able to diagnose her unusual skin *eruption*. In dermatology we refer to all 'rashes' as eruptions. Dr. Frank Parker, our chairman and admitting faculty member at the time, introduced me to Ms. Pritchard. My job was to take a history, examine her, write admitting orders and review all the old records she brought with her.

Ms. Pritchard gave a four month history of red, raw skin sores on her shins—we call them 'erosions'. She had lost fifteen pounds over six months, so we suspected a serious internal disease. She complained of a burning sensation on the skin. Creams had been of no help. She had recently started to get more erosions under her breasts and in the groin. Her tongue was red and painful. Open sores bled at the corners of her mouth and nose. This was definitely unusual. Neither I nor Dr. Parker had seen anything quite like it. A blistering disease possibly? A nutritional deficiency? We would need to investigate. I took a skin biopsy, drew some blood work and ordered urine tests. We started local therapies, whirlpool baths and compresses for comfort while we awaited test results. The biopsy slide wouldn't be out until Monday.

I came in alone on Saturday to make rounds. The lab tests showed anemia and early diabetes. I pondered how they could be related. After finishing seeing my patients, I returned to the clinic where I kept a file cabinet with selected articles from journals. For some reason, an article caught my eye, a case report of a rare disease called 'glucagonoma syndrome' (pronounced GLUE-ka-gone-O-ma). The syndrome was caused by a tumor in the pancreas and consisted of erosions of the skin, sore tongue, weight loss, and an early diabetes profile (sugar in the urine).

It struck me like a thunderbolt. The picture in the article looked exactly like Ms. Pritchard! The patient in the article fit her almost perfectly. I was thrilled. Annie Pritchard must have glucagonoma syndrome! The skin erosions, sore mouth, weight loss, anemia, sugar in her urine—they all fit.

Though somewhat risky for a first year resident, I went back to the hospital ward and wrote an addendum in the chart, proposing glucagonoma as the diagnosis and listing the typical features that fit. She still needed some confirmatory tests (like a glucagon level), and special imaging. Sunday morning, I arrived early for hospital rounds with Dr. Parker and excitedly shared with him my diagnostic theory.

My diagnosis turned out to be correct. Mrs. Pritchard had the highest glucagon level on record. On CT scan, a sizable tumor was discovered in her pancreas and she ultimately underwent surgical removal. The amazing thing was how rapidly her skin healed after the tumor was removed. Within forty-eight hours all the raw skin had healed over with only some slight redness remaining. Her tongue stopped hurting and returned to normal. In medicine, it is rare to achieve a better response to a treatment than what Ms. Pritchard experienced.

Dr. Larry Peterson, my co-resident and highly talented scientist who had worked in Dr. Wuepper's laboratory, took an interest in the case, and carried it one step further. His experiments showed that the high glucagon levels were likely the cause of her skin rashes. The skin healed as soon as the glucagon levels fell to normal after surgery.

I received considerable praise for having made that diagnosis, from colleagues in both dermatology and internal medicine. Dr. Frederick A.J. Kingery, close friend of my father, sent a letter to him acknowledging my diagnostic coup. I realize now that I didn't share with my father my own joy of making the diagnosis. Whether my not sharing came from innate modesty, or the sense I sometimes felt that, in our family, one didn't boast about one's accomplishments, I am not certain. I also don't know whether not sharing was hurtful to him or not. I wish I could go back and do it differently.

One other patient left a huge impression on me during those four months of hospital service. Two months into the rotation, at the end of a long day, I was called in to see Mr. Penny, a very sick man with a new skin eruption. He had acute leukemia and was being treated as aggressively as possible with chemotherapy, for the second time. The chemo had successfully knocked out all of his white blood cells so he had no protection against infections.

My senior resident, Eric Rasmussen, and I went to see Mr. Penny together. We entered the isolation room to see a large-boned man who in better days might have been a lumberjack out of Coos Bay. Instead, his sunken eyes and yellowish skin reflected how dangerously close his illness and treatments had brought him to the brink. His shaking chills also told us he had 'sepsis' (overwhelming bacterial infection in the blood, known incorrectly sometimes as 'blood poisoning'). He had been spiking high fevers all day, with shaking chills and drenching sweats. What didn't fit was that he had been receiving all the appropriate antibiotics. We needed to search for other causes.

The skin findings were subtle. Scattered over his body were multiple small white papules (bumps), individually placed, each bump several inches away from the next. The white papules looked almost like pustules (bumps with pus in them). That couldn't happen, though, because his white blood cell count was zero. We were perplexed.

We took a biopsy using the standard circular cookie cutter shaped 'punch', but knew it would require forty-eight hours before we could review the slide. That was too long. He could be dead by then. We decided to do a scraping as well, to look for fungus. I scraped the top off of several bumps and smeared the whitish material onto two slides, one for a bacterial stain and the other for fungus. We walked across to the clinic, up to dermatology on the fifth floor and into the mini-laboratory where we performed all of our microscopic tests.

I prepared the Gram stain for bacteria and Dr. Rasmussen prepared a fungal prep, known as a KOH (pronounced K-O-H). "Oh my god, there is something here," I said immediately. Within seconds we identified budding yeast, probably *Candida* fungus, on both slides. This was almost certainly Mr. Penny's diagnosis and explained why he was sick in spite of high doses of antibiotics. In less than fifteen minutes with a slide and a microscope, we were able to make a tentative diagnosis of fungal sepsis from *Candida*. Cultures of his blood needed to be done, of course, but we immediately called the oncology team to recommend treatment for disseminated *Candida* infection.

Mr. Penny survived the infection and recovered from his chemotherapy. Blood cultures confirmed our suspicion for *Candida*, but grew an unusual subspecies called *Candida Tropicalis*, a variant that had emerged recently in response to new antifungal drugs. Through natural selection, disease-causing organisms always find a way to survive in the face of new treatment threats.

The picture of Mr. Penny's skin taught me a great deal. It wasn't something I could look up in a text book. To be able to make the diagnosis in fifteen minutes by preparing microscopic tests was a powerful lesson. Also, it may have saved his life. During my career I have seen a total of five cases of disseminated *Candida*, usually associated with leukemia, and every case has looked exactly like Mr. Penny. It still is not in the textbooks, and, sadly, the act (and art) of scraping and looking under the microscope to make immediate diagnoses is being lost. It amazes me that doctors nowadays seem much less compelled than years ago to make a rapid diagnosis on a patient who is deathly ill.

▬ DERMATOLOGY GOES SURGICAL

ON FRIDAY AFTERNOONS the surgery suite in our clinic was reserved for cold steel surgery. Since we in dermatology had no surgically-minded faculty members at the time, we asked plastic surgeons to assist and teach us residents. One such plastic surgeon, Dr. Philip Andrews influenced many residents over the years. A tall, composed man one might expect to speak with an aristocratic English accent, Dr. Andrews had a busy plastic surgery practice in the community where he not only performed nose jobs and breast augmentations but also treated difficult skin cancers and pressure sores in nursing home patients. He came up to the hill every other week and supervised our surgeries. Always a gentleman with utmost patience he would walk us through good plastic surgical technique, taking the lead when necessary.

After each surgery, Dr. Andrews would lean against the counter, lit cigarette held comfortably in hand, and discuss the case, what went well, what could have been done better, surgical pearls from his experience. I ended up spending a month rotation with Dr. Andrews during my senior year, refining my plastic surgery techniques, skills that became highly useful in my practice over the years. Dr. Andrews epitomized the concept of giving back something to the medical community that gave him so much in his career.

Surgery in dermatology was very much in a growing phase during the early 1980s. For nearly two hundred years, the specialty of dermatology consisted mostly of making diagnoses and treating with creams, ointments and a few oral medications. Surgery was left to the surgeons, whether for diagnosis or treatment.

During the prior century we dermatologists had mastered small surgeries. Under local anesthesia, we removed lesions the size of a pea without the need for sutures. Light cautery to stop the bleeding and the wound healed with much less of a scar than if a plastic surgeon had cut it out and stitched it up. Small surgeries on eyelids, ears, noses and lips were our bailiwick. Even today, no one treats small lesions better than dermatologists.

Interest in surgery didn't start in earnest until the 1960s when skin cancer rates began to climb drastically. Dermatologists diagnosed skin cancers all the time; why shouldn't we be able to treat them? Other factors soon came into play, not the least of which was higher reimbursement for surgery. Insurance companies and health ministries paid much higher fees for surgical procedures than for cognitive expertise. They still do, sadly. Dermatologists rapidly entered the pool of surgeons who focused on the skin.

For cancers the size of a grape, an ellipse-shaped excision with suture closure produced best outcomes, but dermatologists had perfected 'curettage', a procedure using a circular blade called a curette to scoop away the softer cancer tissue of grape-sized lesions and leave the healthy dermis in tact. While efficient, this procedure left an unsightly divot for a scar, and in an environment where dermatologists competed with plastic surgeons for market share, a divot was bad for business, so many dermatologists, I included, switched from curettage to excision.

Larger lesions—the size of a lime or lemon—used to be referred to general surgeons or plastic surgeons. In the 1980s, dermatologists began performing these larger surgeries as well. Regional differences in reimbursement determined whether dermatologists performed more or less surgery. If there were too many dermatologists and surgeons in the same town, competition for surgeries could get fierce, and Portland, Oregon in the 80s was vicious that way.

Two major forces continued to push dermatology in the direction of surgery. One was Mohs surgery, a skin cancer technique named after Dr. Frederic Mohs, a general surgeon from Madison, Wisconsin. He developed the concept of microscopically testing margins for residual cancer *at the time of the procedure.* Mohs surgery mapped out exactly where residual skin cancer remained. This new technique increased cure rates of skin cancer to an astonishing ninety-six to ninety-nine per cent, while preserving as much normal skin as possible.

In the early 1980s, Mohs surgery for skin cancers was becoming the standard of care around the country. During my residency we did not have a full-time dermatological surgeon on faculty, but in a few short years, Neil Swanson, a world leader in Mohs surgery, was recruited from Michigan and eventually became chairman of the department. By the mid 1990s, most dermatology programs in North America were training their residents in surgical techniques to some degree.

The other advance that pushed dermatology in surgical directions was LASER. Dermatologists had popularized the carbon dioxide (CO_2) laser which shot a powerful beam of light, vaporizing anything in its way that contained water. It could take your eye out if you accidentally got in the way of even a reflected beam from a shiny object or mirror in the room. Since the skin was mostly water, CO_2 lasers could destroy many skin lesions. Warts were the most amenable to this new modality, but refinements quickly led to a resurfacing CO_2 laser that had an interesting end result: when the skin healed, the wrinkles were gone! You can imagine the gold rush that ensued after that discovery. An entire industry sprang up around resurfacing techniques, both laser-based and other methods.

Throughout the 1990s, laser technology advanced by leaps and bounds. New lasers were designed to treat blood vessels, tattoos, destroy hair follicles to create smooth hairless skin, and tighten collagen fibers for younger looking skin contours. Dermatologists led the way in many of these modalities. The frenzy, however, involved all kinds of doctors. There was big money to be made.

Within two decades, basic knowledge of lasers had become part of the certification examination in dermatology. More and more, newly trained dermatologists adopted lasers as their main area of expertise. Doctors charged high fees and made enormous incomes. I have watched the use of lasers expand during my career to a point where the very specialty of 'medical' dermatology is on the verge of extinction. Fewer dermatologists maintain their expertise in diagnostic and medical treatment skills and instead are opting for cosmetic practices, taking care of non-disease, so called 'beauty care dermatology'. Other specialties are being forced to pick up the slack by learning more dermatology skills. Increasingly, patients with complicated diseases are going undiagnosed and untreated.

My own goals in surgery were pragmatic, to be competent enough to provide the service to my patients, to be proficient with small skin cancers and most non-cancerous growths. I didn't want to have to refer patients to surgeons for every little procedure. I ultimately became quite comfortable with surgeries: the instruments, the muscle memory for cutting and suturing, handling tissue with care. Playing the piano may have helped. I enjoyed the dexterity. I knew, however, that surgery would never fulfill me in the way that it did surgeons. Deep down, my interests never strayed far from the internal medicine arena.

Four months of hospital dermatology came to an end. Wendy was into her third trimester with the due date of our first child rapidly approaching in May. I remained on Dilantin to deal with my head symptoms. I continued to be plagued by them daily, but annoying as they were, they settled into a more predictable pattern that I gradually learned to tolerate. One gets used to most anything.

We were looking to buy a house. I didn't particularly want to keel over dead from a brain tumor or aneurysm right after assuming a large house mortgage. It was not likely, but I thought I should be certain. My neurologist didn't suspect serious illness either, but understood my concern and ordered a CT scan of my head. (MRIs wouldn't be invented for another five or six years). Much to my relief, there was no tumor, no aneurysm. We could proceed with buying a house.

The neurologist reviewed my symptoms again: No headache pain, no visual disturbances, no weakness; symptoms worsened after eating and were possibly better after fasting. No improvement on weekends or with avoidance of alcohol or coffee. I had a history of seeing 'stars' at age ten after getting hit hard in the head with a rock the size of a lime. Probably no connection there, he said.

In passing, I mentioned that the symptoms were worse when I turned my head to look behind me.

"Say that again," said the neurologist.

"The symptoms seem worse when I turn my head."

"That's interesting. I think I'll have you see our neuro-otologist. There may be something going on with your inner ear. We have a new expert in that area, Dr. Owen Black."

I had heard of Dr. Black but had never met him. He had just been recruited to start a research center at Good Samaritan Hospital. Dr. Black collaborated and advised NASA researchers on vestibular (inner ear) function related to weightlessness. Few in the world knew as much about the functions of the inner ear as Dr. Black, and he now lived in Portland. I looked forward to my appointment. Maybe he would be able to figure it out. In the meantime, I began my third rotation of the year: University outpatient clinics.

■ UNIVERSITY CLINICS

DOWN THE BACK corridor from the conference room were our eight examination rooms. The corner room housed the little laboratory where I had made the microscopic diagnosis of *Candida* in the leukemia patient. The most important room was an all-purpose work room nestled in the center between the corridors. This room was like Grand Central Station for the whole clinical operation. We used it to store and wash instruments and equipment, review textbooks and drug manuals, discuss patients without them hearing, schmooze, converse, and flirt, a practice that had not yet become extinct in the workplace as it is today. In that room, medical students presented patient histories to junior residents, juniors did the same to seniors, and seniors to attendings who taught, and elder statesmen who waxed nostalgically about how it was in their day.

Grand Central took on special meaning for me over the three years of residency. Knowledge flowed in and out of that room much like trains at a terminal, some early in the morning, some late, some relaxed, some in a hurry, some elementary, some expert. There had been a rich history behind the evolution of that room. Luminaries in dermatology had stood in that very room and taught over the years.

University clinics functioned at a pace all their own. At the VA, we had done much by ourselves, including escorting patients out of the over-crowded waiting room into examination rooms. We were always behind schedule there. The tempo on the University side was more, shall I say, English. The only elements missing were British accents and ten o'clock tea. University clinics were more organized certainly, than the VA, but in essence, simply slower. We would ruminate over the patient who might have an exotic or rare disease that required lengthy visits with repeated examinations, tests, demonstrations to students, presentations to more and more senior doctors. I recall patients who were there from nine o'clock until noon. Nurses helped with everything if we requested. All of that was a luxury of learning, uncommon to many programs. We were there to think, learn, teach, and conduct research. Patients were supposed to be the beneficiaries, and most certainly did benefit, but so did we residents. Some patients had no tolerance for the slow academic pace and went elsewhere, to private practices off the hill where expediency was king.

■ CHRISTOPHER COLUMBUS'S GIFT

DERMATOLOGY HAS ITS odors. The skin itself has scents, some wonderful such as the sour sweet smell of a breast-fed baby, some disgusting such as the ammonia pungency of urinary incontinence in a nursing home patient in need of a bath, or the putrid smell of infected sores. But there are the chemicals we use as well. Just a whiff of rubbing alcohol strikes fear into the hearts of children because of its association with doctors' offices. Some odors are more specific to dermatology. The smell of cauterized flesh during surgeries becomes commonplace. Some, such as the tar used in ointments and shampoos for psoriasis, we learn to enjoy (at least I did). Some chemicals I never got used to. Formaldehyde, for example. Every biopsy specimen got placed into a small bottle containing formaldehyde. If a specimen bottle spilled, as they did occasionally, the whole room smelled of formaldehyde. It assaulted the olfactory nerve endings high up in my nose. Chemicals in treatments have their smells too: sulfur, trichloracetic acid, thymol and phenol. The worst was DMSO (dimethylsulfoxide), used in some topical formulations at the time. The odor was nauseatingly sweet and rotten, a unique cross between formaldehyde, garlic and almond extract, with sulfur thrown on top. Fortunately I haven't had to smell DMSO in years.

The microscope room contained bottles of brightly colored reagents that lined the shelves, and a subtle but distinct odor of the mix always permeated the air. Hints of almond, sulfur, iodine and tar swirled in low concentrations like the complex aromas of an old wine cellar.

We stood in line to use the ancient microscope. A skilled microscopist with the right equipment could, in a matter of minutes, confirm the presence of fungus, viral diseases of the skin, bacterial infections, infestations, mites, lice, or worms.

For years, the most famous disease diagnosed under a microscope was syphilis. The cause of this disease that Christopher Columbus brought home from the new world in 1493, and which wreaked havoc across Europe for more than four hundred years, was readily visible under the microscope in a test called the dark field test.

By the time I entered residency, the dark field test for syphilis was nearly passé. It had been replaced by blood tests. But my father's generation had used dark field microscopy extensively to diagnose syphilis. One dark field microscope still operated downtown at the Sexually Transmitted Disease clinic. Mostly, however, the dark field for syphilis had been relegated to the history books. In my entire career, I observed only one positive dark field examination under the microscope, but I remember it well: a tiny corkscrew, alive, shimmering fluorescent against the blackness.

We all had the opportunity to become highly skilled in standard tests using the microscope. Ours was the oldest, ricketiest instrument imaginable. It might as well have come from Leuwenhoek in eighteenth century Europe. There was no internal light source, only a mirror to reflect light from, say, a candle, if needed. We used an electric bulb. The microscope was monocular:

only one eye piece. As scientists had done for more than a century, we became proficient at looking through the microscope with one eye, the other eye open but mentally out of service while our brains focused on the other eye.

I took to microscopes like a poet to metaphors. Not every one did. Dr. Storrs, however, was famous for exclaiming Eureka! or Whoopee! every time she found a scabies mite, that evil-looking eight-legged creature that causes the age-old infestation called scabies. She encouraged the rest of us to do the same, and some actually did. I was too self-conscious to scream, but have consistently thrilled at the excitement of a positive slide my whole career, whether it be a mite, fungus, or bacterium.

Using the microscope was not entirely without risk. One time at the VA, one of my co-residents, early on in her rotation there, was making a KOH prep for fungus. The source of flame was an alcohol burner with a wick. When she went to light the wick with a match, the whole burner ignited with that ominous, deep poof sound we love and fear, and she singed off a portion of her eyebrows and eyelashes. Some alcohol must have spilled. She fortunately blinked and averted damaging her eyes and skin, though her pride might have been singed a little.

■ IT'S TRUE: EVERYTHING CHANGES

MY FIRST YEAR was coming to a close. Wendy and I had moved into an old house on Summit Avenue in Northwest Portland, and on Friday the thirteenth of May, Wendy delivered a healthy baby girl. After providing what assistance a father can provide at a delivery, with all parties resting comfortably, I left Wendy and baby Lauren at the hospital to attend the black tie Lobitz Lectureship Dinner at the Waverly Country Club. Dr. Lobitz, now emeritus, had been awarded an annual lectureship funded by members of the Oregon Dermatological Society. As I entered the reception hall as a new proud father, I was greeted by my father's best friend and eminent Portland dermatologist Dr. Frederick A.J. Kingery who said, "Nothing like a little responsibility to keep you out of trouble."

My parents came down from Tacoma to attend the dinner as well. The following morning, they came to the hospital to meet their new granddaughter. My father dressed for the occasion in an olive poplin suit and bow tie, my mother in a bright red blazer and crisp white cotton blouse. For them, it was the respectful thing to do.

Later that morning, I gazed down at the expression of my newborn daughter in the bassinette, her eyes closed, that adorable face with its pouting downturn of the lower lip, and a feeling of sadness crept into my otherwise joyous moment. I thought, "Is this fair, what we've done, bringing this fragile little thing into the world, mostly for our own fulfillment? What if something happens to her? She didn't ask to be here." Throughout Lauren's infancy and childhood, it hurt me more than I expected when I held her helplessly through five days of pneumonia, when she suffered schoolyard rejections that every child gets, when she was overlooked by teachers and peers, and when in high school in Chicago, a careless brute on a mountain bike collided with her, snapping both bones of her lower leg in a clean tib-fib fracture. With her ankle and foot grotesquely askew as if they didn't belong to her leg, Lauren wore the same facial expression I had seen on that day in the hospital.

Having a newborn daughter had a surprising effect on my being a doctor. Six years earlier, I had done my mandatory three months of pediatrics during medical school. It was the rotation where every medical student gets sick two or three times with the local viruses that bathed us every day on the wards. Crying was normal for sick infants and we did our best to make them comfortable. Worried parents needed our support too. I had accepted that. It was part of life. Shortly after Lauren was born, as I walked past the pediatrics ward, an infant rolled by, pushed by the nurse, the distraught parents not far behind. The baby was crying in pain, resigned to life's inexplicable unfairness, while the parents looked helpless. Hearing the infant cry, I nearly dissolved in sympathy for the child and the parents. I felt the pain the parents clearly were feeling for their little girl. The experience was totally different now that I was a father. I would never again be able to detach emotionally from the miseries of a sick infant or child. I would of course need to maintain enough professional detachment to treat patients, but from that point on, I always felt a twinge of tragedy in dealing with sick kids.

CHAPTER 4

Getting Up To Speed

UNDER THE MICROSCOPE

SECOND YEAR KICKED off with four months of concentrated dermatopathology with Clif White. Dermatology residents everywhere love their derm-path rotations. It always comes as a welcome break from seeing patients. Biopsy specimens don't bleed; they don't suffer or complain or need refills of their drugs. Glass slides are never in a hurry.

For four months, I prepared all of the biopsies for processing and read every slide. Every day I gathered up all the specimens that accumulated in Grand Central by the end of a morning clinic, and took them over to the main hospital pathology department for processing. The first step was to 'gross-in' the specimens. Grossing-in was basically extracting specimens from the jars they came in, and cutting representative pieces into postage stamp-sized cassettes. 'Gross' referred to 'large', i.e. visible to the naked eye, in contradistinction to 'microscopic'. Grossing-in was the first step for all tissues, including autopsies. The joke at the time among pathologists, was, "You can gross me out, just don't gross me in!"

Once the specimens were grossed-in, they went to the automatic overnight paraffin imbedding machine. The following morning, the histology technicians used the 'microtome' to cut ultra thin sections from each paraffin block, carefully placed them on glass slides, and stained the slides with various stains. The final product was the thin slice of stained tissue sandwiched between a glass slide and its glued-on glass cover-slip. In the 1980's only the overnight process was automated. The skill of the histo techs could make all the difference between poor and high quality slides.

At around noon, a courier delivered cardboard trays full of pristine new slides, still emitting the intoxicating smell of liquid acrylic that sealed the thin glass cover-slips. It was a present, like Christmas every day. Usually three or four trays of twenty slides each, sometimes more, and I got to study them first, before the 'signing-out' session with Clif White.

Sign-out with Dr. White was a great intellectual exercise. We usually had a full house: one student or resident at each microscope head. Clif looked at the slide 'blind', i.e. without knowing the clinical history. That approach guaranteed an unbiased first glimpse; it preserved academic integrity. We would always go back and read the medical history to corroborate our thinking, but I always respected his academically rigorous approach. Not everyone did it that way. Nearly every general pathologist I worked with read the history first and tried to shoehorn what they saw under the microscope into the suspected diagnosis on the requisition. The end result might be the same, but the process lacked rigor. It seemed almost glib, more technical, to get the job done, than academic, to learn, to grow.

■ BRAIN WORKUP

IT WAS IN the middle of my derm-path rotation that I had my medical appointment with Dr. Owen Black, the neuro-otologist who was going to diagnose and fix my head symptoms. I spent the entire morning at his center. After hearing tests by the audiologist, I underwent a series of tortures designed to test my vestibular system. First was a swivel chair that jerked back and forth while I counted backward from one hundred by sevens with my eyes blindfolded and electrodes glued to my head. Then came hot water injections into my eardrums that caused the room to spin. The last was the standing tilt table that lurched forward suddenly, or backward or laterally, also with eyes closed. I failed that one. They had to catch me from falling on several occasions.

When we were all finished, I sat in an examination room and waited to meet Dr. Black. He eventually came in with his entourage. A respectful man in his forties, congenial without being jovial, thankfully. I abhorred doctors or nurses being jovial. He went over my findings. He said that my diagnosis was something he called 'vestibular hydrops', whatever that was. My inner ear was likely malfunctioning in a way similar to Meniere's disease, whatever that was. Actually, I had read about Meniere's in medical school. My disease definitely was not classic Meniere's because I didn't get vertigo, only the brain fullness and sideways feeling. Dr. Black basically said that he had pioneered a surgical procedure for vestibular hydrops, but if I could tolerate it and control the symptoms through lifestyle and medications, I should continue without surgery.

My appointment with Dr. Black was the closest I ever came to knowing what was happening in my head to cause the symptoms. It was now clear that I would be living with this for the rest of my life. If it turned out to be related to Meniere's disease, the odds were good that the symptoms would get worse over time. Odds were also good that I would go deaf later in my life if it was Meniere's. I didn't like the sound of either prognosis. All I could do was to carry on.

So I left Dr. Black's office resolved to enduring the symptoms. They were an aggravation and a nuisance, but I had no choice. As a doctor, I was fully aware that things could have been so much worse in so many ways. I would cope as best I could. So, *back to work*.

■ DR. STORRS

I SPENT TUESDAY and Thursday afternoons during second year with Frances Storrs, who, despite the twisted memory of my interview with her, was one of the best teachers in the department and a larger than life character, full of ideas, opinion, feminism and energy. Dr. Storrs was one of an elite group of international experts in allergic contact dermatitis, the subspecialty of dermatology that dealt with allergic reactions to chemicals in the environment. Her patients were often extremely difficult to sort out.

An enormous number of chemicals, in the thousands, can cause allergic reactions on the skin. The science is complex, but in essence, an intensely itchy rash develops after an individual becomes allergic to something in the environment that the skin touches—metals, dyes, or a plant, for example. The immune reaction leads to redness, swelling, oozing and excruciating itch where the chemical comes in contact with the skin. Anyone who has had poison ivy or poison oak knows just how awful it can be.

Dr. Storrs taught us that becoming allergic to a chemical sometimes required only one exposure (like with poison ivy), and sometimes more than one hundred exposures. She knew all the chemical names, and pronounced them impeccably every time. She could dazzle audiences during lectures with the way these multisyllabic chemicals rolled off her tongue as a hint of smile came across her face. Some were real tongue twisters, like glyceryl-monothioglycolate; imidazolidinyl urea; methyl-chloro-isothiazolinone; propyl-paraphenylenediamine, to name a few. It was a veritable word orgy in her clinic. Chemical terms were tossed around nonchalantly and if we didn't get the pronunciations correct we were in the dog house until we did. Dr. Storrs was a walking glossary.

Contact dermatitis patients were tested on Tuesdays and came back on Thursday to be 'read'. Up to seventy-five or eighty little patches got plastered onto the back of each patient. Patients had to keep them dry for forty-eight hours. If a patient was allergic to one of the chemicals, we usually knew it by Thursday because the patch created a red swollen area on the skin under the patch. There might be one allergic reaction, or many. Through detective work that occasionally included visits to patient's homes and workplaces, we determined whether a positive reaction might be directly related to the patient's skin rash, or merely coincidental and irrelevant.

Dr. Storrs frequently asked patients to bring in every bottle and tube of cosmetic cream from home, or every chemical from the work place, for us to sort out what might be causing their problem.

Some patients were easier to help than others after an allergy was identified. Let's say a patient is allergic to a chemical in body lotions. She could simply avoid that particular chemical by reading labels on products and do just fine. A hair dresser allergic to a hair dye could wear gloves when working with the dye; a lab tech allergic to a certain chemical could learn to avoid it. Many patients, however, were forced to change jobs entirely. It could be devastating for some patients. A machinist allergic to cutting oils might have to get retrained or, in the worst cases, receive disability insurance payments and remain unemployed. It always made me cringe a little though, when I heard of surgeons who had huge disability insurance policies that paid out hundreds of thousands of dollars yearly when they became allergic to a chemical in surgeon's gloves.

Dr. Storrs pioneered much of the field of allergic contact dermatitis. She was also one of the first woman leaders in dermatology. She mentored dermatologists who went on to pursue careers in allergic contact dermatitis. As a master in her field, and an organizer, she inspired many. In her somewhat imperious way, she intimidated some as well. While I occasionally felt judged by her, I fully appreciated what she gave to me in her role as educator.

She led the way for women in leadership. Where good old boys liked having things their way, she challenged them and held her stance with views that often led to positive change. Effective women in leadership ruffle feathers, and Dr. Storrs was no exception. But just as men and women found inspiration in her teaching and leadership, they repeatedly looked to her as a role model. Frances Storrs will go down in the history of dermatology as one of the great teachers and mentors of the specialty.

THE FUTURE

AS SECOND YEAR wound down, I started to think about what to do after residency. Residents start to get nervous about their futures around that time. I knew my limits. I knew I was not a research dermatologist. I did enjoy teaching though, and hoped to incorporate teaching into my career once I finished.

The first step was to determine where to set up practice. It would definitely be Portland. Wendy was becoming a successful academician, and that plus the joint custody arrangement with our daughter kept us from considering a move to another town. But if one must be stuck in a city, Portland was not a bad choice.

The first offer I received came from the most established and respected practice in Portland, that of Dr. Frederick A.J. Kingery and his partners Paul Russell and Walter Larsen. Dr. Larsen took me aside after a Wednesday morning conference and presented the proposal to join their group.

At first I thought it could be a superb arrangement. All three were highly respected and had contributed considerably to dermatology education at Oregon. Dr. Kingery was the son of one of the founding members of the Oregon Dermatological Society. He had been active on the American Board of Dermatology and was past president of the American Academy of Dermatology. He was as well connected as anyone in the specialty could be. The group practiced out of an office in Northwest Portland, near where I lived and near Good Samaritan Hospital where I had a referral base of doctors. Joining them could be perfect for me.

There was one problem. Dr. Kingery and my father had been close friends since their residencies at the University of Michigan thirty years earlier. Our families went on vacations together. Dr. Kingery had brought my father into the smoke-filled back rooms of dermatology politics. The question swirled in my head that maybe Ted Kingery (as he was called by those who knew him) felt obligated to invite me to join his group. When I shared with my father the news of their invitation, he expressed genuine but lukewarm praise. In his half-joking pig-Latin response, he said "Just don't get ewed-scray."

My father knew I wouldn't be moving back to Tacoma to join him in his practice. The option was open, and I had given it thought. But Tacoma? That blue-collar, Army Air Force, pulp and paper town most famous for Frisco Freeze hamburgers, Ted Bundy, and a toxic industrial stench along the Interstate-5 corridor? I probably had had enough of the Tacoma Aroma for a while. There was too much history. I knew too many people in Tacoma. I preferred the anonymity of Portland.

I began discussions with the Kingery, Russell, Larsen group, to join them a year later. My daughter Lauren had just turned one year old and Wendy, we discovered, was pregnant again. Our eldest, pushing five, was not enjoying the back and forth of joint custody. Nor was I. Neither of her parents was willing to go for full custody because they were afraid of losing her altogether. Judges, in a sign of the times, had started to treat mothers and fathers as equally qualified parents. She had become a pawn in their post-divorce battles, and the tension was bringing us all down. The good news was that on Dilantin, my head symptoms were becoming a bit more tolerable. Life seemed to be rolling along.

■ THE CHAIRMAN

THE LEARNING CURVE flattens out somewhat once we get into third year of residency. We become more confident in diagnosis and treating skin problems. Dr. Frank Parker, as chairman, reserved the privilege of working exclusively with senior residents in his private afternoon clinics. More work got done that way, and teaching took place at the highest level. Dr. Parker, who was the only faculty member shorter than me, was known for his fleetness of foot as he dashed from room to room, patient to patient, in a blur, seeing thirty or thirty-five patients in an afternoon. He could write a coherent, accurate note in the chart at the same time as he spoke to the patient. Though occasionally criticized by other faculty for his lightning pace, he had a depth of understanding of medical dermatology much greater than any of the other faculty. He had trained in internal medicine and endocrinology, and practiced both before entering dermatology training. As a dermatologist at the University of Washington, he continued his internist role by attending on the internal medicine hospital wards! As I understood it, part of his candidacy for coming to Oregon from Seattle was based on his interest in building an electron microscopy program in dermatology. That, unfortunately, never happened. Dr. Parker took on more and more patients. He became the top referral dermatologist in the region for patients who were difficult to diagnose or to treat. He was the only dermatologist in the region comfortable with serious internal drug treatments for skin disease. The entire state of Oregon relied on his expertise.

I worked in Dr. Parker's clinic for four months. One afternoon, he and I went into a patient's examination room together to see a woman probably in her forties, well groomed, healthy and intelligent. I had already taken the history. She had a lesion on one breast to be checked. As we entered, even before we had closed the door, she whipped off her sweater over her head to expose the entirety of both of her breasts. Dr. Parker, always highly professional, was taken aback and quipped, "Geez, I don't get that at home!" In the strictest of terms, a comment like that might have gotten someone in trouble. But given the patient's brazen comfort with the act of lifting her sweater off, her obvious understanding of the facetiousness of Dr. Parker's comment, and our immediate return to clinical seriousness, we all let it ride.

Dr. Parker's working with difficult patients was the part I enjoyed most. Perhaps it was the connection with internal medicine. For the remainder of my career, the patients I found most interesting and most gratifying were those with severe disease or who were difficult in some respect—diagnosis, treatment, or personality. In that regard, it was Frank Parker who had influenced me most. Dr. Parker continued to be supportive of my career for many years, though I never got up to his speed in seeing patients.

■ HIGHLIGHT OF THE WEEK

WEDNESDAY MORNING CONFERENCES continued to be the highlight of the week for me during my third year, as they had during the two prior years. Being senior resident meant that I was often the default resident whom the moderator would call upon after the more junior residents crashed and burned in their attempts at the diagnosis. The junior residents would occasionally self destruct en mass because they hadn't done their own thinking but had formed a diagnosis by committee in the library minutes before the conference. I had always preferred risking a diagnosis alone. One time, I correctly made a rare diagnosis in a patient and received the most disappointing response from my professors. The patient, a pre-teenage girl, had distinct patches of red, thickened skin on her legs that had been present for years. After much thought, I came up with what I thought was the diagnosis (erythrokeratoderma variabilis) and was the only one in the conference room, including the faculty members, to suggest it. When the biopsy report and other tests revealed that my diagnosis was correct, there was no response whatsoever, not then or later. It was strange. I think they must have thought that I had cheated; that no one could possibly have known the diagnosis; that I must have seen the results beforehand and was misrepresenting that I had come up with the answer honestly.

Similar disappointing responses by my colleagues occurred over the years. During one Wednesday rounds, I pointed out a minute feature of a patient's skin lesions that I thought predicted a specific disease entity called Grover's disease (I had compared multiple clinical pictures of Grover's with the biopsy results on prior patients). After the pathology confirmed my prediction, a visiting professor responded, incredulous, with, "Well, I don't know how anyone can predict that pathological finding…etc." He could have asked and I would have explained. Instead, he implied that it couldn't be done, so something must have been amiss. The rigid, inward thinking of my colleagues sometimes was astonishing.

Another time after I had finished residency, during a monthly conference, I brought a patient who had presented with something I had never seen or heard of before: painful joints where the collar bone meets the chest bone (sterno-clavicular joints) which were followed in days by a breakout of pustules on his palms and a worsening of acne on his chest and back. This happened several times per year and lasted a month or two. The entire dermatology community dismissed the unique collar bone symptoms and thought it was just a variant of psoriasis which can also cause pustules on the palms. I was shot down. Interestingly, though, within a year, a group of French researchers published an article describing, for the first time, a new disease identical to the patient I had presented. They named it 'synovitis-acne-pustulosishyperostosis-osteitis [SAPHO] syndrome'. My colleagues had no interest in exploring possibilities of something beyond the familiar.

▰ WHAT WE HAVE HERE IS A FAILURE TO COMMUNICATE

WHILE I ACTIVELY considered the offer from the Portland Dermatology Clinic, a strange turn of events broke off the discussions. I received a call one day from Dr. Parker, asking if I would be willing to help out with a dermatologist's practice in the community. The doctor in question had become sick and was unable to work, but his patients were booked for weeks. His office manager had called Dr. Parker to ask for help. What made this tricky was that just a few months earlier, the dermatology departmental faculty had imposed restrictions on resident moonlighting. But here was the chairman of the department coming to me for help. I let him convince me that he and I would be helping a fallen comrade and that this was an unusual situation and no one needed to know about it, etc., etc. I agreed to spend a few days in the doctor's office over the course of two weeks. Everything went smoothly. I never considered the possibility that the doctors at the Portland Dermatology Clinic might view this as some sort of breach of loyalty, or an example of underhandedness. To my surprise, it was precisely the way they viewed it.

The youngest of the group, Walter Larsen, called me to launch the complaint. In so many words, in their minds, I had done this without their collective blessing. They viewed it as an example of untrustworthiness on my part. He had heard about my being there from a drug representative (those drug reps—gossips one and all!) who made rounds on all the dermatologists in the city.

The fact that Dr. Parker had made the request mattered little. He was not in their political camp anyway. As I write about this now, I can definitely see their point, but there was more diagnostic information that they overlooked. They never had an honest discussion with me to explore how it came about and how they felt about it. Instead, the middle partner, Dr. Russell went whining up the hill to Dr. Storrs—she *was* in their political camp—about how my lack of forthrightness was jeopardizing my chances of joining their practice, and on and on. Dr.

Storrs immediately took their position before discussing it with me. In this case, she made the wrong diagnosis. I had never even considered Portland Dermatology when I agreed to do it. Any surreptitiousness on my part came out of the recently imposed moonlighting ban that I had defied. Nevertheless, for the rest of my career, it felt to me as though I had lost the trust and respect I thought I once had from Drs. Storrs, Kingery, Larsen, and Russell.

On December 13th of my third year, Wendy gave birth to a robust baby girl. We named her Toby, after Wendy's mother, thus going against the Ashkenazy Jewish tradition of naming babies after deceased relatives only. I rapidly learned that her birthday was the same as former chair of the department, Dr. Walter Lobitz, as well as another famous dermatologist from Boston, Dr. Walter Lever. It was looking as if dermatology could make it into a fourth generation of Shaws. Time would tell. We should have named her Walter. A new child meant that life stresses jumped up a notch at home. It definitely was not the time to quit smoking.

DR. A. BERNARD ACKERMAN

MY TWO WEEKS with Bernie Ackerman in New York during third year were among the most interesting and memorable of my entire residency. Clif White had helped me secure the two week elective at New York University.

Dr. Ackerman was, without doubt, the world leader in microscopic diagnosis of skin disease. He had written several of the definitive textbooks on pathologic diagnosis of melanoma as well as the massive group of diseases known as inflammatory diseases of the skin. He had founded the American Journal of Dermatopathology. His editorials reached far and wide in dermatology literature. Though not a research scientist per se, his brilliance and thoughtful approach brought to American dermatology some of the clearest and most innovative thinking in its history. Dr. Ackerman's office, two blocks north of Bellevue Hospital, was the Mecca of world dermatopathology for about twenty-five years. People came from all over the world to study with Bernie.

The day began at six-thirty in the morning, sharp. That meant that everyone needed to be in place well before six-thirty. There was no such thing as straggling in late, having missed a bus or some other lame excuse. I don't recall anyone being late, including Dr. Ackerman, during the entire time I was there. I stayed with a friend in Brooklyn Heights and had arranged a car service to pick me up every day at five-thirty so I would be 'in place' with time to spare.

'In place' turned out to be an interesting concept. The whole morning was spent around a thirteen-headed microscope, a monster of a microscope at the time. Dr. Ackerman sat at the throne, the main microscope, a three foot high tower of precision optics. To his left sat the 'pitcher' and to his right sat the 'catcher', each a fellow or resident studying with him. The pitcher would take a specially selected slide from the collection to be reviewed, and place it onto the stage of the microscope at which point Dr. Ackerman would take over the discussion. When he was finished, the catcher snatched the slide away to make room for the next one. The pitcher and catcher each had their own separate binocular heads to view the slides. The rest of us, twenty in number, sat cheek to cheek, two per head, one eye-piece per person. The room got very warm by the end of the morning.

Dr. Ackerman would start with low power and examine the architecture of the biopsy 'from fifty thousand feet' before going to a higher power. We might spend ten minutes at low power before taking a closer look. Only after arriving at a microscopic diagnosis did he read the suspected clinical diagnosis on the request, which was often correct but many times incorrect. Of course, we only discussed the difficult ones. The easy diagnoses were signed out privately.

When I mentioned to Dr. Ackerman my interest in considering dermatopathology as a part-time career choice, he said, "I spend every moment of every day on dermatopathology and I still don't have it down. I don't think you could give dermatopathology its due with a part-time commitment." I took his comment to heart and redirected my thinking toward clinical dermatology exclusively. Periodically during my career, however, I regretted not having sought further training in derm-path simply because I enjoyed it so much.

TASTE OF REALITY

THIRD YEAR CONCLUDED with four months on the hospital consultation service. I covered all consults in the University Hospital wards: medical, surgical, pediatric, obstetrical, and psychiatric. Inpatient consults were often the most interesting patients I ever saw.

One consultation nudged me further down the dark path of disillusionment and cynicism toward my colleagues and doctors in general. There had been reasons to become cynical earlier, like the sadistic surgeons I had worked with during medical school, irresponsible residents I encountered during internship, the misunderstanding with Portland Dermatology. But this particular case demonstrated to me a degree of glibness and arrogance that I had not before experienced in medicine.

Pediatricians had the reputation for thinking they knew all the dermatology they needed to know. It was as if they didn't want to let go of patients, the way a bratty child doesn't share his toys. So when the call came in, I wasn't surprised.

"Hi, we have a six-year-old-boy with disseminated varicella (widespread chickenpox). We don't want your help with a formal consult. I just thought the derm residents might want to see the patient. It is quite impressive."

I thanked him and said we would take a look. Since I had no pressing business at the moment, I immediately went to see the boy. In the chart, the intern, resident, and attending had each concluded that the patient's diagnosis was disseminated varicella. No other diagnoses were considered. In addition, the infectious disease team had already consulted on the case and concurred. "This is indeed disseminated varicella," the consultant had written. It sounded fairly convincing. No confirmatory tests had been done, but treatment with the antiviral drug acyclovir had been started and the team was resting on its laurels.

I entered the room to examine the patient. Lying on the bed, completely sedated to the point of unconsciousness was a child with a swollen face and distorted, large lips, eyelids, and genitals. Scattered over most of his body were large blisters separating from the skin, some of them two or three centimeters in size. On multiple areas the top layer had peeled off leaving red, raw skin underneath. Some were bandaged with gauze.

This didn't look *at all* like disseminated varicella. Varicella blisters were uniformly small, the size of a pea, and they almost never peeled off in layers leaving raw skin.

The patient definitely needed a dermatology consultation. I had concerns that this was a variant of the condition known as Stevens-Johnson Syndrome which, at its worst, could be fatal. At the time, patients with Stevens-Johnson Syndrome were often managed in burn units the way patients with severe burns were treated. I didn't have authority to change the direction of treatment by myself; I would need to bring in bigger artillery. I asked Dr. Storrs and Dr. Hanifin to look at the patient. They, of course, agreed with my assessment, and diplomatically spoke with the pediatrics team. I then proceeded quickly with two biopsies to confirm the diagnosis, and preliminary discussions about the possibility of a transfer to a burn unit.

The biopsy confirmed the diagnosis of the Stevens-Johnson Syndrome variant, a severe immune reaction to an infection or drug usually. It was *not* varicella. Fortunately the boy stabilized and we didn't have to transfer him to a burn unit. We stopped the antiviral drug and treated him with local wound care until he improved enough to eventually go home. We never identified the infection or drug that triggered his disease.

The pediatrics and infectious disease teams never showed interest in discussing the diagnosis, nor any gratitude for us having corrected their erroneous thinking about the diagnosis. Who was arrogant here? Was I arrogant to think that they should have expressed interest and gratitude? Have I ever made an incorrect diagnosis? Of course I have. It was their glibness that I found distasteful, if not unprofessional. They hadn't even performed the essential tests necessary to prove their working diagnosis. They hadn't considered alternative diagnoses. I would have at least expected the team to be interested in learning how to distinguish between Varicella and Stevens-Johnson Syndrome. As pediatricians, they might be seeing both diseases more frequently than I would over the years so they should at least know how to differentiate the two. It didn't seem to bother them that their cowboy approach had backfired. They had been certain they were right when they were absolutely wrong. Fortunately, in this particular case, the boy would likely have improved with or without a correct diagnosis, but no one could have known that. Nevertheless, my respect for doctors took another nosedive.

I was now two years into my head symptoms. The cause of the symptoms had been determined to be from an ill-defined inner ear problem called vestibular hydrops. In reality, no one really knew exactly what was wrong. And only a few of my closest family and friends knew I had the problem. The symptoms continued to gnaw at me, limiting my stamina significantly. But, other than feeling like hell through most of every day, and as Wendy frequently pointed out, being more irritable than I might have otherwise been, I managed to complete my residency. As I approached the age of thirty-four, it looked as if I might finally be ready to put my education to its proper use. It had already been a lifetime of education. I started planning the next phase of my life, one in which I would be the lord of my hours.

CHAPTER 5

The Real World

Later, everybody agreed that baths should have been closed sooner; they agreed health education should have been more direct and more timely. And everybody also agreed blood banks should have tested blood sooner, and that a search for the AIDS virus should have been started sooner, and that scientists should have laid aside their petty intrigues. Everybody subsequently agreed that the news media should have offered better coverage of the epidemic much earlier, and that the federal government should have done much, much more. By the time everyone agreed to all this, however, it was too late. Instead, people died. Tens of thousands of them.

–Randy Shilts, from And the Band Played On

SCHOOL'S OUT

I NEVER MET A resident in his or her last year who wasn't feeling a bit caged, in need of escape. Residency is not easy. To some degree, *the real world* dangles out of reach throughout medical school and residency, though less so in medical school because it's still light-years away. What exactly the attraction of *the real world* is, I am not wholly certain, residency being that protective environment where we get to do all the learning and someone else assumes all the responsibility and pays all the bills. It probably has to do with autonomy, or greater earning power. Wednesdays on the golf course, perhaps.

As I approached the end, I too was starting to choke on all my residency duties. I wanted out as a trainee, out from under the constant scrutiny of faculty. I was thinking, "I can handle this dermatologist thing all by myself."

Six months earlier, in the middle of third year, I had shared with my close friend and colleague Tony Montanaro the story of the Portland Dermatology Clinic debacle. Tony had recently finished his training at Oregon in rheumatology and allergy/immunology and had joined the undisputed patriarch of Allergy in Portland, Dr. John O'Holleran. Tony thought they could use a dermatologist and that I should be that person. He had made preliminary overtures for me to join them downtown at the Allergy Clinic.

The three of us met in the spring to discuss details. I could see that Dr. O'Holleran had implicit trust in Tony. No written contract was necessary, which was the way I liked to do business. We sealed the deal with a handshake. I would join the group in August of 1985, one month after completing residency.

At the end of the year, Dr. Parker usually put on a graduation 'roast' in which he tarred and feathered the outgoing residents to prepare them for what was to come. The ceremony usually took place over a luncheon at a local restaurant. That year, I presumptuously asked Dr. Parker if the party could be in the evening so we could drink alcohol, and also asked if I could be the M.C. instead of him. He agreed. This time, the faculty were going to get tarred and feathered.

By my assessment, biased as it might be, the evening was a grand success. The month before had been a difficult one for me from the standpoint of stamina and head symptoms, but I nevertheless had enjoyed altering photographs and finding new photos to lampoon the entire department, from the tenured top all the way down to the laboratory mice. After our bibulous dinner, I began the evening with a slide show and overarching Op-Ed on the last three years. I started out with a disclaimer of sorts by showing the cover of *Bad Mood Magazine* which displayed a photograph of an exceptionally irritable man. I hadn't been in the best frame of mind over the last year and I hoped that they would forgive me. I then took on the faculty members. I presented Frank Parker as a young intern wearing nothing but a stethoscope around his neck; Kirk Wuepper at age three, looking at the camera in disgust before and after his first haircut; Fran Storrs in her twenties, a fierce looking, gun-toting hunter (she was rabidly anti-gun); Jon Hanifin in nothing but a raincoat brazenly exposing himself to a nude statue in downtown Portland; and Clif White having grown a full beard for his third grade class photo. Each photo I accompanied with a less-than-flattering tale. Then came the residents. No resident was spared. Finally, co-resident Joel Datloff and I, with the help of several other residents, acted out a semi-cruel parody of Wednesday morning conference, complete with faculty arrogance, senility, and resident ineptitude. We exposed the warts of the department, the *verrucae*, if you will. Judging from the laughter, the catharsis did us well. I think only a few were actually offended. Then it was *back to work*. Three years of residency had come to an end.

▪ DOWNTOWN

REGAL WAS A fitting word to describe Dr. John O'Holleran. Richard II regal, not Louis XIV. He spoke softly in his tenor Irish voice, but with stately authority; held his body erect without effort, dressed elegantly without flamboyance. He spoke little to me except in the presence of Tony. I never quite understood why.

Space was limited at the Allergy Clinic on the thirteenth floor of the medical building. Tony Montanaro's private office faced the West Hills, and he offered to share it with me, a generous offer, considering that there wasn't even space for a second desk. I commissioned a handsome stand-up birch desk, somewhat like a clerk's desk from a Charles Dickens novel: a writing surface just below chest height with a pull-out panel for additional writing, and one book shelf at knee level where I stored reference books and my microscope. It became my entire working area and library for two and a half years. I had always quite liked standing to write and dictate. From the large windows I watched storms blow in from the west.

Room For Examination

Things started smoothly at the Allergy Clinic. I was given two examination rooms and occasionally a nurse. The nurse put patients in rooms now and then when she could escape from giving allergy shots to the hoards of hay fever victims.

The queen bee nurse, Barbara, I had known from internship. She was a head ward nurse at Good Samaritan and I had struck up quite a friendly working relationship with her at the time. Originally a New Jersey girl, Barb had retained nicely her Jersey accent. Tall and elegant, she out-dressed the entire office, flamboyant if she felt like it, and always appropriate for every holiday. Her orange and black couture on Halloween was the best I will ever see. Must have taken her hours. My direct working relationship with Barb at the Allergy Clinic turned out to be limited because she belonged mostly to the allergy side, especially to King O'Holleran, but she added grace and beauty to the art of healing, which was an uncommon amenity for a medical office.

A transcriptionist named Erica had been with the group for many years. Erica, for reasons unclear to me, came in late at night to transcribe the many letters that I, Tony, and Dr. O'Holleran dictated, and was known to occasionally still be asleep on the sofa when the morning crew arrived. Sentence structure meant more to Erica than a paycheck. The final product was perfect. I spelled out words when I remembered—Latin dermatology words could be difficult—but she never made spelling errors even when I forgot. Her grammar was impeccable. I never knew much of Erica's personal life and suspected there must have been a story behind the nocturnal existence, but regardless, she was a gem of a transcriptionist. I have worked with many transcriptionists, and only one—Tina, in Toronto—ever matched Erica in transcribing expertise.

And then there was Howard Wolfe, the level-headed scientist in his oversized lab coat who had run Dr. O'Holleran's laboratory for his entire career. Day in and day out in that agar-smelling lab with its Petri dishes, flasks, and gas Bunsen burners, Howard processed pollen samples that he had obtained from the roof of the building, to create the immune serum used for allergy injections. Howard was a generous man, supportive of me from the start, even carving out a few feet of bench space for my laboratory testing. I have richly fond memories of Howard.

More people passed through that office than I could ever have imagined. The elevator cables in the building had no idea what they were getting into, strained every day by the platoons of patients going to the Allergy Clinic for shots. A separate stream of patients flowed in for visits with the doctors. Our receptionist Becky deserved an award, or a purple heart, for dealing with all those patients.

While my practice was in its build-up phase, I accepted a part-time job offer from Dr. White to teach every week at the newly built VA clinic. I tried to teach residents in the manner Clif White had taught me during residency. Being the physician of record, supervising residents and making sure they didn't kill anyone, was a positive new experience for me. In fact, it was a great pleasure to work beside the fifteen or more residents who rotated through the VA during the course of those two years.

The downtown practice eventually built up to the point where I decided to stop my VA position and concentrate on my own practice. In retrospect, I regret having left the VA. Staying on would have moved me along the path to becoming the academic clinician-educator I eventually became. The VA would have been a good training ground. Would've, could've, should've.

The other teaching commitment I took on fresh out of residency was at my alma mater, Good Samaritan Hospital. Wendy saw her patients in the outpatient clinic there, and we cooked up the idea of a dermatology clinic for the internal medicine residents. Once every two weeks, I saw a morning clinic of patients with skin problems with the residents, and delivered a noon lecture on skin diagnosis and treatment. That exercise got me started on a path of lecturing that I enjoyed throughout my career. The patient referrals from residents weren't so bad either.

THE DISEASE OF THE CENTURY

EARLY INTO MY practice in 1985, AIDS came to Portland, Oregon in full force. In addition to the devastation to patients, AIDS changed the lives of many doctors and profoundly altered the delivery of medicine. Between 1981 and '85, most cases of AIDS had come out of New

York, San Francisco, and Los Angeles. The earliest published reports appeared in 1981, the first New England Journal article in 1982. Young gay men were showing up with a purple-colored malignancy on their skin and internal organs. It was called Kaposi's sarcoma, or KS. In the same community of men, an infection from an organism called *pneumocystis*, known previously in severely immune suppressed individuals only, was causing rapidly fatal pneumonia. The infection filled patient's lungs and killed them before treatments could be started. The cases were baffling because they affected young men who had otherwise been perfectly healthy. For three years or more, doctors could only speculate on the cause. As the sexually-transmitted theory of AIDS gained acceptance, more cases started to show up outside the three main centers, in smaller cities like Portland and Seattle.

It wasn't until 1985 that I started seeing many of the skin diseases associated with AIDS. By the summer of '85 when I finished dermatology training, over twelve thousand patients had already been diagnosed with AIDS in the U.S., and more than half of those were dead from their disease. Skin played a central role in AIDS from the beginning. At the university clinics, high on the hill, I hadn't seen many AIDS cases during my residency from '82 to '85, but had heard about some tragic cases from my wife Wendy Levinson and her partner Dr. John Santa, both internists who had cared for them at Good Samaritan Hospital during those years. Town-Gown was likely at play; inner city gays preferably went to inner city hospitals, not the university. It was true elsewhere as well. University clinics in New York, Los Angeles, and San Francisco hadn't shown much interest at first in caring for patients with AIDS. Ivory towers could be judgmental or, at least, aloof.

I met a patient named Stephen in my first month of practice, August 1985. He had moved recently to Portland from San Francisco and operated an advertising agency not too far from my office. He was referred to me by Dr. Jim Sampson, an AIDS specialist Wendy had hired, and one of a very small handful of doctors beginning to specialize in the care of AIDS patients in Portland.

Stephen did not have AIDS when I first met him. He appeared to be healthy, took no medications, dressed conservatively in the best clothes, and was successful in his work. He merely had some genital warts that I treated over several visits. He was twenty-eight. Several months later, my receptionist put him through to my back line. "Dr. Shaw, I'm sorry to bother you," he said, "but I have a new rash on my chest that's very painful. I was wondering if…"

"One side or both sides?" I interrupted. He said it was only on his left side, in a wide belt of red blisters under his arm. "Can you come to the office today? Like right now?" I was worried about him.

Stephen had 'shingles' on his left upper chest area. One thing we had learned from the early experience of Dr. Marcus Conant* in San Francisco was that an outbreak of shingles (medical term: herpes zoster) was often a telltale predictor of AIDS. The causative virus of AIDS, ultimately named the Human Immunodeficiency Virus (HIV), had recently been identified, but routine blood tests to detect HIV were not yet available, so I couldn't confirm a diagnosis. I let Stephen know my concern about his being infected with HIV. He was fully aware of the risk; he knew that having multiple sexual partners had emerged as the strongest risk factor.

Stephen progressed over several months to full-blown AIDS. He was fortunate to be one of the early AIDS patients to receive AZT (Zydovudine) which was in early development in 1985, and the drug may have slowed the speed of his relentless deterioration. During the next few years, Stephen never lost the pride he took in dressing well and being positive about the future. He ultimately died five years later from multi-organ failure and AIDS encephalitis (brain infection). I must have seen him more than thirty times during his illness, for various skin complications. Always gracious, he unfalteringly showed respect and consideration for our office staff and me. He demonstrated to me that patients with the most life-threatening diseases are often the most appreciative of the care they receive, and complain the least. He never felt sorry for himself or entitled to special treatment. When the end came, it came mercifully: a seizure, unconsciousness, and death within twenty-four hours.

(* Dr. Conant championed good medical care of patients with AIDS from the start of the epidemic. His role in AIDS is portrayed in Randy Shilts's book, *And the Band Played On*),

Another patient, Michael, did not look well from his first visit to my office, his face somewhat sunken, his thinning black hair plastered moist to his head. "I've lost a lot of weight recently. Twenty pounds. I know thin is good, doctor, but this is ridiculous," he said with an attempt at a smile. It was common for AIDS patients to joke as a way of coping with the disaster affecting them and their community. And Michael was an actor.

On Michael's cheeks and forehead were multiple unusual growths that looked somewhat like warts but larger and flatter, with a distinctly different surface contour. "No, they don't hurt at all. They just detract from my…," he framed his tilted face with his hands. "At least they are not on the tip of my nose."

I had never seen anything like it. Had I missed something during my training? Early on in solo practice, the fear of being incompetent always looms. I felt reasonably confident, having passed my board examinations, but it was impossible to know everything. There were always gaps. Now, here was a skin disease I had never before laid eyes on. Michael also had an expanding red rash on his forehead that I tested with a microscopic scraping and proved to be a fungus infection. At least I could confirm one diagnosis. I needed to investigate the other.

I took a biopsy of one of the large warty growths on his face. "I'm terrified of needles," he warned me. When I was finished with the anesthesia, he said, "Oh, that wasn't bad at all, you'll be seeing lots of my friends." The slide came back the next day; it confirmed the presence of a viral infection called *molluscum contagiosum*, but different from any I had ever seen, with thousands of viral 'bodies' on the slide. I was familiar with *molluscum* in children, small flesh-colored bumps, but Michael's lesions were much larger than those we normally encountered in kids. While the usual size in children approximated that of a lentil (about three millimeters), each of his approached the diameter of a dime or a quarter, and he had twenty or more on his face. I searched the literature and, to my surprise, discovered that in November of 1985, some months before I saw Michael as a patient, Dr. Robert Gallo of HIV research fame, and colleagues at Walter Reed Hospital, had published a report of *giant molluscum* occurring in a patient with AIDS.

"Molluscum. Isn't that like barnacles?" he said. "My god, who came up with that name?"

"There is no easy way to treat these," I said. "I can try, but it will require multiple treatments and it will be painful. We might fail. Normally the body's resistance helps, but you don't have much resistance right now."

Michael agreed, and we started a series of destructive treatment sessions using cautery needles and cryotherapy with liquid nitrogen. Despite the tears of pain during each session, he did what was needed to rid his once full handsome face of the alien 'barnacles' that were trying to take it over.

Molluscum rapidly became widely observed in patients with AIDS-induced immunosuppression. While not life-threatening, *molluscum* proved exceedingly difficult to treat. Over the next ten years I must have treated thousands of lesions on the faces of patients with AIDS.

Michael's skin disease demonstrated to me how utterly devastated his immune system had become. Blood tests had by that time become available to look at immune function, and despite his taking AZT, the lymphocyte count remained at rock bottom. It was as if his entire body had been converted to an incubator for the growth of whatever bacteria, virus or fungus he encountered. Michael and I both knew we were losing the battle when he quit joking with me during his visits. "This is getting to be pretty lonely," he once said, his eyes moist. Michael continued to endure the biweekly treatments until a few months into it when he didn't show up for his appointment. I never saw him again. My medical assistant brought in Michael's obituary from the newspaper a few weeks later, one paragraph, 'from complications of pneumonia'. I didn't know she had been watching for it every day.

Terry L. came into the office one day quite distressed, with his partner. Terry carried a known diagnosis of AIDS, and with one look at him, I knew he needed to be hospitalized immediately. His breathing was rapid and strained. He was feverish and clammy. Covering his damp, pale face were numerous flesh-colored bumps, each the size of a pea. He complained of a headache. I had seen him one week before with an unusual open sore on his finger. He hadn't appeared ill at the time and I biopsied the sore, suspecting an unusual infection.

The finger biopsy had shown a fungal infection called *Cryptococcosis*, or '*Crypto*' for short. I discovered a recently published case of an AIDS patient with *Crypto* on the skin resembling Terry's fleshy bumps. It was becoming apparent that many skin infections in AIDS patients were atypical from the outset, much different from textbook cases. Terry's had erupted over his face during the course of one week. It was alarmingly evident that the infection had spread throughout his entire body. The sore on his finger had merely been the first skin manifestation.

For an interminable fifteen seconds in the examination room, no one spoke. My head raced. Terry sat on the examination table, breathing with difficulty. His partner stood with an arm around Terry's shoulder, barely able to hold back tears. Terry looked as if he could stop breathing at any moment, like the worst cases of pneumonia I had seen. This was not good. I jumped into action. "We need to get you into the hospital right away." I made arrangements for immediate transfer to Good Samaritan for treatment with Amphotericin B, the most powerful drug available at the time for *Crypto*.

I saw him in the hospital later that day. He couldn't speak through his oxygen mask and labored breathing. His eyes told of his terror and all I could do was lay a hand on his gown-draped shoulder. A bedside X-ray confirmed that the infection had filled his lungs. Terry died that night. Intubation and treatment with Amphotericin B probably wouldn't have made a difference. His partner stood by him to the end, after which he vanished from the hospital and our lives the way all family members do after the death of a loved one.

No one had ever witnessed anything like this. Less than one month before, Terry was making a good living as a dancer. I was so impressed and appalled by his rapid death and the skin lesions on his face, I took some residents down to the hospital morgue in the basement to show them. I'm not sure which impressed the residents more, the skin lesions on his face or the act of unzipping the body bag in the refrigerated room to expose Terry's colorless corpse.

Stephen, Michael, and Terry L. These were three young men. A business man, an actor, a dancer. I saw hundreds of similar patients over the ensuing decade, nearly all men, with skin manifestations of AIDS. The AIDS epidemic gave me new respect for the fragility of the human body, and how important the immune system was in preventing devastating disease. The AIDS virus destroyed immunity by destroying lymphocytes. If the lymphocyte (CD4) count was above four hundred, patients did well. Once it dropped below two hundred, infections and Kaposi's sarcoma started developing. If it dropped below fifty, life-threatening infections started occurring on top of each other and patients could die in a matter of days. AIDS also gave me a new kind of compassion for those who suffered its ravages. So many people died horrible deaths as a result of infection with HIV, and early on we had very little to offer other than support and compassion. For fifteen years, my medical colleagues and I watched tens of thousands of formerly healthy individuals deteriorate and succumb to the onslaught of infections and malignancies that we were unable to treat.

Itching (medical term: pruritus) became one of the more surprising and profound symptoms from which AIDS patients suffered. Their diseases could be imminently life-threatening but itching might be what tormented them most, intractable, with no obvious cause. I used sedating antihistamines and topical agents routinely with only slight benefit. Fortunately we eventually learned that ultraviolet light was helpful in HIV-induced pruritus. The cause of HIV-itch turned out to be the immune system changes and lymphocyte destruction brought on by infection with the HIV virus. Sadly, many patients with end-stage AIDS died while suffering the most severe itching imaginable. After more than two hundred years of searching for a cure for itch, we can only reduce it somewhat, we cannot eliminate it. The person who designs an effective treatment for itchy skin from any cause will certainly deserve the fame and fortune that will undoubtedly follow.

It took more than five years from the initial cases of AIDS in 1981 to discover the culprit virus (HIV), and close to seven years to market the first drug (AZT) to inhibit viral replication. It was not until around 1995 that HIV drugs achieved enough success that the patients I saw started to reverse their deteriorating course and improve. The drug cocktails had side effects, but they limited reproduction of the virus enough that HIV infection became a chronic disease instead of a certain death sentence. Even more striking to me, with the newer drugs, especially one new class of drugs called protease inhibitors (pronounced PRO-tee-ace), many of the skin diseases of AIDS nearly vanished over night. Dermatologists started seeing the disappearance of Kaposi's sarcoma, the melting away of giant *Molluscum* lesions, a return to normal of patient's resistance to strange infections. Not entirely, but significantly so.

During the early years, I would bring an interesting AIDS patient up to our special Wednesday morning conference at the University, and community dermatologists would stand several feet away to examine him. Gradually, it became clear that exposure to disease was not the only fear. Homophobia, or at least revulsion, was also part of the equation. I recall the story of my wife interviewing an applicant to the internal medicine residency at Good Samaritan Hospital in 1982. During the interview, the applicant divulged to her that he was gay. Wanting to facilitate his coming to her program, Wendy said, "That is the last time you share that information with anyone around here. There are many doctors who have trouble with the concept of gay. Keep it to yourself." The applicant had come from San Francisco. He did ultimately match at Good Samaritan and over the next three years helped to educate doctors about issues related to gay lifestyle and AIDS management.

One internal medicine resident in my office absolutely refused to enter an examination room with a patient with AIDS because she was pregnant. Pathologists at Good Samaritan Hospital refused to perform autopsies on patients who had died from undiagnosed AIDS-related illnesses. They made excuses at first, but then flatly refused. Doctors double-gloved just to enter a patient's room.

Those practices are ancient history now. AIDS taught us the importance of 'universal precautions' for blood-borne diseases. Once those precautions became routine, health care providers of all kinds gradually became comfortable with managing patients with HIV.

Taking care of early AIDS patients caused great controversies in hospitals around the United States. In 1982 at Good Samaritan Hospital in Portland, Dr. John Santa had a patient in an isolation room with probable *pneumocystis* pneumonia. It was one of his first AIDS patients, and one of the first in Portland. Nurses refused to go into the room; they pushed meal trays on the floor in the direction of the patient's bed, and quickly closed the door. John couldn't get a pulmonary doctor to bronchoscope him to make a diagnosis. One of the surgeons at Good Samaritan had started spreading his opinion that there was a new gay infectious disease circulating, and everyone was at risk by exposing themselves to these patients. A meeting was called of all doctors and nurses involved with the case.

At the meeting, arguments flew back and forth about the risks to the doctors and nurses in caring for AIDS patients. Many were vehemently against treating them. Half-way through the meeting, the CEO of the hospital entered the room unexpectedly and took a seat. Everyone shifted nervously in their seats and waited to hear what he had to say. He had heard the rumors and the controversies. He was not a doctor.

"Let me be clear," said the CEO. "In the 1950s, Good Samaritan Hospital took care of patients with polio. In the 1980s, Good Samaritan Hospital is going to take care of patients with AIDS. Now, if any of you feel differently about this, I suggest that you find work elsewhere. Are there any questions?" At that point, the meeting changed its focus from whether or not to care for AIDS patients to how to best care for them. It took the leadership of a non-physician to make it happen.

There have always been ethical questions about the responsibilities doctors and nurses have for taking care of patients with infectious diseases. They arise with every epidemic throughout history, from outbreaks of Plague in the Middle Ages, to the influenza pandemic of 1918, to polio in the 1950s, Legionnaire's disease in 1976, all the way to the outbreak of SARS (Severe Acute Respiratory Syndrome) in China and Canada in 2003. The question is always whether doctors have a responsibility to put themselves in harm's way in order to care of sick patients. I won't pretend to have the answer to that question.

One time I cut myself during a surgery on a patient with AIDS. I was gloved, and was excising a small growth on the foot of a patient with AIDS when his quick movement triggered a reflex by me and I stabbed the palm of my hand with the pointed tip of a small pair of scissors. "Damn," I thought. I took off the gloves. There was blood. And some panic. I excused myself and scrubbed my hands with antiseptic, trying to express as much blood from the wound as possible, before returning to finish the surgery. I put in a call to Dr. Jim Sampson, by then the preeminent AIDS doctor in Portland.

The biggest fear in working with AIDS patients was stabbing oneself with injection needles. A needle stick could penetrate an inch or more, exposing deep tissues to the HIV virus. We used extreme caution with needles, including the small curved needles used for suturing. My scissors injury looked less risky. Even so, I needed to get some advice. HIV and Hepatitis B were the main needle stick risks at the time. I had been vaccinated against Hepatitis B, so it probably was not a concern. Dr. Sampson recommended sexual precautions at home and a blood test in two months. He offered, but did not necessarily recommend, a short course of AZT, the anti-HIV drug, realizing the penetration of the injury was not deep. I decided not to take the drug, and the next two months were among the longest of my life, stressful to both Wendy and me. The blood test ultimately proved negative and life returned to normal.

Some of the saddest patients I saw with AIDS were women. They didn't start appearing until many years into the epidemic. One such patient was Marianna. She had painful small bumps on her face that turned out to be an unusual kind of herpes zoster (shingles) infection that persisted on the skin instead of coming in an isolated episode. She was in misery with pain. She required a slew of expensive drugs she couldn't afford just to keep her skin in check. Not all of her tears came from the pain of her skin lesions. Her anger filled the room.

"Yes, I'm furious. I've lived a pretty clean life, and then I get this… shit…from a husband who pretends to be monogamous with me while he's fucking around with men. For *years*!" she said with a sweeping arm motion.

I could only empathize with her anger. Over the course of a decade, I saw a handful of women who contracted HIV from men who had been living promiscuous gay lives while pretending to be monogamous with them. Another woman took loving care of her husband throughout his decline and death while she herself was under treatment for HIV. He had lived an international life of multiple sexual partners and she had no idea until it was too late for both of them. She went on alone, after his death, to her own demise one year later.

My career interest in immunosuppressed patients grew as I worked with HIV-positive patients. On a path parallel to that of HIV disease, I also became interested in the management of patients with organ transplants who were immunosuppressed by design. They are susceptible to skin diseases in ways similar to patients with AIDS.

Drugs for HIV in the mid nineties nearly eliminated our need to treat the skin diseases of AIDS patients, and in industrialized countries, infection with HIV is now controlled to a large extent, though with significant expense. I now see AIDS patients with skin problems that arise from a return of normal immune function: rashes, eczema, patchy hair loss, all from hyperactive immune systems. I welcome the change. The situation has also improved in organ transplant patients. Drugs are better, less toxic, with fewer side effects. Patients are living twenty, thirty, even forty years with transplanted kidneys, hearts, and livers. However, unlike HIV, where total prevention is the ultimate goal, the numbers of organ transplant patients continues to grow steadily worldwide, intentionally, and we cannot always control the aggressive skin cancers and other malignancies that occur as a result of the immune-suppressing drugs. Nevertheless, most patients fare remarkably well.

Those of us who have taken care of patients with suppressed immunity, be it from HIV or organ transplant drugs, have experienced brilliant successes and dismal failures. We learned as we went along. I tip my hat to my colleagues who were willing to work with dying AIDS patients throughout the early years of the epidemic, and to those that keep them alive today. I salute organ transplant doctors and nurses who guard over the survival of their patients. I salute the donors of organs and their families. And lastly, I am grateful to the researchers who made the discoveries that allowed us to keep immune systems humming along at just the right level.

CHAPTER 6
Getting Established

■ BERNIE

MY PRACTICE BUILT up reasonably quickly. Three months into it, I needed my own assistant. The person I ultimately hired, Bernetta Severson, or Bernie, as everyone called her, turned out to be nothing short of a gift from God (or in my case, its secular equivalent). When I had called the local school that trained medical assistants and enquired about recent graduates, the director recommended that I take one of their soon-to-be graduates in my office for a trial externship. It sounded like an excellent plan.

Bernie was a bit nervous at first, occasionally tossing her blond hair off to one side. It must have been scary to enter the work force after more than ten years at home taking care of two sons and a successful husband in manufacturing. Now that her sons were in school she could look for a new challenge in life, something more intellectually stimulating. It didn't take long for me to realize that I would work well with Bernie. She was perfect for me. She accepted my offer, which wasn't much at first: part-time work, no benefits, unpredictable hours, uncertain future. She started working on December 26, 1985. Why I had patients scheduled on the day after Christmas, I can't imagine, and as I learned later, neither could she.

A dermatologist usually doesn't need an RN (registered nurse). The medical procedures in an outpatient dermatology office don't usually warrant an RN credential or the pay scale it commands. A smart and motivated medical assistant can be taught to do everything a dermatologist needs. Bernie fit right in. She was smart, hard working, and most of all, resourceful. Her knack as a mother must have helped patients feel secure. She was old enough that she felt at ease figuring problems out on her own and implementing the solutions she devised.

Patients loved Bernie. She treated them with respect and caring while limiting the jokes and crossing of boundaries into inappropriate personal areas. She arrived early and left late; she took on every new task I requested; she prepared my KOH slides for microscopic examination; she autoclaved my instruments. For two years, she took surgical towels *home* to launder them (this was before I was busy enough to warrant a laundry service and before public health guidelines for handling blood contamination were introduced). I eventually taught her how to inject patients with local anesthesia for surgeries. She was confident enough to give me advice when I needed it. When I eventually moved out of the Allergy Clinic she participated in the design of my new office. And, she took interest in my personal life and my young family. Generous beyond belief, she sewed professional quality stuffed animals for my daughters for birthdays and Christmas, and knit a beautiful blanket that my wife and I use every night to this day. The only thing Bernie could not do was spell words. It didn't matter; I'm not that good a speller either. I let it slide.

Bernie stayed with me for over ten years, through two office relocations and many changes in office staff. She was a rock of stability. I couldn't have asked for a better assistant.

▰ TOO MUCH TESTOSTERONE

AFTER AIDS, THE second major influence on my career during the early years of my practice came from the adult women I saw with acne. Within months of starting my practice, I discovered something I hadn't learned during residency, that acne in adult women was much more complicated than teenage acne.

I started noticing women patients who had been unsuccessfully treated by other dermatologists. The acne pattern was always the same: involvement of the lower part of the face and jaw line, larger and deeper lesions (pimples), worse before menstrual periods, oily skin on the face, unwanted hair sometimes, on the chin, jaw line, and upper lip. The pattern definitely fit a picture suggestive of testosterone influence, i.e. a hormonal process. Most of these women had already failed standard treatments with topical creams and oral antibiotics. It became apparent to me that we in dermatology had been failing in our treatment of most adult women with acne. This was around 1986. Accutane had become available in 1983 after years of clinical trials, but the drug was kept in reserve for the most severe cases of scarring acne. Also, Accutane caused birth defects, so few dermatologists used the drug in women in their twenties and thirties who might get pregnant, reserving it instead for teenage boys and young men.

One day, a woman with acne in her mid-thirties named Carole came in and asked for a refill of spironolactone, a drug she had been given by a doctor in another city. She had an interesting story. She had tried standard acne preparations from dermatologists, with no help. It wasn't until a gynecologist prescribed spironolactone that she saw improvement. Her face was essentially clear when I saw her. This was a new discovery for me. I had used spironolactone only as a diuretic (water pill) to treat high blood pressure and heart failure in elderly patients. Here, it was being used in a young woman to treat acne? I gave the patient her refill and started looking into published research on spironolactone. There was very little.

Carole's introduction to me of spironolactone in 1985 significantly changed the way I treated adult women with acne. I began prescribing spironolactone to selected patients and discovered unprecedented success. I gradually used more spironolactone in adult women, monitoring their responses, and followed new research on the subject. After four years of building confidence in the use of spironolactone, my success rates were so great that I decided the time had come to write a paper on the use of this valuable drug. No one else seemed to be familiar with it. My dermatology colleagues needed to learn about it.

It is common for dermatologists to discover individual treatment secrets or personally customize ways of doing procedures during the course of their careers. The reason for my particular excitement about spironolactone was this: The women I treated were by far the most grateful and satisfied of all my patients. Many had gone years with unsatisfactory results and were now nearly completely controlled. In addition to the acne improvement, patients felt better, oiliness on the face disappeared, and facial hair, if they had it, became much less of a problem. Women with 'pre-menstrual syndrome' had fewer symptoms. I couldn't wait to share my successes with colleagues.

Spironolactone is not a hormone per se, the way birth control pills are. It was discovered later that it works in skin by blocking the testosterone receptor and thereby prevents the hormone effect of testosterone, which all women produce to a small degree. Testosterone is the hormone that causes acne. The anti-testosterone effect of spironolactone was first discovered when men lost their sex drive and their breasts became tender when they took the drug for high blood pressure. Middle-aged women on spironolactone for blood pressure also reported coincidental improvement in facial and body hair, so-called hirsutism. By the mid-1980s, only a few small studies had been done using spironolactone in younger patients with acne, and while they had shown promise, they were not widely known.

I also became familiar with the prescribing of oral contraceptives (birth control pills—BCPs) in women with acne, and discovered that using spironolactone and BCPs together had better effects than using either alone. There were fewer side effects and better responses. Women felt better and looked better. At the time, I knew of no dermatologists willing to prescribe BCPs. They hadn't been trained in their use, and apparently were not comfortable taking on a new class of drugs that went beyond what they learned during residency. As renowned dermatologists Walter and Dorinda Shelly had quipped, *"If much of what you do in your office today is the same as you did in your residency, you really need a tune-up."*

For many years I published and taught dermatologists at conferences about the benefits of spironolactone and birth control pills in women with acne. Strangely though, I felt alone in this endeavor. Instead of adopting the new treatment modality, my colleagues often challenged me about the safety of spironolactone. Many were reluctant to use it because the Physician's Desk Reference had a warning about possible tumors in mice, and dermatologists were the most timid of doctors when it came to prescribing. I could understand the initial reluctance, but had reviewed the original articles and determined the PDR warning to be misleading. The potential side effects of the drug fell into the 'nuisance' category, easily monitored and without any serious risk. I had quickly become comfortable dealing with the side effects, adjusting doses if necessary. Only rarely did we stop the drug because of side effects.

In addition to skeptical clinicians, there were the academicians in the good old boy acne guild consisting of about six men, mostly older than I, some of whom had conducted important original research on patients with acne. I might have been overly sensitive, but I got the distinct impression that the acne club viewed me as an interloper, an intruder on their turf, and wished that I would go away. Despite my presentations at international meetings being well received, I was never invited to speak about hormonal treatments at the largest venues at annual meetings. Those invitations seemed to go to the dermatologists they had mentored.

No members of this acne mafia, that I was aware of, shared my interest in spironolactone and its effect on testosterone receptors, or 'androgen receptors', as they were called. Instead, with great fanfare and enthusiasm, they promoted a different line of research into an area called enzyme inhibition. In the skin there exists a complex soup of acne enzymes. They wanted to find a drug that inhibited one of the enzymes. The approach was hormone related certainly, but less direct and predictable than receptor blockade by spironolactone. I never thought enzyme inhibition would achieve the kind of clinical success that blocking the receptor did. The receptor was the crucial bottleneck of the entire reaction. Despite hearing my emphasis on spironolactone and birth control pills, they seemed to dismiss that approach to a large degree. The trees apparently were more alluring than the forest.

The acne club always presented the latest research on enzyme inhibitors. After many years, the prime candidate enzyme inhibitor (a 5-alpha-reductase inhibitor) eventually underwent a large, well-designed clinical trial funded by Merck, in which I participated. The drug failed miserably. One member of the acne club was able to get the failed trial published in 2001 (pharmaceutical companies and journals are notorious for suppressing the publication of failed trials), and since that time, work with enzyme inhibition in acne has slowed.

The acne mafia also worked with Big Pharma on studies of revenue-producing topical creams and gels in acne, which, while helpful in mild cases, usually produced incomplete responses in women. At the international meetings, they repeatedly presented party-line recommendations of Cream A plus Cream B, and the dermatologists followed to their drum beat. Long before, I had realized that women with acne usually required internal drugs. Topical preparations usually failed.

It would have been interesting to conduct a large, properly designed trial with spironolactone so it could achieve FDA approval, but I knew why that would never happen. Spironolactone had the remote potential for altering fetal sexual development if given to a pregnant woman, and when birth defects and pregnancy are at issue with a drug, pharmaceutical companies don't go near it. For that reason alone, the use of spironolactone was never going to be approved by the FDA for acne. It would have to remain as an 'off-label' use.

Big pharmaceutical companies eventually got smart enough to recognize the potential gold mine of oral contraceptives in acne, and designed one or two brands to be used specifically for acne. The problem remained, however, that dermatologists had never been trained in prescribing hormonal treatments and were fearful of complications.

Most of my colleagues are still petrified to consider prescribing birth control pills for their patients. And from what I can surmise, very few dermatologists use spironolactone because few faculty members in residency programs are willing to learn about it and teach their residents. That means that about one of every four adults with acne (two of every three adult women with acne) is not receiving successful treatment because the specialists who should know more than anyone else about how to treat it, are too timid to use hormonal therapies. Dermatologists are losing their position of expertise in acne therapy. I guess they are fine with that outcome. They've moved into lasers and Botox.

After twenty years of teaching about hormonal therapies in acne, I decided to quit banging my head against the wall. Perhaps I was impatient. Perhaps twenty years wasn't long enough to influence the conservative thinking of dermatologists, but I had had enough of the resistance and apathy. I continued to treat my own patients hormonally, but I shelved my research and stopped accepting invitations to speak on the subject. Ironically, more and more women now come into the office asking me about whether I know anything about spironolactone and whether it might help them. They have done their homework on the internet and have a better understanding of the success with spironolactone than most dermatologists do.

BREAKAWAY

IN THE SUMMER of 1987, two years after I started practicing in the office of O'Holleran and Montanaro, I made the decision to break out and start my own solo practice. I needed more room, more autonomy. I wanted to be more closely affiliated with a hospital. The free-standing office in the middle of downtown Portland was, ironically, too isolated. The hospital I had in mind was my old favorite, my alma mater of internal medicine training, Good Samaritan Hospital. The renovation of a new office there would take six months and I could move at the end of December.

At precisely the same time I was to move, by pure happenstance, my father was making plans to close his practice in Tacoma. He offered to give me any equipment I could use in the new office: surgery tables, instruments, furniture, autoclave equipment. He and I had long before had discussions about whether I would move to Tacoma and join his practice, and we both knew that wasn't going to happen.

It was sad for me to watch my father close his practice. He gradually had become frustrated with the restrictions imposed by insurance companies, primarily Medicare. Being the staunch Republican that he was, he usually blamed government intrusion for the regulations. The final humiliation came during an audit that forced him to write hundreds of small reimbursement checks to insurance companies and patients. He had had enough. The practice of medicine, in my father's eyes, had lost its charm.

What hadn't lost its charm was the respect he received from his colleagues. The chairman at Oregon, Frank Parker, organized a celebration for his retirement to be held during one of our monthly Oregon Dermatology Society meetings in Portland. Dr. Parker, before becoming chairman at Oregon, had known my father from his days in Seattle. For twenty years or more, my father had driven weekly from Tacoma up to Seattle to teach the residents, and every month to Portland to teach Oregon residents. Dr. Parker roasted him, complete with compromising photos procured collusively with my mother. My father's well known friendship with Portland dermatologist Ted Kingery was recognized at the dinner as well. Toward the end of the evening, the two well lubricated Shaw and Kingery couples stood up and sang their hearts out with an aria from Puccini, or maybe it was a fraternity song from the University of Michigan, I forget which. Whatever it was, they sang beautifully.

My new office got off to a grand start. Bernie's two strong sons and husband helped with the move, and all they got for it, I now recall with chagrin, was a pizza lunch. Once out of the downtown office, an unexpected thing happened to me. It was as if a weight had been lifted. Being my own boss apparently was what I was meant to do all along. At least it seemed that way at the time. Had I been a painter, my patrons would have noticed a lightening of my palette.

In reality, there were more reasons than being in control of my own business. Hospital consultations were now across the street, a sky-bridge walk away. I could run over and do a consultation at lunch, or between patients. I had the space to teach medicine residents in my office on a regular basis. My colleagues—those to whom I referred patients, and those who referred patients to me—were now mostly in the same building. I lived only a few blocks up the hill on Summit Avenue, and walked to work, past an impressive Giant Sequoia and the abortion clinic with its daily vigil of heaven-gazing protestors. If I drove to work, it took less than two minutes.

The new office was in the heart of Northwest Portland where 23rd Avenue had been trendy for years. A few years before, about 1985, while Starbucks was getting started in Seattle, Portland was breaking into a coffee frenzy of its own with Coffee People, whose slogan was 'Good Coffee–No Backtalk'. The coffee scene got even better just as I moved into the neighborhood. The Italian style coffee house Torrefazione moved onto a corner of 23rd Avenue, half a block from my office, so I occasionally escaped from the office for a quick jolt. They made by far the best espresso and cappuccino this side of Rome.

▇ IT'S ALL ABOUT THE PATIENTS

FOR THE NEXT five years, I thoroughly enjoyed my patients and solo practice in general. As usual, the patients made it worth while. One morning, I pulled an empty chart from the rack on the examination room door: a new patient, Ms. Judith Cornish, age forty-seven. I knocked twice and entered.

"Good morning, I'm Dr. Shaw," I flipped open the chart and asked, "You are Ms. Cornish?" (I always used last names only. It was formal, I know, but I preferred erring on the side of respect, not familiarity). I extended my hand. She sat, leaning forward in a chair, one very lean leg crossed over the other.

"Good morning. Yes, I'm Judy," she said in a husky voice. She shook my hand half-heartedly.

In the five seconds it took to introduce ourselves, I had already processed a huge amount of diagnostic information:

One, her hand was cool. Most likely this was poor circulation from anxiety or smoking, though less common causes were certainly possible.

Two, she was thin, and sat with the familiar posture that we in medicine see frequently in undernourished alcoholics. (This may seem presumptuous, and certainly first impressions require confirmation, but experience is a good teacher.)

Three, her voice was raspy. The odds were high that she was a heavy smoker (this was confirmed later by the smell of smoke on her clothes and by my questioning).

Four, her skin was pale and prematurely wrinkled for forty-seven. Again, cigarettes and alcohol were the likely culprits.

Five, the dermatological diagnosis was psoriasis at least. (I could immediately detect telltale signs on her hands and scalp.)

Finally, I could see in her face and body language that she was guarded, as if she wore a sign that said "EMOTIONALLY FRAGILE: HANDLE WITH CARE". I would need to do just that.

"How can I help you?" I asked.

"You can help me with this!" she said, pulling up sleeves and pants to expose her elbows and knees which were covered with large areas of thick, scaly skin characteristic of psoriasis.

"How long has this been a problem?" I asked.

"A few months, maybe a year," she said.

"Any treatments so far?"

"No."

"Do you take any medications?" (Some common drugs can make psoriasis worse.)

"No."

I asked her about other health problems—she had none that she knew of—and whether she had seen her family doctor recently—she hadn't—and after some additional questions, finally arrived at the alcohol and cigarettes.

"About a pack a day," she said. "And I have a few drinks every day."

"Beer, wine?"

"Vodka, mostly."

My preliminary diagnosis, which I didn't share with her at first, was psoriasis with alcohol and tobacco abuse as contributing factors. I asked her to put on a gown, examined her and returned for the discussion after she dressed.

"You have a condition called psoriasis," I said, and went on to explain the disease. "But what I am most worried about is your alcohol consumption. We know that cigarettes and alcohol make psoriasis worse, but my biggest concern is that you are drinking enough alcohol to threaten your general health and your life."

Judy sat back in her chair, folded her arms and turned to the side. Her silence told me she was not pleased with the assessment.

I continued: "I'm going to treat you with these creams, but I encourage you to think about the alcohol and cut down or stop if you can. Your skin might improve on its own. Not everyone can do it alone; you might need help. I suggest that you talk to your primary care doctor, get your liver checked and have a physical examination. I'd like to see your progress in two or three months."

"Well, I'll think about it," she said. Her tone was indignant, and I didn't expect her to follow my advice. I thought she might never return.

Judy did not return in three months, or in six months. It was not until a year later that I saw her again. I looked at the chart before entering the examination room and remembered our first encounter. This could be difficult, I thought.

"Well, hello," I said.

She started right in: "Hi, Dr. Shaw. You know, I'm sorry for not coming back sooner, but I need to tell you something."

I didn't speak.

Her eyes moistened. "You saved my life."

Surprised by her comment, I raised my eyebrows as if to say, "Is there more?" Clearly, there was more to tell.

She continued: "Remember last year when you told me about alcohol? I resented it at the time, and continued to drink—more, in fact—and my skin got worse. But I kept thinking about what you said, until it finally sunk in that you could be right. Anyway, I stopped drinking six months ago, and now I feel great and my skin is much better. I was sliding down a slippery path."

I asked her if she'd stopped drinking on her own, and she sad that yes, she had. I told her that was wonderful, that she must be a strong-willed person and should feel proud of herself. She said she'd been drinking herself to death and didn't know it.

"You were the only person who has ever been concerned about it," she said. "I came in today to thank you."

Her comment made my whole day, my entire week. It is not often that a dermatologist hears the words "you saved my life." Of course, it might not have been entirely true, but it was gratifying to know that my advice about a problem tangential to her immediate skin problem had influenced Ms. Cornish's destructive lifestyle in a positive way.

109

In medicine, we don't expect to receive praise for what we do, and successful treatments are often taken for granted by patients (as they should be, to a certain extent). To hear Judy's appreciation was indeed special.

We went on to address her skin briefly, and at the end of the visit, I couldn't help myself from saying, "Now, how about the smoking? Can you start thinking about cutting back or stopping?"

"That's next, Dr. Shaw. I'm working on it," she said.

We looked at each other. "One thing at a time," we said in unison.

Another memorable patient during those solo years ended up doing the teaching while I did the learning. Howard Backlund, an impeccably dressed eighty-three year-old whose real name I am honored to divulge, first came to my office at the end of a typically busy afternoon. He was a frail man who moved slowly and had a high-pitched, whining voice that grated on my 4:30 p.m. nerves. He was consulting with me because of a tiny lesion on his nose and even tinier ones on his forehead. I used magnification as he pointed out each micro-blemish. I acquiesced to his worries by taking a biopsy of the nose lesion and treating some very early pre-cancers on his forehead with liquid nitrogen spray (we easily could have ignored them for months with no risk to him). He asked to return in one or two months, and with some reservations I agreed to see him at intervals that suited him, thereby adding another high-maintenance patient to my practice.

Two months later, Howard returned, happy with my treatments (thankfully), and showed me new, imperceptible lesions on his face. His tone of voice and plaintive approach had, so far, distanced me from asking about his personal life, so in an attempt to warm up to him, I decided to explore more this visit.

"What kind of work have you done in your life?" I asked.

Howard responded excitedly. "Ohhh! I was an organist and a pianist! I still play the organ at my church! Yes!" His every utterance finished with an exclamation point.

I decided to disclose that I too played the piano, jazz mostly. Self-disclosure during interviews with patients, like humor, must be used cautiously, because what pleases one patient may insult another, and the interview can easily get derailed. Fortunately, this time, it worked. He was thrilled.

We had a brief but delightful discussion about the classical pianists in our city—who played with a good "touch" and who didn't. We both agreed that another physician, Ron Potts, the ER doctor at Kaiser where I had worked, played with wonderful touch. Mr. Backlund had spent an entire year at university working exclusively on his touch, the control and weight of his fingers on the piano keys. He was so appreciative of the lifelong benefit that he said, "You must be exposed to this method! It is something you can learn! It could improve your playing tremendously!" He offered to teach me. In my home, on my piano, as he had sold his years before.

At that point in the visit I'm pondering, "Who is this old guy? Do I want to get more involved with this quirky man?" More important, would I be crossing professional boundaries? What if it were a young woman who wanted to come to my home to give me lessons on touch? How would the medical board view that? What would my wife think?

Nevertheless, after giving the idea more thought I finally decided to take him up on the offer, and before long, there he was, in my living room, assessing my touch on the piano and teaching his method of touch control. It had to do mostly with the weight of my fingers on the keys being supported by the muscles of the fingers, not my arms. Suffice it to say that what he taught me was the most important piano lesson I ever had. What I learned from him had lasting positive effects, and I have been grateful to him ever since.

My professional relationship with Howard wasn't harmed in the least; on the contrary, it improved and we became friends during our interactions. I continued to see him and treat his skin cancers as needed. I even learned to welcome the tone of his voice.

By the simple act of exploring Howard's personal life for a moment, I had the good fortune of turning a somewhat strained professional interaction into a rich and rewarding one for both of us. I don't know which one of us benefited more.

Coincidentally, years later, at the very time I wrote down these thoughts about Howard, my former nurse Bernie emailed to let me know Howard Backlund had died, and that the Portland newspaper had run a gracious eulogy. She thought I might like to know.

■ MY HEAD

IT WAS NOW close to a decade that I had been living and coping with what Wendy and I had come to label as my 'head symptoms'.

They had been continuous, a little better at times, a little worse at times. Rarely did they create such disorientation that I would have trouble driving a car or performing surgery. I was still able to ride a bicycle. The worst times had been when I was a resident back in 1982 and 1983.

I started with a new medical doctor, an internist who worked with Dr. Black the neuro-vestibular guru. The first thing he did was to challenge my taking of Dilantin, the anti-seizure drug that I had been on for several years, and which I thought was helping me somewhat. He suggested that I experiment with a trial off the drug. To my surprise, not much happened. I didn't get a lot worse. So I stopped Dilantin forever. I still have a hard time reconciling the drastic improvement I remember when I first tried Dilantin. I could still be taking the drug today if it hadn't been for my new doctor. One thing doctors usually learn for themselves: it is always best to take as few drugs as possible.

Over time, I learned that a virus such as a common cold would make my head symptoms worse. During the first two days of worsening symptoms, before the stuffy nose kicked in, I would often have fantasies of, *"Okay, this time the brain tumor is going to get out of control or the aneurysm in my head is going to rupture."* Then the cold symptoms would reassure me and I would wait it out.

I experimented with drugs. Antihistamines mostly, which helped somewhat. I tried diuretics once, but they didn't seem to help either. I periodically resorted to stopping alcohol for periods of time, but just like before, there was no help. Mostly, I just put up with the problem.

One thing I attributed to the head symptoms was easy fatigability and an annoying need to take a short nap after lunch. I knew I wasn't alone in the world on this issue: the siesta has been around for a long time, but still, my need seemed pathologically dire. In my view, the head symptoms were to blame. Regardless, whenever I could, I tried to nap in the early afternoon. That plus a double espresso would allow me to squeak through an afternoon. Over the course of my entire career, the best predictor of my being able to function normally was how much caffeine was circulating in my blood. When I happened upon King Louis XIV's putative quotation about coffee, it had special meaning for me: He apparently once said *"What would life be without coffee? But then, what is life with coffee?"*

■ IRONIES IN MEDICINE

MUCH OF MEDICAL practice is predictable. We are trained to handle most situations we encounter. Residents today get taught how to approach specialized situations: the angry patient; how to deliver bad news in a compassionate way; how to disclose a medical error.

Despite this predictability, unexpected situations happen with patients. When the outcome is positive, it's not a problem, but sometimes doing what we think is the right thing leads to a bad outcome. I used to think that bad outcomes could and must be rectified. I now accept that we sometimes have to live with an unresolved conflict; a misinterpretation; a false assumption. These are life's ironies; life's double negatives. That they besmirch our reputation, our integrity, is why they can be powerful. I had my share of difficult patients and misunderstandings. One patient immediately comes to mind.

Malcolm was eighteen years old. He came to me for facial acne. He had taken some of his older brother's antibiotics with some success, but reported having had several 'absent' spells during which he lost awareness of his surroundings for several seconds. The problem had ceased when he stopped the antibiotic, and had not recurred.

I started topical therapy but cautiously added a different oral antibiotic after a few months, and Malcolm seemed to be doing well.

Conversation was not easy for Malcolm, but over time I learned more about his life and ambitions. He told me with pride that his older brother was a fighter pilot in the Navy. Malcolm himself was in the preliminary stages of joining the Navy, and hoped to become a pilot someday like his brother. Months into his acne treatment, Malcolm reported two more episodes of relative loss of consciousness. He thought that the episodes had occurred only after being fatigued, but admitted to having three minor automobile accidents in the last year because of them. "I'm concerned about the cause of these spells," I said, "and I think you need to see a neurologist as soon as possible." I arranged for a consultation that afternoon.

The neurologist ordered an EEG that showed a seizure focus in the right hemisphere of his brain. That alone pointed to Malcolm having a seizure disorder. He set him up for an MRI to confirm the findings.

Malcolm never had the MRI. I saw him the following week and discussed the neurologist's findings. I shared my concerns about his plans to join the Navy. At that point his demeanor changed dramatically. He became resistant to my recommendations to follow up with the neurologist and have the MRI. He said that he had seen another neurologist who thought there was no problem. At the end of his visit, Malcolm told me that I was not authorized to contact the Navy about him.

A few days later, Malcolm's mother called. There was no way I could avoid speaking with her, and she was furious.

"You have destroyed my son's career!" she screamed into the phone. (Malcolm had apparently withdrawn his Navy application). "Your diagnosis is wrong! He saw another neurologist who said there was no problem."

No amount of explaining or recognizing and understanding her anger could calm her. The next day, Malcolm hand-delivered a letter to the office. "Dear Doctor Shaw; You are not to release my medical records, repeat any conversations we have had or discuss with any other physician and/or persons any thing(sic) connected with me."

That was the last I heard of Malcolm. I don't know what became of him medically or aeronautically.

This interaction and outcome might seem trivial to physicians who have been sued by their patients, but for years, the very thought of Malcolm punched me in the gut. It continued to bother me that reaching out to help a patient could be met with such misdirected disdain.

CHAPTER 7
Crawling Back To The Ivory Tower

■ CHANGE IS GOOD

Back in the summer of '85, when I finished dermatology residency, I was completely content with the idea of being primarily a community practitioner, not an academician. In the age-old scrimmage between Town and Gown, I was content with Town. I kept my connection to Gown through teaching and conferences. Over time, though, I gradually took on more academic pursuits—writing and teaching mostly—and after about a decade, buoyed psychologically by the satisfaction of a few published papers (which to my surprise were the most exciting accomplishments of my career), I decided to change course and pursue more of an academic path for the remainder of my career. Research and publishing, even at my clinical level, were more gratifying than taking care of patients.

I definitely came to academics through the side door. Most academically-minded doctors start out gung-ho for academia. They complete residency and immediately pursue a post-doctoral research fellowship and eventually apply for positions at institutions. If fortunate, during their fellowships they work with a mentor who helps open doors to the workings and opportunities of academia.

I had seen a surprising number of doctors abandon academia after a short time. The reasons for leaving were varied: failing to achieve academic goals, not getting research funds, not being treated well by their department chairs, being overworked and underpaid, raising families. I suspect many did not actually have the right mentors to cultivate their true research strengths.

■ GREAT CASE

FOR ME, MUCH of the spurring toward academics came from the patients I saw. One such case was that of Mrs. Shirley Monroe. My partner at the Allergy Clinic, Dr. Tony Montanaro, called me one day to see Mrs. Monroe, admitted two days earlier to a small hospital across the river in Northeast Portland. Tony had been asked to see her with his rheumatology hat on, and an infectious disease consultant had consulted on her as well. Neither had come up with a diagnosis and Mrs. Monroe continued to worsen despite treatment. Because she had some skin findings, Tony thought I might be able to help. I agreed to see her later the same day. Shirley Monroe became one of the best teaching cases of my career.

I entered her room, introduced myself and began exploring her medical history. A few days earlier, Shirley had seen her dermatologist for an acute rash on her hands and mid-section. She had also complained of a headache at the time. The dermatologist (coincidentally the man whom I had helped as a senior resident which led to the Portland Dermatology fiasco) gave her a shot of intramuscular Cortisone. Cortisone injections are bold treatments used to temporarily shut down a wide array of skin reactions. They are frowned upon by academic dermatologists but many community dermatologists resorted to them when they were uncertain about a diagnosis or needed a quick temporary fix. Her dermatologist was famous around town for his intramuscular cortisone shots.

She didn't improve. In two days she had more headache, malaise (general feeling of being unwell), and fevers. She saw her internist who made the wise decision to admit her. I probed more. She mentioned having had multiple previous episodes of a rare disease called acute intermittent porphyria which had resulted in three abdominal surgeries in the past. Could this be playing a role here? She didn't have abdominal pain, so it was unlikely.

I took a break from the history to examine her. In dermatology we often recognize the skin abnormality immediately and make the diagnosis instantaneously (though to express it to patients that quickly can be disconcerting to them). Mrs. Monroe had bright red skin on her hands and feet, as if she was wearing red gloves and socks. She also had intensely red skin across her buttocks and genitals in a bikini distribution. Her throat was inflamed, her tongue cherry red, and her eyes bloodshot.

I immediate thought, "This could be early Toxic Shock Syndrome!" The red hands and feet, the high fevers, the headache, elevated blood count, suggested early stages of toxic shock syndrome. It could rapidly get worse. Toxic Shock was a fatal disease. About one third of the hundred or so patients described with TSS had died.

I took some more history to search for supportive evidence.

"Do you ever use tampons?" (There was strong connection between tampons and toxic shock syndrome.) She was in her late forties so it was not highly likely, but her eyes opened wide with the question.

"Wow. Funny you should ask. I have had vaginal bleeding during the last month and have been wearing tampons almost continuously for weeks." She had been wearing tampons every day, sometimes one tampon for several days at a time! This was the exact scenario that predisposed to toxic shock syndrome. The first cases linked a specific brand of super-absorbent tampons to the disease before it became clear that prolonged use was the critical factor, not the brand itself.

Toxic shock syndrome had only been described less than five years earlier. The cause was *Staphylococcus aureus* infection that grew when women kept highly absorbent tampons in place longer than the less-absorbent models. The *Staph* bacteria in the vagina produced a toxin in the blood that caused the syndrome of headache, rash, and organ damage. A set of diagnostic criteria had been worked out to establish the diagnosis.

Mrs. Monroe's urine culture had already grown *Staph aureus*, the precise bacterial strain that had been linked to the disease. This could not have been coincidental. The positive culture and clinical picture confirmed, in my mind, the diagnosis, even if it was in an early stage. By the time I saw her she had already been started on the shotgun approach of broad-spectrum antibiotics and despite the absence of a diagnosis, appeared for the first time in her three day admission not to be progressing to what could have been full-blown, life-threatening toxic shock syndrome.

Tony agreed with my diagnosis and thanked me for seeing her. The infectious disease consultant, however, was adamant that she did not have toxic shock syndrome. "She doesn't fit enough of the criteria to establish the diagnosis."

I argued back. "The skin changes are classic. And *Staph* in her urine almost clinches it, especially after wearing tampons for a month."

He didn't budge. He wrote in the chart the list of diagnostic criteria for toxic shock syndrome and that she didn't fulfill all of the criteria. How valuable was the opinion of a dermatologist anyway, compared to a 'Young Turk' infectious disease specialist? He hadn't even considered the diagnosis. He didn't have a clue about how to interpret the skin findings, and missed the tampon history entirely because he didn't think to ask. I didn't take it any further. I had documented my opinion; Mrs. Monroe survived, so it didn't matter. What did matter was that the dermatology perspective was the key to making the diagnosis of a potentially life-threatening disease. His rigidity mattered too, but only in its negative effect on my general opinion of doctors.

That's the problem with medical dogma: diagnostic criteria are usually designed to confirm well-established or severe cases of a particular disease. The reality is that diseases usually begin as milder forms, and the criteria might not yet apply. In toxic shock syndrome, for example, one of the criteria for diagnosis was 'peeling skin of the hands and feet'. The mistake there is that the peeling doesn't happen until two weeks after the hand and foot rash is first visible. The patient could be dead in two weeks. Making the correct diagnosis requires recognizing nuances of physical signs and putting them together with historical facts.

The proof of Shirley Monroe's diagnosis would come in two weeks: if the skin of her hands and feet began to peel off in sheets, the diagnosis of early toxic shock syndrome would be secure. I saw her in two weeks and marveled at the thick sheets of peeling skin from her palms and soles, new pink, healthy skin underneath. Fortunately she had recovered completely and had learned how to properly use tampons so she would avoid getting it again.

The case of Shirley Monroe, while not medically groundbreaking, became a high yield teaching case that I used repeatedly. The patient's history, the lead-up to hospitalization, the photographs, the laboratory studies, the uncertainty, plus the arguments with the infectious disease consultant, each carried valuable teaching points about a disease that could kill if not recognized and treated early in its course. She would have been an excellent case to present at M&M conference. Teaching hospitals conduct Morbidity & Mortality conferences regularly to present cases where errors have occurred or something could have been done better to prevent a bad outcome. Since she was hospitalized at a small non-academic hospital, no M&M took place.

GROWING PAINS

MY DAY-TO-DAY PRACTICE of dermatology became busier to the point that I felt it was time to take on a partner and move into a larger office. *Back to work* had grown from jealous mistress into dominatrix with bull whip. It sometimes felt like I was riding a runaway train down a steep mountain side. I needed an associate with whom to share call, share patient load, as well as to share the enjoyment of interesting cases.

Dr. Parker had chosen me to be one of the moderators of the Wednesday morning morphology conference. From the moderator's chair, I got to discuss nuances of skin disease with residents and faculty, while at the same time, assess resident's knowledge. Moderating that conference was one of my all-time favorite activities in medicine. I had been observing the performance of one particular resident, Dr. Bert Tavelli, a balding red-head with a quick-to-smile round face and goatee, and had been impressed with his thoughtful approach to diagnosis. This man I could work with. We eventually got around to having a discussion, and luckily for me, he had been thinking the same thing. We envisioned plans for him to join me in an expanded new office in my building. We weren't buddies socially, but I preferred a good honest colleague whom I could trust, to a good friend as business partner. We ended up sharing an office and worked well together for about five years before I relocated out of Portland. I am not sure how well the arrangement worked for Dr. Tavelli. It took considerable time for his practice to build up, and I suspect he may have had doubts about whether it was a good decision to take on the financial responsibilities of a private practice right out of training. I was not taking a cut of his earnings and had therefore not given him a financial package. He was on his own from the start, to support his wife and children. But Bert always did the right thing, worked hard, and eventually got a solid footing in Northwest Portland.

Having two doctors more than doubled the complexities of our office staff. We both felt the growing pains of having several new hires on board, some more hard-working than others. The hardest working of the newcomers was Kathy, our receptionist. I had known Kathy from the Allergy Clinic years before, and liked how she interacted with patients and doctors alike, always professional but with an edgy attitude, an insult with a wink and smile. She held our front office together in a masterful daily performance that mollified waiting room patients until they were called for their appointments, and then back to check them out, all done seamlessly with a happy face and a sly comment whenever she could.

▪ SPEAKING OF WHICH

I WAS INVITED to deliver my first lecture on spironolactone and acne at the January, 1991 meeting of the Oregon Dermatological Society in Portland. The review paper I wrote, *Spironolactone in dermatologic therapy*, had been accepted and was 'in press' at the time. I looked forward to speaking on my home court about this exciting new treatment. Afterwards, I had doubts about whether any of the doctors in the room actually believed what I said or started using spironolactone on their patients. I understood that it might require some time to become familiar with the drug and its side effects before trying it, but I felt that I could provide the experience, and they could go forth into new territory to discover for themselves how successful the drug could be. Dermatologists had gone forth into new frontiers before, with lasers, with drugs such as methotrexate for psoriasis, and Accutane for acne. Because spironolactone was not a quick prescription for a cream or gel, I figured it would be an uphill struggle to get dermatologists on board. I had learned well by then that dermatologists were a conservative group. Furthermore, spironolactone being the off-label drug that it was in acne therapy, there wouldn't be a cute drug rep bearing gifts and starter samples every week to remind them to use the drug.

The more time I spent writing, the more I enjoyed it. All academic physicians write. Established academicians can easily fall into the situation where a junior person writes the paper and they attach their name to the article because of their position or as head of the laboratory. Many academic doctors have CVs full of papers that contain few or none of their own words and little of their sweat and blood. Years later, I eventually accrued a few of those publications as well in my own CV. It's part of the culture of academia. It is a pleasure and a luxury, though, to have something to say, and have the time to write it and publish it, as I did early on.

By the mid-1990s, my interest in academics grew to the point that I approached our new chair of the department at Oregon, Dr. Swanson, and asked to be considered as a full time faculty member. Neil Swanson had, a few years before, arrived from the University of Michigan to advance skin surgery at Oregon. He was at the time, and still is, one of the leaders of Mohs surgery and general skin surgery in the United States and internationally. He had recently become chairman, replacing Frank Parker.

I had been helpful to Neil. He was by far the best Mohs surgeon in the area, but Portland was tightly controlled by Managed Care, and the three main managed care companies refused to add him onto their panels as a 'provider'. Corporate medical politics had become self-defeating. We were unable to utilize the surgeon we needed most with our complicated skin cancer patients. So, to get around that limitation, I hired Neil as a contracted employee and billed his fees under my name. He would do some of his surgeries in my office, and some at the university. It wasn't an ideal situation, but it was better than not being able to use him at all.

I soon learned that I was rejected in my attempt to join the faculty at Oregon. The way I heard it, Dr. Frances 'vice-on-the-desk' Storrs voiced the dissenting vote. Whether that was true or not, I was disappointed. I would have brought all my experience with AIDS and hormonal acne in women to the residency and medical school. Both of us would have benefitted. Most of my patients, I am certain, would have followed me up to the hill, and the clinic on the hill could have used the business.

■ OUTLIER

BEFORE THE ADVENT of cell phones, I carried a pager every day of my career. My office could reach me, my patients could reach me through the answering service, emergency rooms and colleagues could reach me. I knew I had an over-developed sense of responsibility, but I always felt that if I chose to be in private practice, I needed to be available to the patients and the doctors who might need my help, and once in academics full time, the university and hospital operators could reach me as well for the same reasons. It could be stressful at times, being tied to home, or remembering to inform operators that I would be at a concert for two hours with the pager off, and then remembering to turn it back on later.

Right out of training, it was apparent that I was an outlier by being available and carrying a beeper. Dermatologists, to my surprise, didn't carry pagers. It wasn't as if the concept was foreign. They had worn pagers during residency, and being available was actually considered customary in most medical circles. But I used to be ridiculed for carrying one. "Shaw, you must be the only dermatologist in the world who carries a beeper!" a respected community dermatologist said one time at Wednesday morning conference.

The truth was that many dermatologists were entirely unreachable after hours. Their office phone messages usually went something like:

"This is doctor so-and-so's office. We are closed. If this is an emergency, go to your nearest emergency room (that phrase got them off the hook from a liability standpoint). We re-open such and such a time." Click. Dial tone. No way to leave a message. No way to reach a paging operator. It was an embarrassment to the profession in my view. Not all dermatologists chose to be unavailable, but enough of them did to explain why dermatologists were losing the public's respect. What good, after all, is a doctor who cannot be contacted?

Within a year or two out of residency, practicing in the community, I discovered also that most of my colleagues shirked what I considered to be another responsibility. They turned down requests to see patients in nursing homes. It was too much of a nuisance. It didn't pay enough. They eventually even turned down requests to perform in-hospital consultations. It wasn't worth their time to go to a nursing home or hospital to do a consult, even at the request of a colleague. They could see ten or twenty patients in the same amount of time at the office. Requests for nursing home consultations didn't happen frequently—maybe every two to four weeks on average—but I felt like I was the only dermatologist in my area willing (or foolish enough) to do hospital and nursing home consults. Thankfully, and without the need for any discussion, when Dr. Tavelli joined my practice, he shared my views and gladly saw consults if requested. Hospital consults, I admit, did not pay well, but I always thought they were part of the professional obligation that went with being a doctor.

By not going to hospitals and nursing homes, dermatologists were beginning a slow march into medical obscurity and isolation much the way plastic surgery had already done. By the mid 1980s, many dermatologists had offices that were strictly outpatient enterprises, disconnected entirely from hospitals, with free-standing surgical suites. Many allowed their hospital staff memberships to expire, or never joined hospitals in the first place.

In addition, many dermatologists in Portland refused to see Medicaid patients in their offices. Medicaid reimbursed poorly. These dermatologists apparently only wanted the cream, the highest paying patients, which I found to be not only repugnant but surprising since there were too many dermatologists in Portland and competition was fierce. I couldn't imagine being busy enough with high-roller patients to permit being that selective. I heard the specious argument from them, "I can't take Medicaid patients; they barely pay the overhead"—twisted reasoning based on the fact that Medicaid paid about fifty per cent of normal fees, and office overhead costs often were at least fifty per cent of total revenues. I always thought that practicing medicine should be about the patients to some degree, not just about the doctor, and that reimbursement patterns would probably average out over time. To my knowledge, no dermatologists were filing for bankruptcy. Watching my colleagues reject the undesirables in society offended my sensibilities and set me on a long slow path in support of nationalized health care where all doctors, and all patients, rich and poor, accept the same fee schedule for equal service. Of course, when I voiced those opinions, I became a pariah amidst my colleagues.

At national and regional meetings, dermatologists frequently sounded the alarms. They complained about threats to their reimbursement, how dermatology was crucial to public health, that we were the only ones who did skin disease well, and that the specialty was being eroded by government or insurance forces that were reducing reimbursements, on and on, *ad nauseum*, every business meeting. I once sat on a Medicare committee for reimbursement guidelines, and was accused of 'selling us down the river' by one dermatologist in Oregon. I had been trying for fairness in reimbursement instead of always lobbying for more and more.

I started to become disgusted by dermatologist's incessant whining about not getting the respect they deserved, through reimbursement. The fact was that Dermatology had been losing respect with the public for years, and for good reason. Dermatologists clamored for more money at the very same time as they increasingly shed their responsibilities to patients and colleagues.

Dermatology had quit dealing with entire categories of disease. Sexually transmitted disease had been taken over by infectious disease doctors and public health nurses; diseases such as lupus and its related conditions had been given to rheumatologists; I had watched endocrinologists and gynecologists start replacing dermatologists in the treatment of acne, at least acne in women. Community dermatologists started dumping their patients who might require extra time and effort. "I'm referring you to a colleague with more expertise," is how it usually went. The difficult patients—anything more complicated than a prescription for a cream—got sent to the tertiary dermatology centers or to a few interested individuals in the community. Some dermatologists removed themselves from patient care altogether by turning their offices into drug trial centers for pharmaceutical companies. That was in the 1990s. It is worse today.

During the course of my career, more and more doctors of other specialties also adopted the banking hours approach to practicing medicine. Many doctors demanded the revenue and respect that came with being a professional, but thought they could work tradesperson's hours and turn away all but high-revenue patients. Sadly, this insidious trend continues to build momentum in the U.S. and Canada today.

So, for my entire full-time career, my pager was as much a part of me as my wallet and watch. I felt naked without its little weight and touchpiece feel on my belt. I admit that my carrying a pager went beyond medicine. The pager number was the one my friends and family used, though the vast majority of calls were medical. For twenty-eight years, I had it exclusively on vibrate mode. If by mistake it rang with the full beep tone, it startled me like a hundred volts from a wall socket—not a good thing during surgeries. In the middle of the night I much preferred being awakened by the vibration buzz on the side table than the shrill tone of the beeper or telephone. I would get up and call back from another room so as to not disturb Wendy. Wendy, on the other hand, took her overnight call by telephone, in bed. The obnoxious ring would wake us both. Then she would conduct her business with full voice volume, there in the dark. The things we do for love.

CHAPTER 8

Explorations

■ CORPORATE MEDICINE

THERE HAD TO be a push and a pull for Wendy and me to start thinking about moving from Portland, where we had lived for nearly twenty years. We loved Portland. All of our best friends lived in Portland. Our kids had grown up there. Even so, Wendy and I found ourselves soul-searching. Our professional lives were somehow incomplete in Portland. For Wendy, the pull was the allure of a bigger pond. Portland had shrunk as her research and influence had grown. She had amassed the credentials to look for a larger position at an institution in a big city. For me it was probably more push than pull. I was ready to take on a more academic position, but being turned down at Oregon was the stronger motivator to leave. And then there was 'managed care'.

After ten years, I had become fed-up with the running of a private practice. Doctors had unwittingly allowed for-profit insurance companies to highjack healthcare delivery during the late 1980s and early

1990s. Out of fear of government intervention, doctors rejected President Clinton's attempt to reform healthcare, and convinced the rest of Americans to do the same. The result: for-profit managed care. Now, stock holders, not patients, were the only ones that mattered. An adversarial relationship developed between insurance companies and their clients, the patients. Doctors fell right into step and became greedier. What used to be considered a conflict of interest became acceptable. If corporations could capitalize on their conflicts of interest, why not doctors? The American Medical Association had lost credibility after it seemingly turned into a one issue organization—more money for doctors. I got thinking that joining an academic institution might eliminate some of the frustrations that went with running an office and dealing with the literally hundreds of insurance companies, the claims rejections and red tape.

One patient epitomized just how low health insurance practices had stooped in the Managed Care environment of Portland. This patient, Jane, had insurance with a 'gatekeeper' policy for visits to specialists. That meant that her primary care physician had the power to grant or reject her requests for visits to a specialist. The way gatekeeper plans worked, the fewer referrals to specialists, the more money the primary care physician took home. The incentive was clear.

Jane had recently been discharged from three days in hospital because of a severe immunologic skin reaction. Seventy per cent of her skin surface area had been covered with pustules. She recovered, but what triggered the reaction could not be established initially and she was consulting with me to try to prevent it from ever happening again. Because Jane's primary care physician rejected her request for the dermatology consult, she chose to pay privately, a fact I didn't know at the time.

Two minutes into our discussion, my nurse knocked on the examination room door.

"Excuse me, there's a phone call for your patient."

"Who is calling?" I asked.

"A doctor's office, I think." Jane looked at me quizzically, left the examination room and answered the telephone. For the next sixty seconds, I watched as Jane defended herself against comments from her physician such as, "What are you doing at Dr. Shaw's office? You have no business seeing a dermatologist…you didn't get authorization to see him." Jane defended herself admirably but was flabbergasted. "I am seeing him because my questions regarding my skin problem were not adequately addressed at your office…this does not involve your office…you wouldn't authorize a referral so I am paying out of pocket to see him." Although stunned, we were able to return gradually to our original medical discussion and address her questions.

I was incredulous. How did this happen? There must have been a mistake, or a major misunderstanding. Then I got angry. What doctor could possibly think that calling a patient out of another doctor's examination room to question her reasons for being there was acceptable professional behavior? My third and lasting emotion was sadness. Sadness that the practice of medicine was driven by market forces completely inconsistent with good medical care, and where doctors' offices advocate more for insurance companies (and themselves) than they do for patients. Sadness for Jane, who was put in such a defensive position, and whose privacy and confidentiality were breached. And finally, sadness for myself, that I could no longer trust the intentions of primary care doctors. Perhaps running away, leaving Portland, or affiliating with a large university, might rid me of this distasteful fight over the finances of medicine.

■ BOSTON

WENDY AND I once heard the joke that "Doctors move to Portland to retire." Though only partially true, we were not ready to relax into a predictable professional future with a vacation cabin in the mountains or at the coast. We liked the idea of change, new adventure, and the challenge of a university setting. We had enjoyed the natural beauty of Portland and the Pacific Northwest but had stopped taking advantage of the outdoors. The ocean and mountains had lost their allure. We were becoming inveterate urbanites. Give us museums, symphony, theater, and restaurants. Give us travel. Even our three daughters had started to do more in the city. We decided to start looking elsewhere.

My head symptoms had become a permanent part of my life by then, more than ten years. I had managed to live with them. The only good thing was that they hadn't deteriorated into something worse. I fought through them when they were bad, and enjoyed the good days when they were less severe. Fortunately, it looked as if I would not have to pass up the opportunity for a change in career path if we found interesting jobs in a bigger city.

One of the nice things about practicing medicine in North America is the degree of freedom that exists for moving around. In the U.K., where the National Health Service regulates practice locations, short of a death or retirement of a colleague, a specialist rarely has the opportunity to change locations. In the U.S. and Canada, doctors can go anywhere their credentials take them. Academic doctors move around frequently, some constantly, looking for opportunities to rise up in the ranks. We were not seeking rapid rise in rank, just a larger pond in which to swim, both personally and academically.

Wendy, already a successful academician, was the one who received invitations periodically to apply for positions elsewhere. I would be content with finding an acceptable position in a city where Wendy could land a job, but we had narrowed the choices to only a few. If it couldn't be Boston, New York, or San Francisco, we were content to stay in Portland. It was easy for her to decline offers from, say, Lubbock, Texas, or Tallahassee.

After a few months, Wendy received a call from The Brigham and Women's Hospital in Boston, part of Harvard University. They were looking for someone to lead their new Women's Health program. A new building was being built, and a large support team was in the making. While women's health was not Wendy's primary interest, she had published on women in academic medicine and would be a serious candidate. They also put me in touch with the dermatology division at The Brigham. After reviewing my CV, the dermatology division invited me to visit as well.

The division of dermatology at The Brigham had a new chairman, Tom Kupper, an international expert in lymphocyte trafficking in the skin and lymph nodes. My interview with Dr. Kupper was no less than inspiring. I knew we would work very well together, I as the clinician asking some clinical research questions, he as the scientist (and my boss) investigating them. My experience with HIV and organ transplant patients fit well with his immunological interests. I thought it could be an excellent partnership.

It was also good to be back in Boston interviewing. I had spent six years in Boston, my final two years of college plus four years of medical school. I had lived in Babe Ruth's suite in Myles Standish Hall in Kenmore Square, under the light of the great CITGO sign. I had lived in Brookline, in the student ghetto of Gainsborough Street, in a house off Brighton Avenue, in a tenement apartment off Dorchester Street; I had worked at the New England Deaconess Hospital on Longwood Avenue, the same neighborhood as The Brigham. I felt right at home.

My next interview after Tom Kupper was with Harley Haynes about whom I cannot say enough good things. I felt as if I had met a career soul mate after my interview with him. He certainly was a grand master of dermatology, with unsurpassed clinical expertise in diagnosis and treatment. Some individuals with that reputation could be arrogant, but he had a gentle, thoughtful demeanor. His interest in medical dermatology and disdain for cosmetic dermatology fit perfectly with mine. Here was another excellent partnership in the making.

I met briefly with Dr. Kenneth Arndt, then recognized for being longtime editor of the *Archives of Dermatology* (the leading clinical dermatology journal), and for his dermatology teaching publications and books, as well as his laser expertise. Scattered across a huge desk in the room where I waited to meet with him were hundreds of galley proofs of chapters from the exciting new dermatology textbook he had spearheaded and which was nearing completion. I remember wishing, "If only I had been asked to write the acne chapter in that book, this position would be a shoo-in!"

Overall, the visit to Boston was a huge success, and on the flight home we fantasized madly about the possibility of moving to Boston. It looked like the perfect next move. How could I improve on going directly from private practice to Harvard to work with such an impressive group? Within a few weeks, we both received attractive offers from our respective departments. Everything was moving along nicely and we were getting close to accepting the offers, when our eldest daughter made an announcement to Wendy: "I'm not moving with you. I'll move in with my dad." The floor fell out from beneath us. It turned out that we had not asked the most important question of all.

This was my step-daughter, a tenth grader by then, who was one of the first kids in America to live out her entire childhood in court-decreed joint custody, half at her dad's house, half with us. That has its own complicated story. If we left Portland, we would lose her. This got Wendy thinking in a way she never had before. It took me about thirty seconds to decide. The right thing to do was to NOT go to Boston. The separation and divorce had been difficult enough. To leave her behind and move away just did not seem right to me. Wendy was less certain. She thought that maybe she could visit multiple times throughout the year. After many long hours of agonizing, we agreed not to go. As I write this years later, my thinking has evolved somewhat. Two years at her dad's house doesn't sound so bad now. She would likely have survived. I still suspect, however, that it could easily have been interpreted by her as abandonment. That was the last thing she needed. Joint custody had been difficult enough.

My call to Tom Kupper to turn down the offer was without a doubt the most heart-wrenching telephone call of my entire career. He and I had become so optimistic during the recruitment process, and I now had to throw it all away. It would have been a good match for me, excellent for my career, possibly even a better fit for me than for Wendy. Dr. Kupper shared his disappointment but readily acknowledged that family came first. For months I resented Wendy—the wife giveth, the wife taketh away—for not having addressed the most important question before we got so emotionally attached to the idea of Boston.

■ A LOOK AT CHICAGO

A YEAR WENT by before we seriously explored leaving Portland again. About one year after we turned down the Brigham in Boston, Wendy received a call from Dr. Arthur Rubenstein, Chairman of the Department of Medicine at the University of Chicago. He was recruiting a chief for the 'Section' of General Internal Medicine. The University of Chicago, for its various medical specialty units had adopted the term 'section' instead of 'division', but they were synonymous. The prior section chief had taken a position at Mt. Sinai in New York, and the Chicago position had been empty for over a year.

Wendy expressed immediate interest, primarily because of Dr. Rubenstein. His stature and leadership success during five years as chairman of the Department of Medicine were well known in medicine circles. The concern we had, however, was Chicago itself. Would we consider living in a big Midwestern city when we had learned to love the coasts? Chicago, that town we flew *through* on the way to meetings? That windy, frigid, corrupt, Mayor Daley town of slaughterhouses and trains, devoid of mountains, trolley cars, and Madison Avenues? "Let's not turn it down outright," we said. We decided to take a look.

Again, it would need to be a double recruitment. Double recruitments had by then become a curse on academic departments everywhere. Wendy's own research had shown that the majority of women physicians were married to physicians, which of course meant that the number of husband and wife doctor teams had been growing. Bringing in two doctors when only one is being wooed complicates the process considerably. It more than doubles the effort and probably more than halves the chances of a successful recruitment. Wendy naturally was the one being sought after, and I was the tag-along recruit for whom they needed to find some meaningful academic work.

The University of Chicago presented more uncertainty in my mind, than The Brigham. Harvard was the Mecca of medicine in the world. Chicago was just another leading institution in an elite group of about twenty around the country. I didn't know the dermatology group at Chicago, so it would be new territory. Chicago had once been the Mecca of dermatology for two decades under the leadership of Dr. Stephen Rothman, a Hungarian Jew who left Europe in 1938 as Nazi Germany gained strength, and whose brilliant research in dermatology gave him the title of 'Father of Investigative Dermatology'. He died in 1963, long before I would have had a chance to meet him. My earliest recollection of the Chicago campus was the Gothic stone architecture when I passed through nearly twenty-five years earlier during a drive from Boston to the West Coast. Coincidentally, the building I kept in my memory banks, on Maryland Avenue, was the exact same one that housed the dermatology offices I would be visiting. Perhaps destiny was at play here, challenging my utter rejection of such a silly notion.

Dr. Rubenstein put together the best organized, most welcoming visit for Wendy and me that I could ever imagine. When we were finished, on the plane back to Portland after two days, we were totally enthralled with the place.

The first day, on arrival at O'Hare, we met Gersh, driver and owner of the car service we would use throughout the visit. Seemingly a tough guy turned gentle—was that accent Brooklyn or the Bronx?—Gersh was definitely not from Chicago. I enjoyed our sparring as he escorted us through the streets of Chicago. He assumed responsibility for all of our transportation during the entire visit: shuttling back and forth to downtown hotels, University meetings, dinner and brunch engagements, and everything in between. It's amazing how something as simple as ease of transportation can influence a recruitment visit. I've since observed nightmarish visits where the potential recruit rejects the institution long before any of the interviews take place, because of botched transportation. Ours could not have been smoother.

Melanie, Dr. Rubenstein's executive secretary, was possibly the most effective, organized secretary I've ever met. Professional and confident, elegant in appearance, she personally escorted Wendy and me to each of our interviews, staggered in time so she could manage it. A gentle knock by her on the door when time was up, a respectful introduction to each new faculty member we met, she never showed any sign of being frazzled.

At the end of one of my early interviews there came the knock at the door and there Melanie stood with a thumb gesture to move on. She escorted me through a maze of corridors to the office of dermatology faculty member Dr. Allan Lorincz on the fifth floor of the old clinical wing, formerly the Women's Lying-in Hospital, with its Gothic style gray stone from the 19th Century, and its gargoyles and spires.

Dr. Lorincz's narrow, grotto-like office bespoke a long history in academia—a stuffy feel, poor overhead lighting and dirty windows. The smell of old books hovered close. It was an inner sanctum of cluttered, complex learning, of retained archival records from early projects during a long career of investigation and teaching. Floor to ceiling book shelves lined the left hand wall as I entered, and small desk tops covered with medical paraphernalia and literature led the way to the back of the small room where a heavy desk sat in front of a tall window with a water-stained gray marble sill cluttered with papers. A row of four or five straight-backed chairs lined the other wall leading back to the door. I sat down on one of the stiff chairs nearest to the desk and Dr. Lorincz sat at his throne behind the desk as he had done for a quarter of a century, hands folded, his clean shaven face and completely bald head presenting an almost alien-like picture of high intellect.

In essence, my interview with Dr. Lorincz was an eminently pleasant monologue by him, mostly about his research and new ideas, in full detail. I suspected he had delivered that monologue before. I felt like I had traveled decades back in time. Nothing practical was discussed concerning my joining the U of C faculty.

Other interviews stood out as well. Dr. Keyomars Soltani had office hours once a week at the LaSalle office, a downtown outpost of the U of C designed to capture CEOs, money managers and pit traders at the Chicago Board of Trade. Gersh drove me there, with benefit of sports commentary of the Chicago Bulls. I was greeted by Dr. Soltani, a smiley-faced, somewhat formal looking man with blue eyes at the same height as mine. Dr. Soltani had practiced his entire medical career in the United States. To explain the accent, he said he had come originally from Persia. Iranians usually say they are from Persia, not Iran. Persia carries with it a larger sense of world history and respect. Dr. Soltani had been the section chief of dermatology at Chicago for five years.

He escorted me to the cafeteria for a light lunch. Sadly, what I remember most from the interview was not the substance—there must have been some—but Dr. Soltani's communication style. I could rarely finish a sentence before he would interrupt and hijack my thought in a completely different direction, and then follow it with "yes, you are absolutely right." I gave him the benefit of the doubt at the time— maybe he was nervous. I learned later, after joining the faculty, that interruption was his communication style of choice. A patient, who had switched his care from Dr. Soltani to me, one time expressed it beautifully. He said, "Dr. Soltani walks on my words."

I had lunched the day before with a group of residents. At the time there were a total of six—two in each of three years. We discussed dermatology as a specialty, the University of Chicago, "where fun comes to die", and the pros and cons of living in Chicago, not the least of which was the basketball dynasty of Michael Jordan and the Chicago Bulls at the time. One resident stood out as the most memorable in the group. Unfortunately it was because of his obsequiousness. His fawning agreeability, plastic smile and formal language—"yes, doctor" after anything I would say—threw a large red flag into my view. I'll never forget his saying, "The good thing about this program is that the faculty leave us alone." Another red flag. Sadly, his statement turned out to be true. Worse, though, his comment reflected his own lack of interest in learning any dermatology whatsoever. The resident's name was Francis 'Frank' Lowey. It would turn out that Dr. Lowey would consume an immense amount of my time and energy.

I remember the words of one of the junior dermatology faculty members who later that day walked me down the hall to the residents' room. "The residents are more likely to be playing Tetrus on the computer than studying dermatology. These are not the best residents in the world."

That evening we attended a dinner hosted by Dr. Rubenstein and his wife at their home. Dr. Soltani, as section chief, was the only dermatologist invited to the dinner. He didn't attend. However, Dr. Rubenstein's wife Denise was coincidentally a dermatologist who had trained under Dr. Lorincz. She practiced in central Chicago. I wouldn't be working with her directly if we came to Chicago, but she was a delightful person and valuable contact. She would help introduce me to the local community of dermatologists. Wendy and I both were in performance mode throughout the evening, and fell, exhausted, into the back of Gersh's car as he drove us back to our downtown hotel. From Dr. Rubenstein's home in Hyde Park, past the Museum of Science and Industry, we headed north on Lake Shore Drive. For the first time, we saw the night skyline of downtown Chicago sparkling in the distance like the Emerald City of Oz. All we could do was nod to each other in approval.

Before heading back to O'Hare the next day and home to Portland, I visited the school our kids would likely attend. The University of Chicago Laboratory School, famous for its research in education and academics, was on the U of C campus. Known for its stringent admission requirements, they made every effort to accommodate children of faculty, especially double faculty, which we would be. Then it was north with Gersh to O'Hare along the Kennedy Expressway, known affectionately as the Kennedy Parking Lot.

Winter was winding down, so a dirty March afternoon surrounded us. Mostly, however, we were oblivious to the traffic and the weather. We combined our thoughts about the move. There were pros and cons to this move. We had become more circumspect after having turned Boston down. We would be leaving all our friends in Portland, uprooting our two younger daughters Lauren and Toby, our eldest off to college by that time. I would be abandoning a ten year practice to leap off a cliff into the unknown of academics. Wendy's job as chief of the Section of General Internal Medicine seemed fairly structured, if multifaceted. Mine was less certain as a faculty member, with multiple open avenues for academic work. I saw room, though, for huge growth and possible leadership.

▰ TAKING THE LEAP

ONCE BACK HOME, we began the long process of obtaining Illinois licenses and collecting materials all the way back to high school for our academic appointments. Dr. Rubenstein, determined and supportive at every step, remained the mastermind behind the move. We got a lesson in recruitment by paying attention to his skills in communication and how he dealt with us, mostly through frequent telephone conversations. He outlined every step of the process and kept encouraging us along the way. His soothing South African accent became a pleasant addition to our lives.

In essence, we both were ready for a change. And Chicago? It would be okay. We were willing to give it a chance.

It is a daunting task to relocate one's family, to sell a house at one end and buy a house in unfamiliar territory at the other, get kids into schools, leave longstanding friendships behind, meet new friends, learn the new day-to-day routines.

After several more visits, we ended up having a lucky break in the purchase of a house we loved, a Georgian townhouse on Blackstone Avenue, eight minutes by foot from the Medical School. Walking distance from work had always been a priority for us. The purchase itself, however, was touch and go. It hinged on a five by seven foot contemporary aluminum sculpture in the back yard. There were two competitive bids for the 100-year-old house. Our offer stipulated that we keep the sculpture. Theirs said take it out. The sculpture, it turned out, had sentimental value to the sellers because it had been made by a family member. "We are working with the two doctors," the sellers said to the agent. A lucky break for us, since none of the other houses we had seen in the neighborhood had interested us in the least.

Wendy and I started to make final preparations. In addition to leaving private practice, I would be leaving twelve years as a volunteer at the Wallace Medical Concern, a free clinic for the homeless and poor. The clinic had an interesting history. Near the end of my residency twelve years earlier, Dr. Jim Reuler had approached me. An internist at the VA Hospital, Dr. Reuler had taken care of a patient named Mr. Wallace who, before undergoing heart surgery, made Dr. Reuler promise that he would not forsake the homeless of Portland and requested that a will be drawn up posthaste. He died the next day from complications of his surgery. A few months later, Dr. Reuler received a letter that Mr. Wallace had left a total of one thousand dollars to him in support of the project. Dr. Reuler, true to his promise, named the clinic after him. Not bad for a gift of one thousand.

It began as a single room in the Estate Hotel, a flop-house in Old Town Portland. I agreed to participate, and together with fellow resident Joel Datloff, began a long commitment to one evening per month. The patients we saw at first were drug addicts and schizophrenics who couldn't cope at all in society. I treated their skin problems; an internist or family doctor attended to their general medical problems. I recall one patient with open sores on his arms and face that might have been mistaken for deep infections but were from amphetamine-induced gouging of his skin.

Dr. Reuler eventually came up with enough funds to hire an executive director named Kathy who oversaw our activities and kept the place solvent. Volunteer nurses staffed each clinic. We used drug samples to stock our makeshift pharmacy. Instruments had been donated for minor surgeries. We even had a microscope to examine skin scrapings and smears. There were three examination rooms with poor lighting, and the whole clinic smelled of the musty hotel and the men who stayed there. While totally a shoestring operation, not infrequently we saw remarkably sick patients, new cases of AIDS, acute pneumonias. We would have to scramble to find hospitals around Portland that would accept them.

During the first six months, word got out about the free clinic and I started seeing sad young single-parent mothers with children and no health insurance. I recall walking to every clinic angry that the American people and American government refused to do the right thing in healthcare, thus necessitating volunteer clinics such as Wallace. At the end of each clinic, however, I usually felt somewhat better, invigorated about having helped a few patients in need. My partner Bert Tavelli also donated his time to Wallace Medical, as did several other dermatologists.

As I write this, Wallace patients have become somewhat of a blur: Scabies, boils, infections, AIDS, sexually transmitted diseases, Herpes, Shingles. What isn't a blur in my mind is the cake Kathy made on my last evening there. It was the absolute best cake I have ever eaten, a vanilla layer cake from scratch, silken and moist, bittersweet chocolate frosting. It was her mother's recipe. Or maybe her grandmother's. I remember standing there after we finished, the three of us—Kathy, the nurse, and me with our mouths full of cake— enjoying her exquisite labor of love.

▰ PREPARE FOR TAKEOFF

THE MOVE TO Chicago was imminent. My bonsai trees, foster children in a sense, had to remain on the West Coast. They wouldn't survive Chicago winters without a greenhouse. It was painful—I had trained and nurtured about fifteen trees over as many years—but I found good

139

homes for them with friends, especially long-time high school friend Steve Anderson from Tacoma. Steve was the one who had most influenced my interest in bonsai and who took most seriously the care of his own collection of trees.

I arranged to sell my practice to esteemed colleagues in the neighborhood—my partner had made his own plans to start a private office in an adjacent building. I then had the privilege of composing a goodbye letter to my patients which stated, in essence, that I felt I had become as close to many of them as professional limitations permitted. I would truly miss them.

The move happened mid-December, 1996, coinciding with an early Chicago snowstorm. Moving day happened to be on our daughter Toby's birthday, a fact of which she reminds us now and then. An icy wind whipped up the snow as we entered our empty house on Blackstone Avenue. Vacant as the house was, everything seemed to be intact, no leaks or broken windows. Within minutes of our arrival, Wendy's colleague, Nicholas Christakis, a brilliant social scientist and internist who lived in the neighborhood, dropped by with a care package of food staples. Our entire neighborhood was full of University of Chicago faculty members, all with prodigious IQs. In our row of five townhouses alone lived four Chicago faculty members, three in medicine, two in psychiatry, one in the math department. The whole neighborhood was a veritable faculty ghetto. We became friends with Nicholas and his family. He was proud of his Greek heritage and we will always remember him fondly for the comment he made to us two years later as we passed him on the street on our way to eat Italian food with my parents who were visiting. With his nose slightly in the air, he said of the Italian food, "A derivative culture."

We had made plans to spend our first night in Chicago with Sharon Gilmore, long time artist friend of Wendy's, in her bungalow north of the city. Gersh picked us up and drove north on Lakeshore Drive, past the stunning Christmas Chicago skyline and into the town of Evanston. On a narrow plot of land, Sharon's cottage, a house legendary for The Eagles and Linda Ronstadt having jammed there on several occasions in the past, was nestled between two large apartment buildings. The house barely had room for her and Lucky, but she had made lavish arrangements to accommodate us for a night or two until our moving van arrived. She even kenneled her beloved Lucky to make room for our black Labrador retriever.

Wendy and Sharon had been friends for twenty years. They met at McGill and had coincidentally both moved to Portland back in the late 1970s, Sharon first, then Wendy a year later. The friendship grew for years in Portland until Sharon moved to Chicago to study at the Art Institute. One could have thought we were following Sharon around North America.

Nurse by night, talented artist by day, Sharon sculpted found objects and fabrics into powerful pieces of emotional and political import. She periodically showed around Chicago, and sold her work regularly, though not enough to allow her to give up her nursing job.

Sharon's broad accepting smile, her tall slender stature, together with her prematurely silver hair flowing past her shoulders, portrayed the mysticism that was her essence. Hope and belief flowed out of Sharon as honestly as joy exudes from a happy child. In the thirty years I have known Sharon, going back to the Portland years of broken marriages and renewals, she has always been a great emotional support to us both.

After a near-blizzard night of howling wind and snow, Sharon came with us to our new house in Hyde Park to lend her artistic eye to the arrangement of our furniture and effects. She had always been there for us when we needed her. In the uncertainty of having just uprooted our family, we definitely needed her those first few days.

CHAPTER 9
Chicago Beginnings

"No realistic, sane person goes around Chicago without protection."
-Saul Bellow

■ DRINKING FROM A FIRE HOSE

WENDY AND I and the girls dived headlong into our new lives in Southside Chicago. I kicked through snow ten inches deep every day along East 58th Street to the medical school, past Frank Lloyd Wright's famous Robie House, past the Rockefeller Chapel with its massive carillon of seventy-two bells, largest in the world. We made an effort to walk home from the University together most evenings. Those winter walks, snow sparkling under the streetlights, the carillon bells ringing their discordant tunes, became an enchanting part of living so close to campus.

It was complicated, though. Wendy could never walk home alone, especially at night. Almost everyone we knew had a story to tell. One colleague had come from Portland for a visiting fellowship and on his first day was held up at knifepoint in broad daylight on our street. One young physician on faculty was mugged on her front porch as she and her husband brought their newborn baby home from the hospital. Our daughter's pediatrician, a Chicago faculty member, was accosted at gunpoint in the parking lot of the grocery store where we shopped. She was lucky to distract the perpetrator long enough to extract her belted-in child from the car seat before he drove away in her car. A man was shot dead by a cab driver in that same parking lot a year later. Two eighth grade boys, classmates of our kids, were robbed and beaten up by older boys fifty feet from our front door. Shouts from a man running down our street woke us at two o'clock one morning with "Help! Call the police!" The following year, the brilliant seventh grade son of a faculty member survived a violent break-in of his house while his mother stepped out for a short errand. He was battered and shut in a closet. Ten years later, his mother says he has never fully recovered emotionally. Yes, life in Hyde Park could be complicated.

The University of Chicago boasted having one of the largest private police forces in the nation. Emergency blue-light telephone stations with direct connections to university police adorned most street corners throughout our neighborhood. I don't know how secure they actually made us, but the phones did give us a sense of connection with security. University security warnings started popping up on our emails weekly, telling of the latest muggings, stabbings, or shootings. It wasn't until after a year of being bombarded by these emails that some clever person had the wisdom to recognize the negative effect the announcements were having on faculty morale, and discontinued them. It was better not to know how bad it was out there.

"I wonder if we will leave Chicago before or after our violent event," I said to Wendy a few months after arriving.

Perhaps we were paranoid. One side of my brain said, "This is a big U.S. city: get used to it." Our immediate neighbors in the attached townhouse, the luminary and longtime University of Chicago internist/ethicist, Dr. Mark Siegler and his family, seemed to flow with the uncertainties of the neighborhood. The Sieglers had lived on Blackstone Avenue for over twenty years. They had raised four children, and had never been victims of violence to my knowledge. They left their front door unlocked most of the time. They did however have Cleo, a waist-high black Lab with a convincing bark, just inside the door.

The street-wise side of my brain kept antennae out at all times. Late at night I used to walk in the middle of the street, thinking that being in the street itself was somehow less vulnerable than being on the sidewalk. One incident confirmed that we weren't just being paranoid. Our daughter Toby and a friend one time missed their stop on the southbound train from downtown Chicago. Both tenth grade girls, they had been yakking too much about their makeovers. The next few stops took them deeper into unfamiliar south side neighborhoods as they became more frightened and uncertain about what to do. One rider advised that they get off at the next stop, switch to the northbound track, but NOT to go into the neighborhood to use a telephone. A security officer on the train, a woman, advised the same thing. They got home safely, but were shaken, and it confirmed to me that the rest of South Chicago shared our concerns. It was not a pleasant way to live.

In spite of South Chicago angst, we took great advantage of the culture of the city. Sir Georg Solti conducted Stravinsky's *Symphony of Psalms* at Symphony Hall early in our stay. Solti died within months of that concert, but the power and beauty of that one performance will haunt me forever. Toby, our youngest daughter with near-perfect pitch, got selected by Bobby McFerrin to sing a close-up improvised duet with him during a Chicago Symphony Orchestra concert he was conducting at Symphony Hall. At Chicago museums I discovered the contemporary paintings of Gerhard Richter, the disturbingly symbolic paintings of Philip Guston, the photographs of Cindy Sherman. I deepened my enjoyment of Rene Magritte's surrealism at the Chicago Art Institute to the point of recreating in our house a 3-D simulation of his painting of the train coming out of the fireplace. We had a nonfunctioning fireplace with a white mantle piece in the bedroom of our one hundred year-old townhouse. It had immediately reminded me of the Magritte painting, *Time Transfixed*, of the train coming out of a fireplace, white mantle, clock and candle sticks. One day I secretly bought a large scale electric train engine about eighteen inches long, and when Wendy was away at a meeting, suspended it so it came out from our fireplace just like in Magritte's painting. I placed some old candle sticks on the mantle that matched those in the painting. A clock needed to be found. When Wendy returned from her meeting, she said, "Look at what they gave me. It's nice enough, but I have no idea where to put it." She unwrapped the gift, a heavy rounded desk clock, at which point I silently beckoned her upstairs with my forefinger. "I have just the place for it." We enjoyed that kitschy little homage to Magritte for years.

And there was jazz. At the Green Mill, that intimate art deco jazz club of the Al Capone era, I first heard Kurt Elling's hip, satin voice, close-up drumming of Paul Wertico, as well as many other fine jazz musicians. Despite Chicago's infamous underbelly, in many ways this great city was delivering where Portland had fallen short, and overall, we were pleased that we had moved.

Wendy's position as Chief of General Internal Medicine, under the mentorship of Dr. Rubenstein, was giving her invaluable leadership experience. I would frequently meet her at the end of the day so we could walk home together. One evening, I asked how her day had gone. Her eyes widened. "Like drinking water from a fire hose," she said. At least we wouldn't likely get bored in our new jobs.

In the years before we moved to Chicago, Wendy had risen within the ranks of General Internal Medicine in Portland and around the country. Her research in Portland had focused on residency training and doctor-patient communication skills. She had completed a large survey study of women in medicine that found its way into the New England Journal of Medicine, quite a feat for a women's study, that journal being the stalwart guild of alpha-males that it is. After that, she started directing her research to doctor communication styles and how they influenced malpractice suits, patient satisfaction, and physician satisfaction. She had won awards and taken on leadership positions in medical societies. Wendy's career was clearly on the rise, and her leadership talents had been constrained in Portland. Chicago had all the potential for her to grow.

My position in Chicago started slowly but became more fascinating every day. I found myself in new territory, having just abandoned private practice for a life in academics. The biggest adjustment was not doing the hiring or firing of people who worked with me. Whereas Bernie and my other employees had been trained specifically for my needs, I was now a cog in a large wheel and had to play by someone else's rules. I knew from residency that medicine in large institutions could be frustrating, and Chicago reaffirmed that. While the nurses and secretaries were mostly excellent, they could be spread thinly at times, or could call in sick unexpectedly, and we had to do much by ourselves. It brought back memories of being a first year resident at the VA.

Teaching residents is all bedside and very little classroom. Doctors in universities see patients just as community doctors do in private practice, we just do it less. We earn less as well. Someone like me with the title of *clinician-educator* sees patients about fifty per cent of the time, whereas a *clinician-scientist* might see patients ten to fifteen per cent of the time, with eighty-five per cent time for research. Students and residents learn by shadowing us, by seeing patients and presenting their findings to us for discussion. Protected time—the hours we have to ourselves, apart from clinical care and teaching—becomes one of the most sought-after components of an academic doctor's week. That's when we do our research, writing, committee work, and administration. The more grant funding we have, the more protected time we have. The best *physician-scientists* ultimately see a minimal number of patients, and many give up clinical activities altogether.

My entourage in the clinic consisted of one or two dermatology residents plus a few medical students or general medicine residents. Clinics were busy, twenty or so patients per afternoon. I would try to teach a little with every patient—a diagnostic pearl here, a therapy pearl there.

▆ THE STARTING LINEUP

THE SECTION OF Dermatology at the University of Chicago was a mixed, if not mixed-up group, despite their strong medical credentials. I soon discovered that I was, by my way of thinking, one of the least dysfunctional members of the whole section.

Dr. Keyoumars Soltani, the chief, had had a steady academic career with enough publications to gradually work his way up to full professor. Unfortunately, though, he was marginalized at the national level, possibly because his English was not strong enough to speak effectively at meetings. He had found a niche, though, in immunofluorescence (specialized testing for auto-immune diseases). He had also become an efficient dermatological surgeon.

Dr. Soltani's main fault as section chief was his strong aversion to conflict. He found ways to extricate himself from a controversy, if not an entire relationship, to avoid conflict. Dr. Soltani freely admitted that being chief did not suit him well. I suspected that it was because of his aversion to the political conflict that came with the job.

In Dr. Soltani I detected and admired an inner peace, his 'Persian' accent, always pleasant, irrespective of content, his habit of drinking tea—"Yes, nice flavoore, more ceeveelized" he would say with a broad smile. In his spare time, he was a sculptor.

Dr. Alan Lorincz, the most senior of the group, should have retired years before I arrived at Chicago. He still used body wraps with ointments and gauze as therapies, treatments that, while somewhat effective in their time, were much less effective than newer systemic therapies. He shunned the use of mainstream drugs such as Accutane for acne and methotrexate for psoriasis, and discouraged residents in their use. I found it deplorable. I fear there are thousands of patients around the country with poorly treated acne or psoriasis because their dermatologist was trained at Chicago. There was, however, one exception. Dr. Lorincz published the first reports of oral nicotinamide and tetracycline in the treatment of a severe blistering skin disease called Bullous Pemphigoid. For that we were all proud.

Dr. Lorincz is revered by his former residents. Their loyalty to him is among the strongest I've ever witnessed. He is deservedly recognized for his diagnostic astuteness and encyclopedic knowledge of dermatological science. He taught, though, by detached monologue, as if everyone should already know the material. The disappointing part was that the residents ate up being spoon-fed. Residents quickly learned that, once accepted to the Chicago program, they could get by with little effort. I suspect former residents of Dr. Lorincz strongly disagree with my interpretation. There had been, after all, some hard-working residents over the years. When I arrived, however, the motivated ones were the exception.

Dr. Maria Medenica (Americanized to 'med-a-Nee-ka' from the Serbian 'ma-Denit-za') was a dermatopathologist extraordinaire, venerated by Chicago dermatologists for her pathology reports and teaching. Doggedly diligent in her interpretation of each pathology slide, she could make diagnoses where many other dermatopathologists couldn't, but the time spent on each slide was more than anyone else could spend. It was not uncommon to find her asleep on Dr. Soltani's office couch when the early team arrived in the morning. She could get lost in the far reaches of her own office, her petite frame obscured behind her microscope and mountains of papers.

Nazi soldiers had burst into her home in the early 1940s—her mother was Jewish. She only referred to the trauma occasionally in short outbursts more like expletives than commentary. I suspect she suffered from post-traumatic stress disorder most of her life. Just my entering her office with a question, she would jump. It was sad.

Drs. Soltani, Medenica, and Lorincz represented the old guard of dermatology at the University of Chicago. All had tenure, all had had illustrious careers, and all would likely continue on as long as their intellects allowed, maybe longer.

Three additional faculty members filled out the dermatology section. Dr. David Pezen had many of the characteristics of a successful academician: intelligence, ambition, basic science experience, special skills in information technology, and good inside knowledge of the University of Chicago infrastructure and faculty. The first in his family to go to college, his talent had landed him a research fellowship at the National Institute of Health during the international race to discover the AIDS virus. He actually held in his hand the 'blot' that proved, to the shock of the scientific world, that the AIDS virus being studied extensively in the United States by Dr. Robert Gallo's laboratory was the strain that had been first isolated by Dr. Luc Montagnier in France.

When I came to Chicago, Dr. Pezen had just become an important right hand man to Dr. Soltani, who needed a strong phalanx. The two played good cop, bad cop very well, Dr. Soltani dodging conflicts while Dr. Pezen laid down the law.

Dave Pezen became an important supporter of mine during my time at Chicago, and I always appreciated his astute perspective on the politics of the place. He could be petulant, however, and found university politics aggravating to the point of ultimately rejecting academic life for a practice in the community.

Dr. Scott Phillips had been hired to start up a center for pharmaceutical drug trials. He was famous around campus for running through the basement mazes of hallways during frigid winter months when he was on call, training for marathons. At a faculty meeting, Dr. Phillips became the unlucky recipient of one of Dr. Medenica's outbursts. He had made some remarks about a disciplinary action concerning a resident, and Dr. Medenica was such a loose canon that she blurted out to him, "Sometimes even a Jew can be part Nazi!"

The sixth, and by no means least, faculty member in our section was Dr. Shail Busbey. She had been hired by the internal medicine faculty a few years before my arrival. She saw dermatology patients in the medicine clinic, not ours, and was the favored clinical dermatologist for most faculty members and their families. She had created a loyal following. She gradually fell more into the fold of our group, became a full-time member of the dermatology section, and took an interest in research, teaching, and publishing.

So, that was the dermatology family of the University of Chicago as I found it at the end of 1996. A dysfunctional family, to be sure, but not entirely so, and not a great deal more dysfunctional than other departments of dermatology I had known and would learn to know. Residents came and went, teaching continued as it had for close to a century, and we diagnosed and treated patients in the best way we knew how. Some research took place, with the odd article getting published now and then. But it was far from the academic jewel it had been in the era of Stephen Rothman. There was room for improvement.

■ OPPORTUNITY CALLS

ABOUT SIX MONTHS into our first year we received the surprise announcement that our chairman of medicine, Arthur Rubenstein, would be leaving to become dean at Mt. Sinai medical school in New York City. While disappointing to me, the news devastated Wendy. If we had known he was going to leave after six months, we would never have moved to Chicago. What was worse, his decision was driven by a lack of support from our dean who had made Dr. Rubenstein's position so untenable that he felt he must leave. That's how it's done in academic medicine. Doctors are not usually fired; they are marginalized to the point of choosing to leave. Dr. Rubenstein had been too successful. He carried too much power and respect from his faculty for the dean's comfort. We felt sorry for ourselves, though. We were losing a mensch, but Arthur was going from a chair of medicine to a dean position, a significant upward move. We would miss him.

Greater Chicago, with its eight million inhabitants, provided much more variety when it came to patients and skin disease, than Portland had with its less than half a million. Each of five Chicago academic institutions drew patients from surrounding neighborhoods. Chicago has long been known for its colorful neighborhoods. Northwestern University saw affluent patients from the Gold Coast, the Loop, the Magnificent Mile all the way up to Lincoln Park. A bit to the west, Rush University, University of Illinois, and Cook County were clustered together and got their patients from the central neighborhoods of Pilsen, Little Italy, the West Loop and Garfield Park. The ethnic mix, heavy on Polish and Hispanic, self-selected where they went. Those with money ended up at Rush, those in between used UIC (U of Illinois at Chicago), while the destitute gravitated to Cook County Hospital. Further south, we at the University of Chicago took care of Hyde Park, Lincoln Park, McKinley Park and Englewood all the way past Midway Airport. The majority of U of C's patients were of African-American descent, though not all. And patients got shuffled around the entire city based on a particular doctor's area of expertise. The Chicago Dermatology Association had been hosting world famous meetings every month for over one hundred years, meetings where wild and wonderful patients and their diseases were put on display for teaching purposes, and each institution, in a healthy competition, tried to outdo the other.

One sizable segment of patients at the U of C came from its alumni and faculty, many of whom lived in Hyde Park. The Chicago faculty had always been an impressive lot. University tour guides made regular use of the fact that Chicago boasted a disproportionately high number of Nobel Laureates. The best Nobel Laureate story I heard was the doctor who was reviewing his resident's admission note. The note began, "This seventy-eight year old N.L. with new onset chest pain, etc., etc…"

At Chicago, the term Nobel Laureate had been transformed into an acronym!

Around Thanksgiving, toward the end of our first calendar year at Chicago, Dr. Leif Sorensen, the acting Chair of Medicine after Dr. Rubenstein's departure, called me into his office. Dr. Soltani had just tendered his resignation as chief of dermatology, and Dr. Sorensen was offering the position to me. Earlier, Dr. Soltani had expressed to me his reluctance about being section chief. He apparently thought I had brought enough fresh thinking and organization to the section to permit him to step down. It made perfect sense for him to resign the position. As he also had tenure, I silently hoped this move might mean that he was planning to retire soon.

"I'd like some time to think about it," I told Dr. Sorensen.

"I'll need yo ansah within the week," he said in his soft Scandinavian accent.

The time-honored approach to choosing new academic leaders is to form a search committee of a few people from within and outside the division in question, advertise in journals, review CVs of interested parties, and interview a select group of applicants. The committee makes a non-binding recommendation to the chair, who concludes the search with a unilateral decision. In institutions with budgets too small to run a full search, or when chairs care more about loyalty and control than about bringing in new talent, division heads are sometimes hand picked without the full vetting and selection process.

Dr. Sorensen offered the position of chief directly to me because the section of dermatology was insignificant in the grand scheme. Compared to the budgets of larger sections like cardiology, we were irrelevant. Our training program was manageably small. More importantly, it would have been costly to conduct a search which could easily have failed to yield a new chief, especially since our section was a fixer-upper. I was the new kid in town, Dr. Sorensen knew I could probably handle the job, and by choosing me, he could fix the problem of Dr. Soltani stepping down. All respectable rationales.

I gave the offer serious thought. I could have benefitted from sage advice from someone who had been in similar shoes, but no one materialized to provide it. What resources would I need to move the section ahead academically, to recruit good people? On the other hand, such advice might not have helped because our section contained three tenured professors who, despite slowing down, could not be fired to make room for new faculty.

I examined the pros and cons. In the positive column were leadership experience, interactions with a new chair of medicine, rubbing elbows with heads of dermatology departments around the country, and most importantly, having some influence over what was taught in my residency program. Residents needed to learn about the use of oral medications that the senior most professors refused to use; they needed surgical training; wound care; more exposure to ultraviolet light therapy. The list went on and on.

In the negative column was mainly my dread of working with the senior trio of Soltani, Lorincz, and Medenica, set in their ways, and who had already shown signs of resistance to my leadership. "We've always done it this way" was alive and well at Chicago. Why humans latched onto beliefs that closed doors to progress had always baffled me. I'm sure all humans do it to some extent, but the insular thinking at Chicago was definitely a negative.

I added more columns. In the anxiety column was the administrative arm, the daunting responsibility for the success of the section and the training of residents that I had never before administered. It would be like inheriting a large family over night. I would be in charge of six faculty, six or more residents, ancillary staff numbering about twelve, a busy clinical operation, a dermatopathology lab that processed fifteen thousand slides every year, and a budget that I had not yet scrutinized.

In the uncertainty column, my health was pretty good—the head symptoms fluctuated as they had for years. So far, no major neurological disease had declared itself. Urgency and stress, i.e. adrenaline, actually lessened the symptoms, so taking the position might keep them at bay. My own doctor had done routine blood tests. He had said, "Your cholesterol profile is so good that if you die of coronary disease, it's publishable, and I'll even put your name on the article." Family life had stabilized since the move, the kids were thriving at Lab School, and Wendy, though unhappy about Dr. Rubenstein leaving, seemed to be enjoying her work. We had started to build friendships. We hadn't been mugged yet. We even hired a chef to cook dinner for us three nights a week. Life was good.

    I decided to accept. I think I made the decision more out of curiosity and a sense of adventure than anything else. Though inexperienced and naïve in that kind of leadership, I felt energized about the work to be done, and comfortable enough with my people skills to make it happen. No big recruitment package fell into my lap. Perhaps a savvier manager could have negotiated one, but Dr. Sorensen offered to work with me on recruitments, so I hadn't pushed it. I outlined the projects I thought were important for the next few years. I remembered that Dr. Rubenstein had made two million dollars available to Wendy when she took over as chief of general internal medicine (a much larger section), and in retrospect, I should have tried to secure at least $300,000 or $500,000 from Dr. Sorensen. In the end, it probably didn't matter. I brought in new people and built infrastructure anyway.

CHAPTER 10

My New Family

■ THE PLOT THICKENS

I BEGAN MY NEW role as Section Chief in December 1997, exactly one year after we arrived in Chicago. A few congratulatory letters came in from those who felt they needed to make contact, i.e. those connected to Wendy or to my father from an earlier time. My friend Josh from Portland painfully hit the nail on the head when he asked, "Did no one else want the job?"

I knew where I stood in the ranks of dermatology chairs around the country, but I also remembered the words of Dr. Zbinden from Good Samaritan Hospital who said that it is not the geniuses of the world but those who work hard in the trenches that often accomplish more. I knew I could improve the section, not likely to Stephen Rothman stature, but at least to a point where we were more mainstream instead of the backwater we had been for the last twenty years.

I needed first to have the faculty work together, and to spur the residents into action, to perform, to adopt some critical thinking skills. During the prior year, I had observed each faculty member operate in a bubble, and residents coasted. I repeatedly told the residents, "Your duty is to question everything you hear from us and confirm its validity yourselves. Go to the literature. Look up the study." There were practical housekeeping matters too, such as a dire need for a library/conference room of our own. And then there were fiscal problems. There were always fiscal problems.

Shortly after my being installed as chief, a colleague said, "The first thing you need to do is to fire somebody. Then they won't fuck with you." I knew we were long on superannuated faculty, but short of poisoning one of them, I wouldn't be able to get rid of anybody. They all had tenure, which at Chicago often meant until death us do part. Instead, I worked more closely than ever with them. As the saying goes, organizing doctors is like trying to herd cats, and in my section, the aphorism fit well. Nevertheless, I set up regular faculty meetings, instituted a lecture requirement for residents, and designed surgery lectures. I cancelled Saturday clinics so residents had a full weekend off. These and many more immediate changes were miniscule, but collectively, I hoped they might create some semblance of camaraderie and set the stage for greater performance.

Within the first month, an email landed on my desk from the chief resident. One of our on-call residents had refused an after-hours request by the emergency room physician to assess a patient with disseminated herpes infection (a potentially fatal condition). In fact, the patient wasn't seen by the resident until the middle of the following day. I knew enough about this resident to know that it was not about bad judgment; it was about his familiar pattern of shirking responsibility. I would need to deal with the problem. I would be dealing with residents for three years that I had had no input in selecting, and I wouldn't be able to fire any of them without huge cause. They were the appurtenances that came with the job.

We are told to expect the unexpected, but what happened next was something I would never have imagined. About two months into it, I received a call from one of the attorneys from University Legal Affairs.

Our secretary Yolanda had filed a suit against one of our residents and against the university. She had already been gone for a month of medical leave. We heard she was quite sick, but now Legal Affairs was learning that Yolanda had launched the suit because her illness had been caused from a drug prescribed months earlier by Dr. Frank Lowey, the resident about whom I had had so many doubts on my first interview day. He had prescribed the drug as a favor to her, and had done it alone, with no medical record or staff supervision. The drug had caused severe lung disease, and if Yolanda survived at all, it looked as if she would never be able to work again. Unfortunately, I wasn't at liberty to make contact with Yolanda to lend my support. Lawsuits prevented such personal gestures.

Any doctor might have prescribed that particular drug to Yolanda. Her lung disease was an unpredictable complication of a drug that eventually affected hundreds of patients, a complication that turned into a national class action suit against the drug maker. The problem was that Dr. Lowey had prescribed the drug outside the legalities of a residency contract. Yolanda had asked Dr. Pezen to prescribe the drug too, but he had been wise enough to insist that she get it through her family doctor or internist.

As a faculty group we discussed what should be done. Dr. Lowey had already been the topic of many of our faculty meetings. He was chronically unavailable, didn't answer his pager. "I'm so sorry, doctor. It won't happen again," he would say, repeatedly. Dr. Pezen once discovered Lowey hiding in a utility closet during clinic to avoid seeing patients. Weeks earlier, as director of the clinic at the time, Dr. Pezen removed Lowey from all clinical activities because of his unprofessional behaviors. In a letter to Dr. Soltani, section chief at the time, he said. "Francis Lowey has repeatedly shown the inability to assume responsibility for the care of patients assigned to him…he has on numerous occasions pawned his patient care responsibilities to his fellow residents…blatant disregard for patients…has refused to work with certain attendings…"

I raised the possibility of his being 'impaired', the politically correct term for drug or alcohol addicted. Some of the faculty thought he didn't look well, had lost weight, looked tired, supporting the 'impaired' theory. We couldn't prove it though. During prior administrations, the culture of leniency had prevailed and no action had been taken against his irresponsible behaviors. Now, with this rogue prescription, Dr. Lowey had put the whole university at risk.

I presented what details I knew to the faculty. I emphasized that something formal needed to be instituted to monitor his behavior. The junior faculty agreed with me and shared their own experiences with Lowey's incompetence. Drs. Lorincz and Medenica disagreed, thinking we were persecuting Lowey for personal reasons. Dr. Soltani remained silent. After much contention between the two camps, we arrived at a decision. I, of course, was the evil one in the eyes of the senior camp, for pushing for disciplinary action. We placed Frank Lowey on probation for the remainder of his residency, approximately four months.

I drafted a formal probation letter and had it reviewed by Legal Affairs. The annual meeting of the American Academy of Dermatology was about to begin, so I delivered the probation letter personally to Lowey in Orlando at the February meeting. He and I met outside on an empty terrace like two secret agents exchanging information. The letter stipulated, among other things, that he was allowed to write prescriptions only with staff supervision, and that further independent prescribing of any kind would be grounds for expulsion. He agreed to the conditions of the letter. He also agreed to be tested on his dermatology knowledge every two weeks, by me, with Dr. Lorincz in attendance as chaperone to ensure that I was fair.

What I knew about Dr. Lowey up to that time was that he was at least six years older than the rest of the residents. He had originally come from Hyde Park and had attended Lab School through grade twelve. He lived alone with his mother. He had started medical school at the University of Illinois but transferred after two years to St. Louis. After one year of surgery residency in Cleveland, he dropped out of medicine entirely for reasons that were never clear, and from what I could gather, spent the next six years in England, at Oxford, in an area of economic studies. For reasons that were also never explained to me, he eventually chose to leave Oxford and try to return to medicine. Why anyone might have thought that a doctor could reenter medicine directly after a hiatus of six years, I didn't understand. I recalled, with acid in my stomach, the visceral alarm I experienced when I first met Lowey, that something was amiss with this man. Whether it was fixable was rapidly becoming doubtful.

EX LIBRIS

WE RETURNED FROM the AAD meeting, back to the tasks of treating skin disease and minting new dermatologists. Maybe the Lowey issue would blow over.

In the meantime, I had a library to create. For years, what the section of dermatology had called their library was largely overtaken by resident desks, computers and file cabinets. As a resident room it was extravagant compared, at least, to what I had during my training at Oregon, but in the gradual transition, the library had been usurped. The main science library—The Crerar Library—had everything ever published in medical science but was a fifteen minute walk from our offices. And despite each faculty member having small private collections of journals, access to those wasn't easy (this was before journals went digital). Dr. Lorincz talked students to sleep in his dark office, Dr. Medenica taught at the six-headed microscope, a method I favored, but there was no equipment to project pathology slides to our whole group during conferences. We were sorely in need of a larger library for communal learning and conferencing. I started considering ways to create such a room.

I had introduced the idea to the acting chair of medicine before accepting the section chief position. Surprisingly, after two months he committed fifty thousand dollars to the project and I immediately began working with building planners. We first had to find space. Dermatology lived on the fifth floor of what earlier had been a maternity hospital. The halls were rock solid, fully tiled, with curved granite floor moldings and heavily plastered walls. Our individual offices were once birthing rooms, large enough for a group of doctors and students to deliver a reluctant baby. Each door had a push plate instead of a doorknob, and opened only with the help of a shoulder. We wouldn't be tearing down any walls to design a library.

It is amazing, though, what hidden rooms, lost and neglected, can be discovered in the halls of a century old medical center. By poking around and opening locked doors we discovered, in a corridor just north of the main dermatology offices, a room that must have been in disuse for over twenty-five years. It had formerly been a maternity operating theater, complete with a raised dais at the back for students and residents to observe surgeries, not with the grandeur of the Johns Hopkins surgical amphitheater, but with historical charm nonetheless. When I first saw it, the room was nearly impenetrable, packed to the jambs with discarded medical equipment, desks, chairs, and antiquated surgical devices of all sorts. A thin beam of sunlight coming through a torn black window shade highlighted dusty cobwebs that laced every post and chair, as if out of a Dickens novel. How this room had remained unused for so many years at a time when space was so scarce completely mystified me. But there it was, and we would gladly take it. It was perfect for our library.

During my weekly thirty-minute commute up to Weiss hospital on the north side, I got a brilliant idea that might improve my relationship with Dr. Medenica. Perhaps, I thought, she would be pleased to have the library named in her honor. I actually thought that both Dr. Lorincz and Dr. Medenica could be jointly named. *The Lorincz-Medenica Dermatology Library*. It had potential. They certainly had earned the honor. Using their names, I might be able to raise funds from former residents who loved them both. I went to her the following day, couching the proposal in the most respectful language I could muster without being obsequious. Her answer was immediate. She didn't express gratitude or ask for time to think about the proposal. She said instead, in slow staccato, with her nose curled, "I don't *want* a library named after me." So much for that. I should have known.

In three months, the *Rothman-Lorincz Library*, as I had decided to name it, was in full use as a conference room. To make it a state-of-the-art library would require at least another fifty to one hundred thousand dollars in fundraising revenues or endowment, for books and electronic equipment. That would take some time. The only new piece of furniture was a lovely wooden conference table, but the room was newly carpeted and the smell of fresh paint still lingered. Our first lectern was a black music stand I brought from home.

As I write this, more than a decade later, I realize how fortunate we were to have built such a room, especially given our low position on the university totem pole. The current trend in academic medical centers now is to build multi-use conference rooms where one must reserve time slots far in advance. New buildings don't have the space for dedicated departmental libraries.

▪ MUSICAL THERAPY

A MONTH HAD passed since we placed Dr. Lowey on probation and no new breaches of responsibility had occurred. Legal Affairs was handling Yolanda's lawsuits. There was talk of Yolanda needing a heart/lung transplant. It was looking as though Lowey might complete his residency requirements, though whether he would pass his certifying examinations was another issue entirely. The system in the U.S. is such that even those who fail their credentialing board examinations can claim to be dermatologists by using the term 'board eligible'. I know of no other country that condones that sort of incompetence. Nevertheless, for the moment, our section was on a relatively stable course.

About that time, I met a fine saxophone player on the medical faculty who gravitated to the same kind of jazz as I did—never an easy find. Peter Friedman was an internist who worked in Wendy's section. He played tenor saxophone very well and loved the compositions of Wayne Shorter, a favorite composer of most tenor players. Peter lived in Hyde Park only a few blocks away from where I lived. We started to play as a duo and made some rather decent music together. Life, though, had become much busier in Chicago than what I had left in Portland, and neither of us ever considered doing gigs. Nevertheless, my time rehearsing with Peter was musically rich. He introduced me to *Infant Eyes*, a painfully beautiful Wayne Shorter tune I knew but had never played.

When musicians are playing, all mental energy focuses on the music. The rest of the world drops out of existence. Girlfriends and wives are all too aware of this fact. While exhilarating, the playing is also therapeutic. For me, it was particularly so in the turbulent waters into which my career had waded of late. The Lowey untidiness was one thing, but I was also putting in fifteen hour days as section chief (as did all doctors in similar positions), and while I enjoyed most of it, my family detected the strain. Piano helped that somewhat.

My main source of joy and gratification in medicine, namely, my patients, continued to deliver. I had recently seen a patient in consultation and received a letter of thanks from the referring doctor. A sixty year old man had been referred with what I thought was an early form of a disease called dermatomyositis. I had recommended that his doctor order a chest X-ray because dermatomyositis could be associated with lung cancer. The doctor was writing because the man did turn out to have lung cancer. Fortunately, the cancer was successfully removed surgically and when it was gone, his skin problem disappeared. Occasionally we were lucky to catch cancers before they spread. He was a good teaching example of how skin was the window to his internal disease.

THE PLOT THICKENS MORE

ONE DAY IN March, Dr. Lowey reared his head again. The pharmacy had called Legal Affairs to report that he had prescribed the same weight-loss drug to one of our receptionists in the clinic, again without a medical record and without supervision. It had been less than a month since Lowey had been placed on probation. I immediately called him to my office and asked whether it was true. He denied the accusation.

"I'll need your keys and I.D. I'm suspending you from the residency until I get more details." Beads of perspiration were visible on Lowey's upper lip when he left my office.

Within thirty minutes, I was interrupted by a call from the head of outpatient pharmacy services. Dr. Lowey had gone directly from my office to the pharmacy, claimed to be the section chief, and asked to see all dermatology prescriptions in the last twenty-four hours. The pharmacist immediately recognized the fraud, and denied him access.

Later that night, I heard from the receptionist involved. Dr. Lowey had been harassing her throughout the afternoon and evening. He insisted that she come to the clinic to create a retroactive medical record. After several hours of refusing to come in, she decided to call me at home.

"Call the police if you feel threatened," I said. "Tell him that's what you intend to do."

"I will if he doesn't stop," she said. "It's more mental abuse." She could handle it, but wanted my approval. She went on to request some emergency personal time off. She was innocent; to my knowledge she hadn't known about the situation with Yolanda or the lawsuit against Lowey.

The next morning on my desk was a stiffly worded medical chart note written by Dr. Lowey, dated the previous day. It was written in self-protective, legal-sounding language entirely uncharacteristic of a medical chart entry. "Are you serious?" I said aloud. But I nearly jumped out of my seat when I noticed directly below Dr. Lowey's signature at the bottom of the page, the co-signature of Dr. Maria Medenica.

I showed the document to the legal affairs attorney who immediately called Dr. Medenica into my office. Within thirty seconds, the attorney extracted a confession from her. "They have persecuted Dr. Lowey for two years," Dr. Medenica said. "I was only trying to help him."

"And you thought that committing fraud yourself was going to help him?"

"Yes!" she said in typical defiance.

Later the same day I summoned Dr. Lowey to a meeting with me and two members from Legal Affairs. I presented our joint decision to expel Francis Lowey from the residency program, effective immediately. All the appropriate documentation had been laid out in the terms of the probation letter and the advice and consent from Legal Affairs. A termination letter still needed to be drafted. As I was newly installed as section chief, Dr. Soltani was still the residency program director of record, and I requested his co-signature on the letter. Dr. Soltani refused.

I had inherited this Lowey mess after only two months as section chief. While I fully concurred with the expulsion, it did not feel good to have to get rid of a resident three months shy of finishing his training. The risk of legal action after firing a resident was almost certain. I would be relying on Legal Affairs a great deal to manage the legal issues.

I will forever be perplexed by the relationships Dr. Lowey developed with the senior faculty members. Somehow, despite his obvious deceit, he had managed to get them all on his side. He was known to adulate anybody in a position of authority, including me. He actually was quite helpful to me on a trip to Oxford by loaning me his library card to enter the beautiful private library at Magdalene College, and recommended some sites to visit at Oxford. I had had no problems with any of that, despite the irony of my misrepresenting myself as him! Unprofessional behavior, like everything else, has two sides to each story, and maybe there were reasons I didn't know to explain the senior trio's reluctance to act. I even considered cultural differences. Perhaps they considered any discipline a form of oppression. Whatever the reasons, their protective stance eventually led to inappropriate if not self-incriminating behaviors.

ONCE IN A CAREER CASE

WHILE THIS WAS going on, patients continued to keep me sane. In the middle of a busy afternoon clinic, my resident presented a new patient who became a once-in-a-lifetime teaching and learning case.

Mr. Cannondale, an otherwise healthy man in his thirties, had come into the clinic appearing 'Cushingoid', i.e. puffed up in the face like a balloon. He had been on large doses of steroids (prednisone) for over a year. At first look, I understood why his dermatologists had tried to treat him aggressively with steroids, but even so, the drugs weren't working. In addition to his having a balloon face, he was covered in painful open sores over his body, mouth and lips, as well as the inside his penis (urethra). He couldn't eat, and it hurt to urinate. The man complained little, but I could see that he was in pain.

We started over, as one often must with difficult cases. We repeated biopsies, blood tests, and a comprehensive review of his history. I suspected several types of blistering diseases with names like Pemphigus and Behcet's disease, but it was unusual that prednisone hadn't quieted down either of those. Something about Mr. Cannondale was not typical, and the blood tests showed no abnormalities. The next day, two biopsies came back from Dr. Medenica without a specific diagnosis. When I was a resident, Dr. White had taught me that when the clinical picture is unusual, the biopsy often is unusual too. There was no support under the microscope for the blistering diseases I had suspected.

I couldn't continue with prednisone because he was at risk for serious complications from the drug. Besides, the drug wasn't working. We needed a diagnosis. I needed to have a look at the biopsy slide.

I requested the slide and slipped it into place on the multi-headed microscope. To my surprise, I immediately saw something subtle that I had learned from Dr. White. There were several subtle features present that created a distinct picture. "This could be Erythema multiforme!" I said to the resident. The diagnosis would definitely fit with Mr. Cannondale's sores and blisters. The biopsy wasn't classic for the disease, but neither were his blisters, or his whole year of illness.

We had known by then that the most common cause of erythema multiforme (EM) was an infection with herpes. I called Mr. Cannondale and asked whether he had ever had herpes cold sores on the mouth, or genital herpes. He said no, but maybe his wife had had cold sores in the past. It was possible that his EM had come from herpes that never appeared on his skin, so-called subclinical herpes. I ordered blood tests on Mr. Cannondale and his wife, and both came back highly positive for herpes antibodies, which meant that Mr. Cannondale had been infected at some time in the past, but never knew it. The information supported my theory. I immediately started him on anti-herpes drugs. Within two weeks the sores on his penis and in his mouth were completely healed, and the skin blisters stopped forming. We tapered the prednisone over the course of a few months and his balloon face gradually returned to normal. Mr. Cannondale remained on anti-herpes drugs for the next few years with no recurrence of his skin blisters. He would probably need to stay on those drugs for life. Once again, the success of treatment could not have happened without a correct diagnosis. Dermatology was all about making the correct diagnosis. In the words of the illustrious dermatologists Walter and Dorinda Shelley, *"Therapy sails on the winds of diagnosis."*

■ ...AND THICKENS

ON THE DAY Dr. Lowey got expelled, the first thing I needed to do was to notify the Chair of Dermatology at the University of California at San Francisco. Lowey had been accepted into San Francisco's Mohs surgery fellowship. How that could have happened in the first place was astonishing to me. Someone in our section must have written a stellar letter. I suspected who it might have been. Here was a resident who hid himself in closets to avoid seeing patients, whose knowledge base was entirely inadequate for his level of training, and who had been put on probation for inappropriate prescribing. Now he had been accepted into the prestigious San Francisco surgery program. I reached the chairman and informed him of Dr. Lowey's expulsion. He was supposed to begin in July, only four months away. I could not legally divulge the entire story, but the terms 'breaches of integrity' entered into the conversation. Though somewhat bewildered by the strange news, the chairman thanked me for the call.

Portland Josh said, when I shared the details with him, "See what you've gotten yourself into? So you expelled someone. Move on. Let the university attorneys deal with the mess." This was Josh, the attorney, speaking.

"It's bigger than that, Josh," I said. "No one expels a resident these days. I don't know a single instance of a resident being expelled, and I've witnessed some terrible residents. They usually get coddled. It wouldn't surprise me if convicted felons have been allowed to complete their residencies before they go off to prison."

Within a few weeks, I received a call from the program director of the dermatology residency program at the University of Pennsylvania, a man I had known to be of highest integrity. Dr. Lowey was now applying to Penn to complete his residency.

"I've spoken with Dr. Lowey and Dr. Lorincz," he said. "Lowey says that he voluntarily left the program because of personal issues with you."

"Did Dr. Lorincz agree with that statement?" I said.

"He didn't correct it."

The program director at Penn appropriately wanted to verify the story, as well as Dr. Lowey's performance at Chicago. I told him what I had told the chair at San Francisco: it was expulsion, not voluntary withdrawal; it was sanctioned by Legal Affairs; he had fraudulently misrepresented himself and had breached the articles of his probation.

"Would you like to speak with one of the attorneys?" I asked.

"That won't be necessary."

About that time, Dr. Soltani reported to me news that Dr. Lowey's mother had suddenly died. It wasn't until a month later that we learned that his mother had not died. Dr. Lowey had fabricated the story, apparently to summon up our sympathy. It was pity, not sympathy for Dr. Lowey that I was beginning to feel. I also tried to find out more about his history. I called the University of Illinois to see if they could shed any light on why he had transferred after his second year of medical school. I had known medical students who got asked to transfer for cheating. Illinois told me they could not release any information without Lowey's approval in writing. I called the surgery program in Cleveland where he had left after his first year. According to the program director to whom I spoke, Lowey had successfully completed his internship and had made a personal decision to pursue a career outside of medicine. Strange, but no smoking gun there.

One of my junior residents came to me a few weeks later. She was always so wonderfully open and friendly. "Dr. Shaw, guess what? Lowey got into Brown (University)."

"How did you hear?"

"A resident in another program."

I wasn't sure that was true.

"He told them that getting kicked out of Chicago was because you didn't like him, personal issues, nothing more. Rumors are going around now that you and he were lovers and had a falling out."

I laughed. She smiled.

My suspicion was that Dr. Lorincz had made all the arrangements for his acceptance at Brown, and supported the lie about personal issues, although I didn't have direct proof of that. The chair of dermatology at Brown had contacted my secretary to request copies of Lowey's faculty evaluations. He never tried to reach me to discuss the case. Only later did I discover that the former provost at Brown University was the son of former Chicago chief of dermatology, Stephen Rothman, and that he and Dr. Lorincz had jointly written an obituary on Stephen Rothman. Clearly, there was a strong connection between the two.

There was not much more I could do at the time. As far as I was concerned, Brown could keep Lowey. He would be out of my hair. It was only a matter of time, I figured, before he would burn bridges there as he had at Chicago. I had other fish to fry at home, so, *back to work*. If I didn't have to deal with Lowey again, I would be happy.

■ RECRUITMENTS 'R' US

THE PRIMARY ACTIVITY of all divisional and departmental leaders at medical institutions is to recruit new faculty. One of my first goals as chief was to recruit a pediatric dermatologist. Chicago had a reputable children's hospital with good funding and researchers. There were plenty of pediatric patients with skin disease and we frequently were asked to consult on hospitalized kids with skin disease. But Northwestern University had cornered the market on pediatric dermatology in the Chicago area. Dr. Amy Paller, who would become their departmental chair, was indisputably one of the top pediatric dermatologists in the world, of which there were only a handful. She had expanded pediatric dermatology at Northwestern over several years through excellent recruitment, and every year trained one or two pediatric dermatology fellows.

We would never be able to compete with Dr. Paller's shop, but even so, needed our own pediatric dermatologist, if only to expand the robust citywide energy. Having a pediatric dermatologist had become an essential component of every respectable academic center. Our chair of pediatrics agreed to split the cost and give whomever we recruited a joint appointment in Pediatrics. It wasn't going to be easy to hook such a fish, and even more difficult to land it, but we needed to try. In the end it took close to three years.

I placed advertisements in dermatology journals and had some nibbles. We held some recruitment dinners, made some offers, received some rejections. I thought we were close with one applicant from Wisconsin, but in the world of academic recruiting, one can never be certain until the ink is dry, sometimes not even then.

Dr. Sara Stein was about to finish her dermatology residency at Northwestern, and we ultimately were able to attract her. She had completed her training in pediatrics before training in dermatology, an alternative approach from the usual route which was to finish dermatology first and then do an extra year fellowship in pediatric dermatology.

However, she was well trained and we were thrilled to hire her. The fact that her husband was an internist on faculty at Chicago probably didn't hurt our chances.

Dr. Stein immediately became an integral part of the section and provided a much needed connection to the Department of Pediatrics. Our residents started getting involved in clinical research projects with Dr. Stein, and she began to build our pediatric dermatology activity into a respectable entity.

While it had taken three years to hire Dr. Stein, I did manage to add one faculty member during my first year. Dr. Anne Laumann had had an interesting career path beginning in England where she grew up, through internal medicine in the U.K. with special training in nephrology, and finally dermatology training at Chicago in the 1970s under Dr. Lorincz. For years, she had practiced in Chicago, primarily at Michael Reese Hospital at the sexually transmitted disease clinic there. Michael Reese, however, was struggling in the vicious health insurance battles going on at the time in Chicago, and Anne saw the handwriting on the wall. She came to me with an interest in moving over to our section. That recruit turned out to be easy. Anne continued with her fascination with STDs, and went on to develop a research niche in tattoos, piercings, and other body art.

Now all I needed to do was to attract a topnotch research scientist to raise the stature of the section. That might be more difficult.

About half a year into my new position, in early summer 1998, we got a new chair of medicine to replace Dr. Rubenstein. It turned out not to be who we thought it would be. The dean's selection process was coming to a close toward midsummer, and the heir apparent, an insider who, as an endocrinologist, had worked closely with Dr. Rubenstein, had been hammering out the final details of an offer from our dean. The entire faculty was optimistic about our chairman-to-be. We then started to hear ominous rumblings of uncertainty from the future chair, and within a week, he walked away from the negotiations. The move surprised us all; he clearly was the best choice, but the dean's package must have restricted his ability to grow the department. He knew he could take his research operation elsewhere if he needed to (and did, a year later).

With egg on his face, the dean needed to act quickly to find a new Chair of Medicine. It had already been a year since Dr. Rubenstein had left, and the provost's office was getting impatient. Second best would have to suffice. Within less than a week after the rebuff of the heir apparent, without benefit of interviews or any traditional vetting process, the dean appointed an insider from the section of oncology. I had only recently met him, and Wendy had had only minor dealings with him. A new chairman makes everyone a little nervous, especially someone less well known by insiders and hand-picked hastily without an open selection process. But we carried on as best we could, being good citizens of academia.

Soon after assuming the position, he held a weekend leadership retreat at his summer home in Michigan. Wendy and I attended with our section chief hats on, and everything went as it should. Although some section chiefs privately expressed reservations about working with him, I thought I could probably pull it off. The main slogan from the retreat was No Deficits. We would need to cut costs, possibly freeze hiring altogether for a while. He directed us to see more patients and do more teaching, near contradictions in terms. Emphasis on reducing costs and increasing revenues smacked more of a business initiative than academic vision. Apparently, times were getting tough.

■ ...IT JUST NEVER STOPS

ONE DAY IN the summer of 1998, after Lowey had apparently joined the Brown University program, I received a thick packet in the mail from the California Medical Board. It outlined charges against Dr. Lowey for his inappropriate overprescribing of narcotics, dishonesty, falsifying records, among other charges. The forty-two page packet included page after page of his prescriptions for large quantities of Dilaudid, a potent oral narcotic with high street value. He had falsified entire medical records. In retrospect, it made sense. Lowey went to California during his vacations every year, and had a license to practice medicine in California. What didn't make sense was why he would do such a thing. Was he doing it as a business or was this his idea of helping patients? Why would he risk his career on a stranger's narcotics for some spending money? This behavior seemed sociopathic. I had suspected that he had a sociopathic personality disorder all along.

At our next faculty meeting I presented the information to the rest of my faculty. The senior trio didn't seem to be fazed. Dr. Medenica said something to the effect of "Other criminals are given second chances through rehabilitation. I *don't* see why he can't as well!" Dr. Soltani remained silent. Too conflictual, perhaps. Dr. Lorincz at least expressed his disappointment.

I thought: Something is systematically wrong when a person as unethical as Dr. Lowey can be expelled from one residency program and accepted at another without there being some form of official exchange of information between the two programs. In Lowey's case, it had happened through insider trading by a network of good old boys who bought into the story that Lowey's circumstances at Chicago had somehow been trumped up unfairly. I decided I needed to try to create a systematic change that might prevent such recycling of reprobate residents. It was, after all, about maintaining high standards and protecting patients.

Through the American Professors of Dermatology (APD), of which I was a member, I introduced a policy proposal stipulating that in cases in which a dermatology resident desired to change programs *for any reason*, the program directors or department chairs would be obligated to discuss the conditions surrounding the transfer. I had heard that a similar policy existed through the American Board of Internal Medicine.

The APD leadership turned down my proposal. The formal response from the president conveyed an executive committee opinion implying that the Lowey case likely was based on a need for better communication within my section at Chicago, and did not warrant introduction of new policies. They too, like the program director at Brown, chose never to discuss the details with me. At a subsequent meeting of the APD, the chair of dermatology at SUNY Downstate stood at the floor microphone and addressed the issue briefly, stating that 'we' in dermatology had a long and successful history of being able to discuss issues among ourselves when necessary, and that formalizing requirements was not necessary.

Okay! Right! Long live the old boy's club mentality! At that point, I dropped the issue and was prepared to try to forget about Francis Lowey altogether. To my disappointment and frustration, he wouldn't go away.

I next heard that he was preparing to write the American dermatology board examinations. I had no idea how this could be, since he had not received credit for any of his third year at Chicago. Was it possible that someone at Brown was unilaterally altering his Chicago records for accreditation purposes? I decided there was one more thing I needed to do for the benefit of patients and the specialty. I spoke with the President of the American Board of Dermatology (who had known my father well and, to my surprise, immediately recognized my voice as nearly identical to my father's over the telephone). I told the story of Dr. Lowey, and followed up by sending a package that included a review of the events leading to Lowey's expulsion, the California Medical Board narcotics charges, plus my strong opinion that he was not ethically fit to be certified as a dermatologist. Ever.

I never received any follow up from the American Board of Dermatology concerning their actions or decision, or even that they had received the package. The whole process was entirely unsatisfactory, and unprofessional in my view.

To jump ahead, the Lowey case continued to fester. More than a year later, I finally heard, second or third hand, that a committee had been formed at the American Board of Dermatology to deal with Lowey who was suing to write his board examinations. After a long battle with his lawyers, the board finally refused to allow him to sit for the examination. There was hope for humanity after all.

Jumping ahead further, I continued to hear about his misrepresentations and lies. In 2006, I received an email from a former co-resident with me at Oregon. He was contacting me in his role as medical director of a multi-specialty clinic in California. Dr. Lowey was applying for a position as a Mohs surgeon in that clinic (he had never trained in Mohs surgery). Understandably, he found Dr. Lowey's C.V. intriguing: economics at Oxford after medical school, then dermatology; a stint in the U.S. military, etc. He wondered if I had ever worked with Lowey, or knew anything about him, since Chicago was on his CV. I had plenty to share, and his application was ultimately disposed of appropriately.

In 2007, he floated to the surface again. He tried to become a member of the American College of Mohs Surgery, claiming that he had been honored with medals in the military and completed a fellowship in Mohs surgery at Northwestern, neither of which was true. He reached the final stages of acceptance before being exposed as a fraud and rejected. The same year, I discovered also that he had started a cosmetic dermatology practice in Carmel, California and was advertising himself to the public as a board certified dermatologist. I notified the American Board of Dermatology of his false representation, and though my letter was handled appropriately, I got the distinct sense that the Board viewed me as the trouble-maker, not Dr. Lowey. At least this time they wrote a letter informing me of their actions. They contacted Lowey, and he agreed to remove the board-certified claim from his website. No other actions were taken.

The case of Dr. Francis Lowey taught me a great deal. It taught me that doctors will not likely ever be able to police themselves when it comes to unprofessional behavior or conflicts of interest because they protect their own guild more than they protect patients. I remain dismayed at the ease with which Dr. Lowey, through gifts and adulation, was able to gain the continued support of our three senior faculty members who appeared otherwise to be highly ethical. I wince with disillusionment over the club of old boys in dermatology and the degree of resistance I experienced from the American Professors of Dermatology when attempting to introduce a modest policy change that would likely have protected patients by preventing training programs from having to deal with disasters like Lowey. I remain impressed and disappointed by the extreme caution exhibited by the American Board of Dermatology when dealing with the ethical challenge that Lowey presented.

If Lowey or doctors like him end up harming someone, it will be because we as a profession are afraid to control individuals like him, either out of fear of losing a law suit, or, simple spinelessness when it comes to disciplining our colleagues and putting our patient's well-being before our own.

CHAPTER 11

Chicago Endings

"Loving Chicago is like loving a woman with a broken nose."
–Nelson Algren

■ PAIN CAN BE A GOOD THING

It wasn't until my second year at Chicago that I finally quit smoking. The habit, of course, is taboo these days in medical circles, but smoking had been an on and off thing most of my life since the eighth grade when I tried to emulate a fellow trumpet player in eighth grade band class. Actually, that's not entirely fair. I can also blame my parents. My mother smoked cigarettes and my father smoked a pipe. They smoked and drank martinis throughout all six of my mother's pregnancies. I can only imagine what might have resulted if they hadn't. By the time I moved to Chicago I was well aware of the research that had proven that the primary indicator of whether a person smoked or not, was whether the parents smoked. But everyone, it seemed, smoked in the 1950s and 60s. Be that as it may, I smoked. Everyone in my rock band smoked. I smoked through high school and two years of college, stopped for four years during a bout of clean living only to restart during medical school in my third year surgery clerkship at Boston City Hospital. Surgeons typically smoked. The habit fit the métier and the temperament. My surgical intern smoked, so we smoked together in the resident's lounge. My good friend Kevin from college smoked, and he became a surgeon. I could never bum a cigarette off him, though, because he smoked Tareytons, a wretched brand that tasted like old bread and dirty socks.

Lucky Strikes and Camel straights were best, though I didn't smoke them much because a very close family friend had died of lung cancer at an early age from smoking Camels. In his last days in the hospital, in true form, my parents gathered in his hospital room to share one final very dry martini, straight-up, together. That's bedside manner.

My first fiancée Mimi smoked. We smoked together all the time. During our difficult times, and there were several, that's all we did. We wouldn't talk; we would just chain-smoke.

Miles Davis smoked.

Wendy, of course, never smoked.

So, I was a closet smoker throughout our marriage: back porches, garages, up the flue. Always furtive. I remember one time waking up early one hot summer morning to the smell of burning wood coming from outside our house, and panicked, knowing precisely from where it was coming. I had dropped a lit cigarette on the wood bark groundcover late the previous night, thinking that it would burn out on its own as it always had in the past, but the summer had been a dry one, and it had smoldered throughout the night, expanding into a three foot symmetrical ring of glowing, smoking embers ready to burst a tree into flames at any moment. I doused the incipient fire but privately hung onto my chagrin for years over that carelessness. In Chicago, I made sure my cigarettes were out, cold-out, down there in the basement tinderbox wood room, before returning to domestic life upstairs.

I would probably still be smoking today if I hadn't started getting pain in my gut every time I inhaled. That started in Chicago. I didn't smoke very much by then—one or two per day, maximum—but with each inhale, I received a kick in the gut and pictured some important blood vessel constricting blood supply to my stomach. I knew that cigarettes were one of the most potent constrictors of blood vessels ever identified. I didn't particularly want to choke off the blood supply to anything, and if it was doing that to my gut, think what it must be doing to my heart! And besides, pain, that great motivator, took away the pleasure of servicing my addiction. I stayed off cigarettes and felt good about it. I no longer had to be a hypocrite when I recommended quitting to my patients. Instead, I switched to cigars which I discovered were much better quality tobacco, better aroma (no cigarette paper), and I didn't inhale them so I didn't get the pain in my gut. I started to enjoy smoking a cigar now and then. The trouble with cigars was that women are able to detect one part per billion cigar smoke in a house. In our house, old cat urine and rotting garbage had a better chance of going undetected than a cigar smoked three weeks ago. More than a few discussions have taken place between us on that subject.

■ GHOST BILLING

THE SECTION OF Dermatology at Chicago had run a deficit for decades, but we now had a new Chairman, and he was determined to eliminate deficits. I spent hours with the Chairman and his advisors, to search for ways to claw back twenty-five years of operating under water. Years before the advent of antibiotics, several million dollars had been donated to the University of Chicago to support a department conducting research in syphilis, and for some years the section of dermatology was the beneficiary of that endowment, but after syphilis became a treatable disease, those funds were directed elsewhere. This fund, which could easily have erased our deficits (fiscally irresponsible or otherwise), had been usurped by other departments, possibly to erase their fiscally irresponsible deficits. I tried, but failed, to have some of those funds returned to their rightful owners.

An experienced manager might have reviewed all the finances before agreeing to take over as Chief, but in my usual perverse fashion, I had taken the risk without knowing the details. What I found was a fiscal operation badly in need of repair. New annual budgets were due soon, and for starters I had to find a way to shave off one hundred thousand dollars from the prior year's budget.

There is a widely held perception that in large universities, we doctors are flush with money and don't ever have to worry about revenue. I frequently have been told by community dermatologists that "it doesn't matter how many patients you see because, don't you get a salary from the university?" Not so. Universities are businesses like any other. We eat what we kill. The problem is that Cardiology and surgical specialties are filthy rich from all their procedures, but poor cousin specialties such as pediatrics and rheumatology and, believe it or not, dermatology, are paupers. Without some form of departmental communism to spread the wealth, some of us are always struggling. I was rapidly discovering that much of my time as chief would have little to do with academic vision and everything to do with money management.

I discovered that dermatopathology was the only revenue producing operation within our section. This was despite an on-site laboratory, three full-time technologists, a manager, and Dr. Medenica's salary. When I looked closer, I learned we were charging much less than anyone else in the country. How could that have happened for so many years? By merely correcting the Medicare charge codes, our revenues increased by more than fifty per cent.

The real eye-opener came, however, when I uncovered something that completely astounded me: a covert practice rampant throughout Chicago. The practice was known as Ghost Billing. It went like this:

Dermatologists would set up an arrangement with our section of dermatology whereby Dr. Medenica would process and read a biopsy for a fee of ten ($10!) dollars. For each biopsy, the community dermatologist would turn around and charge the insurance company or patient the full pathology fee of fifty to one hundred dollars per specimen. Dr. Medenica received thousands of specimens per year under this arrangement from private dermatologists, mostly former Chicago residents. Specimens arrived by courier from all over the country. She would send the slides and pathology report back to the community doctors and they would plagiarize the report. By billing insurance or Medicare the full fee, they were claiming to be the dermatopathologist of record. Why Medicare auditors had never discovered this fraud (or was allowing it) baffled me. Dr. Medenica put her heart and soul into her dermpath reports. She came to work early, stayed late, overnight sometimes.

She could spend hours on a difficult slide. Referring dermatologists enjoyed her expertise, plus open access to discussion with her at any time, all for ten dollars per slide while they raked in multiples of that.

How dermatologists thought that it was okay to bill as the dermatopathologist of record when Dr. Medenica did the work, I found incomprehensible. Estimating conservatively, five biopsies per day, four or five days per week, forty weeks per year, at fifty dollars per slide would be fifty thousand dollars to the dermatologist, with only ten thousand going to us for processing and Dr. Medenica's expert interpretation.

Once I found out that we were essentially giving away expert dermatopathology services, I immediately increased our fees from ten dollars to thirty dollars, with plans to increase them further in the future (most similar consultations were well over one hundred dollars around the country). The ghost billers were outraged—"We're trying to make a living out here!" one dermatologist said to me. Dr. Medenica was also outraged. She had always thought that no fees should be charged for any medical services, that departments ran on funding from the heavens.

Ghost billing had been the norm in Chicago for years. I don't know if Northwestern, or Rush, or the University of Illinois had similar arrangements with their former residents, but I learned from the dermatopathologist at Cook County that he had had a similar arrangement for years and implied that ghost billing was widespread throughout Chicago. It probably still is.

Every time I increased our fees over the next three years for ghost billing, I received angry phone calls from dermatologists. They didn't feel it necessary to actually know dermatopathology, just to bill for it. I couldn't sympathize with them.

■ 200 TO ONE ODDS AGAINST

"HOW MANY APPLICANTS do we have this year?" I asked my secretary in January of 1998, one month after assuming the Chief position.

"Four hundred. Or thereabouts. And that's for how many positions?"

"Two," I said with rolled eyes.

Dermatology residency programs are among the most competitive. Derm usually gets the cream, the straight-A students, AOA members (alpha omega alpha, the prestigious medical organization). Top applicants try for Harvard, Penn, New York University, San Francisco, and a few others. We at Chicago had to settle for applicants down one notch or two. In addition we received huge numbers of international applicants, mostly from Middle Eastern countries. Interpreting an international applicant's credentials was difficult at best because of language barriers and unknown standards. After each applicant made a huge effort to compile the documents, we had to eliminate most of them in the first round. I felt sorry for them, but we would never be able to properly assess their potential, and with so many well-qualified Western applicants, we had to reject them.

Every year we devoted two long months to the selection process. We read all four hundred applications to pick the top one hundred which we scrutinized to select thirty to interview for a total of *two* available positions. Dr. Soltani and I each took two hundred of the initial tidal wave of files. This was before the process became electronic. We waded through reams of paper files, each with a comely photograph of the applicant. The following year the process became electronic, and the photograph was eliminated, having been viewed as a potential source of bias. It was a good thing too, because once women doctors started choosing dermatology in the 1980s, some programs had become notorious for accepting a preponderance of good-looking women. Of course, eliminating the photograph never prevented program directors from ultimately choosing the good-looking women, but at least the runners-up in the glamour department weren't eliminated in the first cut.

After we sifted through the piles of applications, we invited about eight applicants on each of three successive days, and spent the entire day with them. Eight to ten dark blue suits milled around in our new library conference room, pretending to nibble on croissants. I always viewed that breakfast socializing exercise as cruel. Here they were, each applicant competing with every other applicant for a lifetime career and they were trying to be cordial with one another? They probably wanted to kill each other!

I began the day with some introductory remarks, extolling and exaggerating the virtues of our program. Then we faculty went into our respective offices and waited for the applicants to come in, one by one, as we conducted a rotating series of twenty minute interviews for the remainder of the morning. With some applicants, the twenty minutes flew by in a matter of seconds. With others it seemed like three hours trapped in an elevator. The applicants then had deep dish Chicago pizza with our residents who also were instructed to extol and exaggerate the virtues of our program, after which we conducted an afternoon set of interviews.

Ranking the interviewees was not easy. Most were highly qualified. By the end of the day, the first interviewee, even if the top of the group, might be supplanted by the last applicant who was almost as good, but made more of an impression because he or she had been last. After the three interview days, all thirty had to be ranked. Collating three sets of ten into one ordered set of thirty was even more difficult. It often got down to nearly arbitrary ranking for the top ten and the bottom ten, making the middle ten just as arbitrary. I would likely have been happy with any of the top ten and would have been unhappy with any of the bottom ten. Each faculty member, a total of six when I first joined the Section of Dermatology, ranked the applicants in a similar manner. We were then ready for the marathon event, the formulating of the official rank list that we sent to the Resident Matching Service, known simply as The Match.

We were fortunate to have Dr. Pezen around during those epic sessions. He knew how to take each of our lists and combine them electronically into a master tally of our preferences, in order. We parked ourselves in the conference room at the end of a Wednesday afternoon and didn't come out until the final list was completed.

Systematically, we reviewed each applicant, discussed pros and cons, and moved names up or down as we saw fit. I have fond memories of those final sessions. With every name, Dr. Pezen would move the person up or down, asking how they compared to the person above and the person below. I then submitted the rank order to the University office that handled our match lists. Then we waited. Throughout my time at Chicago, I enjoyed those meetings, late into the evening as they usually went.

■ A NEW COLLEAGUE

ONE DAY, DR. Lorincz walked into my office holding some papers. "This is someone you might want to seriously consider as a resident." He handed me the file. I looked at the name: Aleksandar Krunic.

"How do you pronounce it?"

"Krunich, I think." Dr. Lorincz said. "I worked with him briefly a year or two ago."

I had my secretary set up a meeting.

"What is the correct pronunciation of your name?" I asked upon meeting him.

"Doesn't matter. However you like to say it," he said with a big smile.

"How do *you* pronounce it?" I asked, just as I asked all new patients with unpronounceable names.

"Krunich," he said. "Sasha Krunic." He had completed medicine and dermatology in Belgrade and was finishing a Mohs surgery fellowship at Duke with plans to return to Belgrade and start a program in Mohs surgery at the University of Belgrade.

"Now I cannot return because of the war." It was 1999. Serbia and Kosovo were at war, and life in all of former Yugoslavia was in turmoil again. Dr. Krunic needed to find a way to practice in the United States. He needed a Green Card. "What I have to do in order to practice dermatology in the States, which I would like very much to do, is repeat my entire dermatology residency." He already had published an impressive number of papers. This was a highly motivated person. I jumped at the opportunity to bring him into the Chicago program.

We started the process. After considerable negotiations, my chairman found the funding to give Dr. Krunic three years of residency as one of the additional positions I had secured from the accrediting body that year. The bureaucrats at immigration eventually came through with a new visa, and Dr. Krunic was set to begin in July of 2000. He became one of our best residents and teachers ever.

Before Sasha started his residency with us, I had envisioned that his presence might permit me to create a Mohs surgery service. It would require Dr. Soltani's collaboration, but if successful, we would boost the academic, clinical, and financial credentials of the section considerably. Having just completed a residency and Mohs surgery fellowship, Dr. Krunic was completely up to date in diagnosis as well as medical and surgical treatment. He was not afraid to use the treatments that

Soltani, Lorincz and Medenica avoided. He would be a collaborator with me instead of saboteur. As soon as he began, I set up a meeting in Dr. Soltani's office with the three of us. I proposed that Dr. Soltani be the supervisory surgeon of record, and Dr. Krunic would 'assist' on every case. Dr. Soltani, to my surprise, appeared to be enthusiastic about the plan.

Mohs surgeons were relatively few in number throughout greater Chicago, some in private practice and some in academic centers, but Dr. Krunic was one of the best trained. A university-based Mohs center would definitely benefit patients. And because fees for Mohs procedures were high, the program would be lucrative for the section of dermatology.

I presented the idea to my chairman and his business managers. "What revenue potential is there?" they asked. I presented some details, and they bought into it. We moved ahead quickly. The project required investing in new equipment, space, instruments, and one dedicated lab technician. Dr. Krunic organized the new surgical suites with confidence and expertise. Before long our Mohs service was up and running successfully. Within a few months, the business managers were coming to me celebrating the improved revenue numbers, which was all that mattered to them.

In addition to Mohs, Sasha became an integral part of the residency program, volunteering his teaching expertise and informally overseeing residents even though he was technically a first year resident. My facilitating his joining our residency program had been nearly as valuable as a new faculty recruitment. We discovered one more hurdle, however. In order to be a certified Mohs surgeon in the U.S., he had to also repeat his Mohs fellowship. The Duke experience apparently was a limited fellowship designed for foreign doctors planning to bring their training back home. It was not recognized by the American College of Mohs Surgery. Sasha smiled when he told me the news, in his not-yet-perfect English. "I don't mind. I am so appreciative for what you have done. It will be happy for me to do another Mohs fellowship." I had been looking forward to recruiting Dr. Krunic when he finished to build the surgery component of our section and residency. Now it would have to wait an extra year or two.

■ UNPROFESSIONAL

FOR A YEAR, Wendy had been having some trouble in her position. The new chairman had difficulties with Wendy's vision and leadership; he preferred having a loyal following, right or wrong. I wish she had stepped down immediately when he took office, but we were fairly ensconced in Hyde Park by then. Our daughters would be finishing high school over the next three years, and Chicago had a benefit for faculty known affectionately as 'golden handcuffs': They paid full college tuition for children of faculty members, or an equivalent amount for any other college of their choice. It was difficult to walk away from a benefit like that. If Wendy went to a different institution in the city, I could have stayed on and received the benefit, but leaving the University of Chicago was not a good option for her. She had leadership projects to carry forward. Her staying resulted in many sleepless nights for both of us. The wife giveth, the wife taketh away.

One day, Wendy received a call from a physician whom she had recruited a year before. "Wendy, I thought I should share what just happened. The chair called me into his office today. I had no idea what he wanted. When I got there, he said he was conducting your performance review, and asked my views of you, which of course were all positive. He pressed me on areas where you might have room for improvement. As the interview progressed, and he pressed more about the negatives, I got the distinct impression that this was an attempt to create some dirt about you that he could use."

It turned out that the chairman of medicine had, with no prior notice, called several members of Wendy's section that same day and grilled them under the false pretense of a formal performance review, on what Wendy might be doing wrong. It was as shady a move as I had ever seen in academia.

Departmental reviews are normally conducted as formal procedures where all parties are aware of the agenda, and voices are heard from across the department. They are not interrogations by despots. This was the chair trying to find something negative he could use to justify his not supporting Wendy.

That behavior toward Wendy, we both suspected, had been actionable on several occasions. After having a private discussion with a group of select leaders, Wendy decided to explore the issue, more for the purpose of reining in the chair than to file a claim against him. She met with the provost to discuss how she was being treated by both the dean and the chairman.

The provost listened, but his main concern was whether Wendy thought she had a solid legal case. He was protecting the dean and chairman. Clearly, the writing was on the wall in bold lettering. It was time to start thinking about leaving Chicago.

The final interaction related to two of Wendy's recruitments, one a man, the other a woman. The woman had more advanced training and more academic experience. The conversation between Wendy and the chair went something like this:

You may offer Dr. A (the man) $100,000 and Dr. B (the woman) $85,000.

Wendy said, "I can't do that. If anything, Dr. B should have the higher salary, with her advanced training. At the very least, they should be equal."

You *will* do it. Let me remind you that you serve at my pleasure.

This was the final violation. Ethically and personally. Wendy retreated to her office where she shared the conversation and commiserated with one of her most trusted section leaders, a stalwart faculty member whose car license plate had read 'UC 1980' for nearly twenty years. Soon after that meeting he, too, made the decision to leave the U of C, and within one month, was happily installed at Northwestern University, downtown. Our best infectious disease specialist did the same. This chairman was turning out to be the most effective recruiter for Northwestern University they could ever have hoped for.

▰ SKINNED ALIVE

TAKING CARE OF patients continued as it always had. One hospitalized patient affected me profoundly. The University of Chicago performed many bone marrow and stem cell transplants, mostly for leukemia. During the recovery period, patients often had rocky courses and, though most survived, they were at risk for several serious diseases. One of the worst was graft-versus-host disease (GVHD, as it was known) which occurred when some of the transplanted bone marrow cells attacked the normal cells of the patient. Skin was often the main target of damage.

I watched one such patient, an attractive brunette in her mid thirties named Patricia, struggle with graft-versus-host disease following a stem cell transplant for leukemia. It is always difficult to watch patients develop GVHD after they have already suffered from the leukemia that has sapped the body's strength before the diagnosis, and the chemotherapy after diagnosis that removes any remaining strength, leaving only hope in those who can still muster a thread of it. Patricia tried to be a 'good patient', stoic and friendly to the squadrons of doctors who descended upon her daily. When I first met her, she smiled calmly with an acceptance of her situation and the task ahead, despite the fact that nearly all the skin on her back was peeling off, down to raw bloody flesh. It was as if she was being skinned alive. GVHD typically produced large blisters, separations in the skin, as well as damage to liver and intestines. She was constantly nauseated from the intestinal part. The oncologists pushed maximum immune suppression drugs intravenously, but couldn't control the process. We began topical dressings to promote healing and minimize her pain, but every day the involved areas expanded. Patricia tried to endure. After two weeks, her eyes welled up more and more easily when we asked how she was feeling. She knew the recovery was not going well. The oncologist and I conferred frequently, but had little else to offer.

"I can't see clearly today," Patricia said one day when my residents and I went in. "I woke up with only part of my vision". She had mentioned it to the other doctors as well.

I asked some questions. Was there blurring? Pain? Any other abnormalities? It seemed to be visual field loss, not blurring, and there were no other symptoms. Neither I nor the oncologist could detect anything grossly wrong by examining her. We weren't aware of GVHD affecting eyes and vision like this. We suggested waiting one day to see if it cleared. The next day, she reported that her vision was no better. She said it was like having blind spots. "We'll get an ophthalmology consult right away."

Patricia never saw the ophthalmologists. She died suddenly that same day. The cause of her death was a complete mystery, so the medical team asked her family if they would authorize an autopsy. They agreed, and to our surprise, the autopsy showed a large stroke in the part of the brain that controls vision. She had not died from GVHD, as severe as it was. Her blindness had come from the stroke, i.e. in her brain, not her eyes. Patricia died when the hemorrhaging from the stroke extended beyond the vision part of the brain to the part that controlled her breathing.

For reasons I don't fully understand, Patricia's death affected me far more than I expected. Perhaps it was her young age, or her beauty, juxtaposed with the cruelty of relentless disease. Mostly, I think it came from her attempts, genuine or contrived, to have a positive attitude when it was apparent that she was in pain and losing her fight to recover. Patients are not permitted to express their despair. It labels them as bad patients. It upsets the nurses and the doctors. Patients are expected to be hopeful all the time. It is a failure of medicine, that inability to accept the inevitability of death. Regardless, Ms. Patricia died a miserable, tragic death that exemplified the horrors and unpredictability of disease even in this 'modern' era of advanced knowledge. Her deterioration and death inspired me to compose a musical piece several months later that I called *Requiem dance for a dying young woman*. I am still haunted by her death and the suffering she endured.

■ WRITING ON THE WALL

IN THE FALL of 2000, we made the decision to leave the University of Chicago. The dean and chair of medicine had made Wendy's life too unpleasant. My own relationship with the chair, in spite of his somewhat Stalinist style, was not at issue. He and I, for the most part, had worked collegially together. I had brought some new energy to the section and he had been supportive of most of my initiatives. He even understood how troublesome some of my faculty could be. Under the influence of our new resident, Dr. Krunic, Mohs surgery was thriving. Dr. Soltani seemed to be going along with the new activity. I had managed to expand the residency from two to three residents per year, giving it the critical mass so important in residency programs. Dermatopathology revenues were up. The Lorincz-Rothman Library was fully functional. Academic and clinical activities of the section had improved noticeably with the addition of our two new full-time faculty. Overall, the experience as chief had been a good one for me.

Despite that, I had soured to the University of Chicago. Wendy's battles with the chair and dean consumed too much of our energy. Once again, after Wendy's career had enabled our move to Chicago, it was her career that was now forcing us to give it all up. I had issues but they weren't as dire as Wendy's were. The Dr. Lowey affair had caused me to lose respect for some of the dermatologists in my section. At the same time, I was not able to get rid of them because they were tenured. I welcomed the idea of leaving Chicago. We began the search for a new institution.

■ THE SEARCH...AGAIN

I WASN'T SEEKING leadership, though I did enjoy it and would have accepted a leadership position. Any faculty position would suit me fine. One thing I knew: I probably would never return to private practice. I had learned to like the teaching of residents, of being part of a university. For Wendy, everyone in academic medicine in the U.S. had heard how she had been treated at Chicago. Many sympathetic chairmen of departments of medicine (they were all men at the time) offered to accommodate her search for a leadership spot. After some scouting, we settled on three to investigate further: New York University, the University of Washington, and the University of Toronto. I had family in Seattle, Wendy had family in Toronto, and as for New York, it just sounded thrilling.

I called Irwin Freedberg, Chairman of the Department of Dermatology at New York University. A vacancy had opened for the dermatology director at the Veterans Administration Hospital, a huge operation just south of the NYU hospitals on First Avenue. The former VA director had left to join forces with Novartis Pharmaceuticals in Illinois. Dr.

Freedberg set up a visit coinciding with Wendy's interview with the Department of Medicine.

I have met only a few leaders in my field or any other with the gentle strength that Dr. Freedberg embodied. He displayed a welcoming confidence and encouragement, so important in a leader. His accomplishments in dermatology were peerless: longstanding chair of his department, lead editor of the principal dermatology textbook for many years, successful researcher. When, a few years earlier, he failed in his bid for president of the American Academy of Dermatology, losing to a private dermatologist, I not only was saddened for him but for the specialty. It looked to me, right or wrong, as if the academic and patient care missions of dermatology were being supplanted by the priorities of private practitioners, revenue preservation, and lobbyists in Washington D.C.

Nevertheless, my day at New York University was a grand success and I looked forward to the possibility of working with Dr. Freedberg and the rest of his large group.

"My one request, if we end up coming here," I said to Dr. Freedberg at the end of the day, "is that you would be willing to be a mentor to me. I have never had a mentor."

Irwin said he would look forward to mentoring me, that mentoring was one of the things he did best.

Wendy's day was also fruitful. The chairman offered to create a vice chair position for her. We returned to Chicago fantasizing about living in New York. We still needed to work out details including a place to live. While we did that, we had two more cities to investigate.

My Seattle contact was Dr. John Olerud, division chief at the University of Washington and father of the famous baseball player of the same name. He led me in the direction of Dr. Greg Raugi who practiced at the Seattle VA. It was looking very much as if Veterans Hospitals were going to have a role in my life again. I had seen Greg only at meetings over the years, but had always remembered his being my very first dermatology teacher back in 1977 when I spent that impressionable month in dermatology at Oregon as a fourth year medical student. His entire career had been at the University of Washington where he had become a master teacher and innovator, but was in dire need of a partner. I thought working with Greg could be an excellent fit.

Typically, a recruitment visit includes one or two presentations by the candidate. The talk I delivered at Grand Rounds in Seattle was about blistering diseases of the skin and precisely how they occurred at the sub-cellular level. At the end of the talk, in a time-honored custom, the medicine residents presented a 'stump the professor' case for me to try to unravel, or become unraveled in the process. The case was that of a hospitalized patient who developed unusual blisters that didn't fit a typical appearance or biopsy picture. Luckily, I nailed the diagnosis. I identified the man's antibiotic as the trigger of a unique type of blistering disease. Vancomycin was the antibiotic, and the disease it caused was called *linear IgA bullous dermatosis*. Most dermatologists would have recognized it, but the medicine team and audience were impressed. Seattle was in the running.

Toronto came last. Months earlier, I had sent my CV and letter to the division director of dermatology. I heard later from the division secretary, that after sending back a quick letter to me indicating that there were no open positions and he would "keep me in mind if something became available", he had thrown my file directly into the trash. Michelle, the secretary, told me she had retrieved and kept it.

The city of Toronto had grown on me over twenty years of visits to my in-laws with our children. I found appealing the idea of living and working in Canada. The politics of medicine in the United States, with doctor's lives being overrun by insurance companies, had definitely become tiresome. I was willing to try something different. Having just witnessed the Supreme Court's foray into partisan politics with their decision to elect George W. Bush only served to strengthen my interest in Canada.

▆ TRUST ME, I'M ARROGANT

MY FIRST DIRECT exposure to the medical community in Toronto was inauspicious, to say the least. We met with someone with whom Wendy had worked occasionally during her career. The meeting took place on one of our family visits to Toronto. Wendy had asked him if he would join us for breakfast one morning so that we could get the lay of the land.

It is remarkable that I didn't flatly reject the idea of Toronto after that first meeting. Wendy and I sat at a small table in the café at The Four Seasons Hotel. The doctor waddled up to the table, sat across from us on Wendy's side, and started talking about himself. I was impressed by the fact that he made eye contact exclusively with Wendy. He did not once look in my direction the entire breakfast, nor did he direct any of his speech toward me as he boasted about his conquests. I turned this strange behavior into a game, a challenge to try to detect any hint of a glance in my direction. He proudly told Wendy of his ruthlessness, about how, when a doctor had come to him asking for a raise, he had decreased his salary. "Not only that, I decreased his salary a second time a year later when he asked me again for a raise." Throughout this Doctor Scrooge monologue, he kept smiling at Wendy and chuckling. No discussion took place about how academics functioned at the U of T. or anything else of practical use about the academic community in Toronto. I couldn't wait to peel away from that breakfast meeting, leaving Wendy to continue on her own for another hour. He never once looked in my direction.

We continued to explore the University of Toronto, but not because of Doctor Scrooge. Instead, we worked with the chair of the department of medicine, in which dermatology was one of the divisions. After Wendy met with the chair (and he consulted Dr. Rubenstein who was by then dean at the University of Pennsylvania), he must have been impressed because he immediately started to shape a job for her. This meant of course, shaping a job for me as well. He connected me again with the head of dermatology (who had thrown my CV away). Before long, we were headed up to Toronto for a two-day visit of interviews and presentations. I spoke to the dermatology division about my favorite topic—hormonal treatment of acne in women. At the end of a long day and dinner with our respective groups, we added Toronto to the list of potential moves.

▰ UNEXPECTED DEATH

IN FEBRUARY, 2001, amidst job searches, I was laid low by the unexpected death of my father. The final event, as often happens in death, was a shocker. He had developed fevers and night sweats around Thanksgiving. His doctors were either unable or unwilling to search for a diagnosis. "We'll watch it," they said. After several weeks, Wendy persuaded him to ask his doctor to get some blood cultures. "Oh, that's probably a good idea," the doctor said when my father used the word 'endocarditis' (infection of heart valves) as a possibility. The cultures came back positive, proving the diagnosis of bacterial endocarditis as Wendy had suspected, and he started a month of intravenous antibiotics. The upshot, however, was that the reason he developed endocarditis in the first place was discovered to be a severely constricted heart valve (medical term: aortic stenosis). Once the endocarditis was appropriately treated, his doctors recommended an aortic valve replacement.

In early February he underwent open-heart surgery to replace the valve. I remember my brother, Will's recollection of a brief dialogue he had with my father on the eve of the surgery. He said, "Dad, we are all optimistic about this surgery, but I want you to know also that you have been one of my best friends." I imagine that was not easy for a youngest son to say calmly to his father. This was the closest anyone got to expressing a concern for the outcome of the surgery. Will later reported to me that "Dad spaced out for a second at first but realized that the comment probably should elicit a response, like a 'two no-trump' bid in bridge, and said "It worked out pretty well, didn't it." Emoting didn't come naturally in our family.

He was home from the hospital in three or four days, and enjoying a small martini by day five or six. That was a good sign. On day seven, Valentine's Day, my secretary walked down the hall to interrupt me. "You have a telephone call. It's your brother."

I felt pre-car-crash nausea.

It was my younger brother Dave with a solemn voice on the phone. "Hi Jim, I think you should talk to Mom."

My mother took the phone but only spoke three words. "We lost him," she said.

Dave, who lived in Tacoma, had been the first to respond to my mother's call. He had been there to support her. He had laid eyes upon the corpse of his dead father. The rest of us were spared that unpleasantness.

I groaned into the phone for several seconds before managing to ask for some details. Dad had been in the bathroom and collapsed. Still conscious, he said his legs felt very heavy, like dead wood, and asked my mother for help to get back in bed. Once there, he turned pale, lost consciousness and stopped breathing. It took about ninety seconds. "I'll be there by tonight if I can get a flight out of Chicago," I said.

I first called Wendy who immediately terminated a meeting to come over to my office. Then I crossed the hall to Dr. Soltani's office and shared the bad news.

Dr. Soltani jumped up from his desk and wrapped his arms around me, squeezing tight for a long time. "I'm so sorry for you." It was the closest I had ever felt to him. Here, in the finality of death, there was no controversy, only genuine caring.

Wendy and I both suspected initially that the new valve and support ring must have dehisced (separated) from the aorta. Post-op day seven was when surgical wounds were weakest, when sutures start to dissolve but wounds are not yet strong. Wendy had implored my father to get a second opinion from the University of Washington, the center in the region where the largest number of aortic valve surgeries were performed, but Dad wanted to stay in his own neighborhood in Tacoma for the surgery. Wendy's suggestion created some tension and controversy within the family, especially with my brother Josh, an experienced internist in Everett. Was Town/Gown rivalry taking place within our own family? It was possible. I thought it stubborn of my father to reject the idea of a second opinion. I also privately thought that he might have been dismissive of my wife, this aggressive, Liberal, divorced, Jewish, Canadian, academic daughter-in-law of his. I secretly thought also that Dad may have had a death wish, not particularly wanting to go on with life. He must have known that wounds were weakest at seven days post-op. Could he have tried to cause the dehiscence? It might have been possible by bearing down in a Valsalva maneuver. Wendy thought that was a crazy notion, and after discussions with cardiologists who said that artificial valves are secure and never dehisce, I dropped the theory. His death must have come from something typical seen in postoperative complications such as a pulmonary embolism. Sadly, my father's last few months, in spite of his playing the good patient, were not happy months. He had never feared death.

■ CHOOSING TORONTO

LIFE CONTINUES FOR the living, and Wendy and I carried on in our searches for a new University, a calm port away from the shark-infested depths of the University of Chicago. I worked on details of the offers from each of the three Universities. All three were top notch.

The argument against New York and Seattle for me was that both offers came from VA hospitals, and both would have hindered my interest in the treatment of women with acne. Women are a rare species at VA hospitals. I would need to carve out a presence at a different site, or abandon hormonal acne altogether. On the other hand, either New York or Seattle would have placed me in superb departments. The argument against Toronto was the uncertainty of working with some of the characters I had met so far. But that is true of every major move.

By the end of March, the time had come to make a decision. We were used to those conversations, having agonized over Boston and Chicago years before. The positives and negatives, on paper, two columns, over a bottle of wine. By then, I had learned to enjoy the exercise. Housing had also tipped the scale away from New York. Wendy looked at NYU housing and just couldn't stomach it—low ceilings and cockroaches in the best apartments they had to offer. We could have done better on our own but the effort seemed daunting and we didn't have the time. Seattle seemed less secure for our academic futures, and despite the draw of my family now that my mother was a widow, we leaned away from Seattle.

We ultimately chose Toronto. The chair of medicine had created a vice chair position that would give Wendy good leadership training. And her mother lived in town. Toronto mothers had always been viewed by the chair of medicine as the best recruiting devices he knew to entice doctors to return to Canada. I decided to join one of the three downtown hospitals that had recently merged into a new conglomerate called University Health Network. I had always preferred inner city espresso-drinking, sushi-eating communities to fast food, strip-mall, suburban-style hospitals which is what Sunnybrook Hospital, the competition, seemed to be. Working with Dr. Freedberg in New York would probably have been better for my career. He had all the right connections for my research, speaking, and writing. But I whole-heartedly looked forward to living in Toronto, and it looked as if there were plenty of opportunities there. Toronto would be another adventure, another city, another country.

The only potential problem with my choice of hospital came with the words "remember who signs your paycheck," which I heard had been spoken to a colleague by Doctor Scrooge, the one who never looked in my direction but to whom I would report on occasion. I would be taking my chances with him. I felt confident, however, that I could start filling the relative vacuum in academic dermatology that existed at the hospital I chose, though it was only one of several core dermatology groups in the university system. Like our move to Chicago five years earlier, this move would have uncertainties, but Wendy and I had never had problems with the concept of uncertainty. In fact, we rather enjoyed it.

As soon as I submitted my resignation, the chair of medicine at Chicago began speaking disparagingly about me to the dermatology residents I had helped to train. They were appalled.

Chicago had been such an emotional roller coaster. We had arrived full of anticipation and hope but were leaving with some bitterness. We had loved our home in Hyde Park for its proximity to campus and the intellectual feel of the neighborhood, but we hated the constant threat of violent crime. The leadership experiences for Wendy and me had been ones of learning but also of disappointments. I had started out so proud of my new affiliation with Chicago, but ultimately had to agree with the comment by a former graduate student, that "The University of Chicago is fratricidal." Friends from out of town raved about how much they liked visiting Chicago, and I had to agree that the downtown corridor was exciting. Day to day tasks in Chicago, on the other hand, were a struggle. Once we were out, I didn't miss Chicago at all. I felt instead a sense of relief. Our decision to move turned out to be a good one.

≋ CHAPTER 12 ≋

Toronto Beginnings

"Toronto had rules before it had people."
–guy at an ATM machine

■ CANADA *IS* A DIFFERENT COUNTRY

THE DAY BEFORE we drove out of Chicago, as the fully-loaded moving van pulled away from the house, Gersh pulled up with Wendy in the back seat. She was returning from delivering our daughter Lauren to college at Pomona, in California, where she would be starting as a freshman. Lauren would lose something with this move. Both Lauren and Toby would lose something, but Lauren would never get to return during school breaks to her own bedroom, to her school friends, the way most kids do when they go away to college. Her home in Toronto would be more hotel than home; she would be using the guest room. I felt a bit sorry for her. She was being pulled up by the roots again. Any emotional connections to Chicago Lauren and Toby had made during the last four and a half years would require much more effort, and prior connections to Portland had already faded considerably. Lauren was becoming a wandering Jew, an Army brat without the health insurance. At least Toby would be living with us, though her roots were being pulled as well, and friendships would become long-distance relationships.

We drove out of Chicago with a trunk full of the wines I didn't want to cook inside a moving van during the September move. I thought I had navigated through all the red tape required to bring my small wine cellar from Chicago to Toronto. One has to have priorities, and close behind gathering all the medical credentials necessary for the move, wine ranked right up there. One of my first discoveries about Canada was the fact that if the Province of Ontario doesn't get its nickel out of every drop of alcohol sales and trade, it gets very irritable. I had submitted a list, paid a fee, about one or two dollars per bottle, and had the documentation to show for it.

At the border, when we entered Canada as 'settlers' and disclosed having some wine in the trunk, the officious border guards leaned back in their chairs, and said, "Oh, we'll have to look into this further. These fees are transfer fees only, eh? There would still need to be sales tax, PST, and GST on this wine." I thought Wendy would have a stroke on the spot. "How much wine would you be bringin' in today?" they asked.

We ended up paying about five dollars on every bottle of wine, about ten cases. It could have been much worse. They could have searched the car themselves for an accurate count which was more than ten cases. They could have gone online to evaluate the value of each bottle. As it happened, they accepted the lowball dollar value we gave them, and for their purposes, we made sure they were worth little more than the glass in which they were bottled.

Before moving, I had been informed that with all the paperwork in place, an Ontario medical license would be waiting for me when we arrived. Not so. I was met with an unpaid sabbatical of three months, or as they say in Canadian British style, 'three months time'. I would have been more than willing to personally courier documents anywhere in the province, but the snail's pace seemed to be an essential part of the process in Toronto. Efficiency, to Canadians, apparently was viewed as someone stepping out of line, jumping the queue. Letters sat on desks for weeks before being mailed to the next bureaucrat to sit on that desk for weeks before the sign off. It was my first taste of the Canadian way of doing business. I tried to be patient.

The moving van pulled onto our street and began to unload the same day we arrived. The movers asked Wendy, "Where would you like these items, ma'am?"

"I don't know. This is the first time I've seen this house."

It was true. We had purchased the house without Wendy ever seeing it. We had searched Toronto neighborhoods together for months, without success; had put in full-price bids on other houses and lost in bidding wars. This house had become available suddenly and only I could free myself to fly up from Chicago and look at it. It was pure genius by our realtor that the house landed in our lap. We had made an overpriced bid with no conditions. Our competitor massively overbid us, but with the condition that they had until eleven o'clock that night to confirm. The seller naturally took the higher bid. Our realtor, in a brilliant move, changed our contract deadline at the last minute, to 11:15, so the seller could come back to us in the unlikelihood of our competitors capitulating. It turned out that our competitors, who had flown in from Montreal and didn't see the house until after dark, were unable to commit by their deadline of eleven o'clock and the seller accepted our offer. The flurry of midnight phone calls to learn of our prize was laughable and memorable.

After unloading at our new house, the movers drove to my office on the west side of town, and Wendy's office on the central east side. Like a kid, I rode along, high up in the cab of this huge moving van, through the skinny neighborhood streets of Little Italy and Chinatown, gears shifting five times just to get up to ten miles per hour.

Everything seemed to be in order. It wasn't until weeks later that I realized my most valuable box of personal effects was missing. I had packed a box with many of the important parts of my adult history, and labeled it something uninteresting like 'electronics' or 'miscellaneous' instead of 'most important!' so no one would want to look inside. It contained all the negatives and proof sheets from my early years in photography. It had all my records from medical school, internship, photographs from dermatology residency in Portland, photographs of the Section of Dermatology in Chicago each year. It contained my file on Dr. Lowey, including the California charges for overprescribing narcotics. That box never surfaced. Fortunately, the Lowey documents turned out to be in the public record and email backup files.

■ SEPTEMBER 11, 2001

WE ARRIVED IN Canada one week before September 11th, 2001, that black-hole day in American history. I was at home that dreadful Tuesday morning when I received a call from my father in-law. "I think you better turn on the television." Every American recalls in his or her own way, and with perfect clarity, the rest of September 11th. The bringing down of the Twin Towers by Islamic fanatics made me wish, for the first time in many years, that I was younger so I could go off and fight. Unlike Viet Nam, this was a fight worth fighting. The practice of medicine, my career, seemed irrelevant. If younger, I could have enlisted in an organization that would fight to rid the world of the beliefs that gave birth to such evil doing. While friends and relatives worried about their own friends and relatives who might have been hurt or killed in New York, I felt this act was much, much bigger than individual loss. As inconceivably horrendous as it must have been for the victims that day, this was going to be a fight for who inhabited the world.

I had trouble with the anti-American comments I at first heard that day from many Canadians, on radio and in newspapers, some in person, that Americans deserved it, had asked for it. Anti-American sentiment had been thriving in Canada at least since the Viet Nam war. Canada has always been more liberal-minded than the United States. President Bush was not popular in Canada, and President Reagan probably hadn't helped any. I also had trouble with the standard American media approach of concentrating on the praising of firemen, Mayor Giuliani, and everyone who came together in this time of tragedy. They all certainly deserved praise, but it seemed as if the entire event was treated as a natural disaster, not an attack by fanatic religious terrorist murderers. Few in mainstream media examined the evil-doers and their ignorant, destructive beliefs. My anger and frustration ate at me for the entire three months of waiting. At first, when I finally started seeing patients, despite knowing it was wrong, I had to struggle to be professional with my Muslim colleagues, students, and patients.

Why? Because I never once heard a Muslim colleague, student or patient express any outrage or even disapproval over 9/11. I worked with enough of them that I thought someone should have had trouble with the violence of 9/11. Instead, they were silent. The only sentiments I heard came from newspaper columnists who, if Muslim, wrote about unjust Islamophobic backlashes and, if Canadian, wrote of their country of 'moderate' peace-loving Muslims. How could we know whose side these 'moderate' Muslims were on when they were silent? If there were moderate Muslims out there, they chose not to be heard. How could one embrace the concept of moderate Islam without hearing Muslim leaders publically condemn 9/11, denounce terrorism in general, and support peace in the Middle East? It wasn't happening. Doctors are trained to use evidence to influence their thinking. The evidence was lacking.

A few months after 9/11, a friend and his wife, both Jewish, were invited to dinner at the house of a colleague and his wife, both Muslim, educated, affluent and fully assimilated into Canadian life over thirty years . The foursome had long ago agreed to disagree about Israel. They avoided contentious subjects. The two men had been occasional partners in business. The Muslim man even drank wine. During dinner, his wife came out from the kitchen and said, "Wasn't that great what Osama bin Laden did to the World Trade Centers?" My friends were too dumbfounded to react. They finished the evening without challenging her comment. This woman, a Canadian citizen and wife of a professional, was precisely the peace-loving moderate Muslim everybody was assuming made up the vast majority of Canadian Muslims. From that point on, I would need much more evidence to convince me that the notion of moderate Islam was real. It seemed to be too much the wishful thinking of politically correct Westerners.

▰ INSTALLED AT THE UNIVERSITY OF TORONTO

WITH MY FREE time during those three months of waiting, I prepared several dermatology talks, wrote papers, played the piano, and worked on a book project. Autumn in Toronto was glorious that year, and my love for the city deepened. We lived in a beautiful neighborhood in

Toronto, with winding streets lined with massive Silver Maples and Oaks. One easily got lost in the tangle of its circuitous tree-lined streets, streets into which unsuspecting drivers were fabled to have ventured and, as legend had it, never found their way out.

I finally started seeing patients in December. Later that month, Wendy experienced another Canadian surprise. On about December 18th, she went down the hall to see her boss, the chair of medicine.

"You wouldn't believe the funny thing I just heard from the secretaries," she said. "They said the whole department is closed for the next two weeks for Christmas and New Years."

He looked up at Wendy and said, "Welcome to Canada."

In the U.S., we had been used to employees having only the afternoon of Christmas Eve, plus Christmas day off. Doctors were back at work on the 26th of December and bright and early on January second, so ancillary staff better be there as well. We immediately noticed that doctors worked much harder as a rule in the U.S. At least we had worked harder, and we didn't view ourselves as outliers. We eventually got used to it. We learned to appreciate the holiday down-time in Canada, to be able to work in our empty offices or undisturbed at home.

In retrospect, it was no wonder that our children rejected medicine. Our enthusiasm apparently had not been good role modeling for them becoming doctors. "No way," Toby said at age thirteen about considering medicine as a career. "You guys work way too much."

"I want to be there when my kids come home from school," Lauren once said. It felt like a knife in Wendy's side, she told me later.

What I rapidly discovered in Toronto was that not being in charge, as chief, or chair of something, had more advantages than disadvantages. I didn't have to manage other people's problems and negligent behaviors. I had responsibilities for the teaching and evaluations of residents but could work more on my own research and writing instead of organizing the education of our residents, arranging on-call schedules, and going to endless committee meetings. I had known those activities well in Chicago and didn't miss them in the least. I had been told that the residency directorship might become available because the residency director was considering stepping down. After I moved, however, a new division head was installed, and the residency director changed his mind. He had disliked working under the prior leader, but worked well with the new one. That was fine with me. I had no need for titles that added layers of responsibility.

For the third time in my career, I started over. This was a new community; I had to build trust with patients and doctors, learn local customs, local geography. Toronto Western Hospital became my new home base. Toronto Western Hospital was an old hospital, like most hospitals in which I had worked. Three generations of friends and family in Toronto seemed all to have been born there. Maternity services had long since moved to other hospitals a few blocks away, but dermatology had taken over the maternity ward on the eighth floor of the old tower, with its heavy doors, high ceilings and thick walls for every room. If you looked south out our windows you could follow Bathurst Street all the way to the lake, past Queen Street with its Bohemian squalor, the old banks and warehouses on King Street and over the railroad yards to Lake Ontario. From the windows to the east, the hospital looked down upon the one-story shanties of Kensington Market, Toronto's oldest market neighborhood, where Peruvian, Thai, and Rastafarian restaurants comingled on the aromatic one-lane streets. Alongside the restaurants stood fish mongers, dry goods stands from central and South America, and third generation butcher shops where beheaded chickens hung by their feet over blood-spotted sawdust, a reminder of an earlier time, of eastern European Jewish immigrants who had first settled there in the early nineteen hundreds. Carry your gaze further and the streets became a neon circus of Chinese characters lighting up the sides of every building in Chinatown. The broader view opened up to the financial towers of Bay Street, Toronto's answer to Wall Street, and the CN Tower (built by Canadian National Railway), the tallest structure *in the world* at the time, which looked down upon the entire city. From Toronto Western Hospital you could also see the University of Toronto campus and Hospital row that included Toronto General, Mt. Sinai, Princess Margaret, Women's College Hospital, and Sick Kids (Hospital for Sick Children), all part of the University system. It seemed to me that Toronto Western, while known for its expertise in many areas of research and clinical medicine, could not shake its 'poor cousin' image when compared with hospital row on University Avenue.

Over fifteen languages were translated at Toronto Western Hospital, and that was just for the telephones. Many of my patients spoke only Portuguese, Italian or Chinese. It was strange to take a medical history from grandma with her six year old granddaughter doing all the talking, with no detectable accent. We were surrounded by Chinatown and the largest Italian and Portuguese neighborhoods in Toronto. The city of Toronto boasted the largest Italian population outside of Italy itself. During international soccer tournaments, the surrounding neighborhoods went completely insane. World Cup week was the most out of control, with a succession of flag-waving, horn honking street celebrations by each victorious immigrant group immediately following every game.

About one hundred dermatologists practiced in Toronto to cover the five million inhabitants of Greater Toronto. Most of them chose to affiliate with a hospital, five of which were part of the University of Toronto system, and about five which were not. At Toronto Western, we had close to fifteen part-time dermatologists. When I came on board, I doubled the number of full-timers. The only other active full-timer had been appointed division head a few years earlier but had not expanded the operation. In fact, it looked as if they were struggling a bit, just the sort of practice I enjoyed building up. It was only because I preferred the inner city and culturally rich markets, to a suburban existence, that I joined Toronto Western Hospital. I figured I would accept whatever happened.

Over time, I regained my old reputation as a dermatologist willing to take on complicated or difficult cases, hormonal treatments of acne in women, and the person most interested in working with organ transplant patients.

■ REFLECTIONS ON MY FATHER

LESS THAN A month into practice, I was flipping through the Journal of the American Academy of Dermatology and locked onto the name John M. Shaw, at the top of a page, in big lettering. I had stumbled onto my father's obituary. I didn't know one had been written. His dearest friend and colleague, Dr. Frederick A.J. Kingery, had written the warm and appreciative piece. I felt a strange mix of emotions as I read the succinct tribute. I knew I would never be as respected in dermatology as my father had been. He knew everybody, it seemed, and his gregariousness had brought him into many inner circles. At the same time, I felt strangely liberated from his shadow. It had not been a dark shadow, but sons and fathers can have complicated relationships, and his death, in a small way, simplified my relationship with him. He could now be the father who taught me to chop wood, build fires, and catch fish instead of the doctor father everyone praised, and who, because of my own insecurity, made me feel less significant. Mostly, I felt fortunate to have had a father to introduce me to medicine, dermatology and so many other life experiences. I recalled his asking, some years earlier, whether, if given the chance to do it over again, I would choose music or medicine as a career. My answer was medicine, without any doubt. Few careers offered the constant intellectual stimulation that medicine did, and I felt grateful to him for making that opportunity available to me.

With my father gone, it occurred to me that I never really knew how he felt about my joining the ranks of dermatology, whether he was proud to have his son follow in his path, or whether I might have been an embarrassment to him. I know I embarrassed myself on occasion so it stood to reason that I might have made him cringe a time or two. We weren't exactly buddies. Fathers and sons rarely are. I often felt like he didn't want to discuss details of dermatology with me, or the political struggles within organizations. Those discussions, and the uproarious laughter that they elicited, I observed, were between him and his cronies. I did feel a sense of camaraderie with him about the specialty of dermatology, the shared knowledge, the jargon, but personally, I felt an absence of his being proud of me. It was expected in our family that we were to be successful in our careers in our own respective ways, but unfortunately we didn't know how to celebrate it together. Other things got in the way, too, of our sharing the joys of our profession. I had strayed from his right-wing, almost libertarian way of thinking. I had gone so far as to become a proponent of *SOCIALIZED MEDICINE*. I had published on the subject. I think it broke both my parents' hearts to observe their politically wayward son. We shared the pleasures of food, wine, and music, but he liked Teddy Wilson's piano playing, I liked

Herbie Hancock and Keith Jarrett; he played Dixieland jazz banjo, I played modern jazz piano; he snapped his fingers on one and three, I snapped on two and four. We couldn't really share the language of my music. Perhaps we were competing with each other.

I asked Wendy if she thought my father had been proud of me. "Are you kidding?" she responded. "Of course he was extremely proud of you. Your problem is that you don't appreciate when others appreciate you." She may have been correct.

CHAPTER 13

O, Canada

WHOA, CANADA!

In 2002, one year into our new life in Toronto, I attended the Gairdner Awards banquet. Winners of the Gairdner, Canada's highest scientific award, often went on to become candidates for the Nobel Prize. While seated at one of over one hundred dinner tables at the black tie affair, James Orbinski, recipient of the 1999 Nobel Peace Prize on behalf of Médecins Sans Frontiers (Doctors without Borders), posed a question to me. He said, "Now that you've worked here a year, do you miss the U.S. healthcare system?"

That simple question crystallized my year of weighing differences between the new Canadian healthcare system and the U.S. system I had known for over twenty-five years. While each had its own advantages and disadvantages, I was much preferring the Canadian approach. "Surprisingly, I don't miss it at all," I said.

There were so many reasons, but the primary one was that healthcare in Canada was a moral enterprise, not an entrepreneurial venture: everyone had the same insurance coverage, in Ontario at least. All medically necessary diagnostic tests and treatments were paid for out of provincial tax revenues. The Canadian design was so liberating compared to the way doctors in the U.S. treated every patient with caution because every patient had a different insurance plan with its own rules, or no insurance at all. In Canada, I never had to worry that a chest X-ray or MRI wouldn't get done because insurance might deny it or the patient couldn't afford it. Whereas my two-doctor Portland office had dealt with hundreds of insurance companies, my practice in Toronto (fifteen doctors) spent a fraction of the billing time we required in the U.S. Canada had retained fee-for-service payment to doctors, albeit with fixed fees, and revenue potential remained high, but all charges went to one office and payment arrived within six weeks. Billing in the U.S. was, and still is, a complex nightmare of rejections and resubmissions, necessitating the full-time efforts of entire billing offices.

We Canadians paid a little more in taxes than Americans, but any increased tax, I felt in my economically naïve way, was well worth it for the services we received, especially healthcare.

My patients continued to be a steady source of professional gratification, though often a challenging one. Cindy was one such patient. The first time I met her, I got that sinking feeling that came with the most complicated patients, the ones where the chances of making any progress seemed nearly impossible. Here was a woman in her forties, confined to a wheelchair, immobile and obese, moaning in pain and covered in small red pustules over her entire skin surface. She was addicted to narcotics because of the pain of her disease. She had been suffering with this condition for a decade and in spite of seeing all the academic leaders in Toronto dermatology, apparently couldn't be brought under control.

Cindy came with a diagnosis, an obscure and rare one called subcorneal pustular dermatosis (SPD). She had failed all the standard drugs used to suppress it. What I did was to start over with her, confirm the diagnosis with biopsies, and review whether she had taken appropriate doses of prior drugs. Fortunately, I discovered that she never had been treated with the vitamin A-related drug that we used in severe psoriasis. Why she hadn't been put on that drug I didn't know, since several reports had shown its success in SPD since the mid-eighties. She had been on everything else without success. I started this drug, called acetretin.

Cindy's moaning, despite fairly high doses of narcotics, was going to be a big problem. Doctors frequently suspect that patients who are dependent on narcotics avoid getting better so that they can continue to receive them. The addiction can be too strong a motivational force. I thought that might be the case with Cindy. All I could do was to try. Her skin would need to show signs of improvement before we even started to taper the narcotics, and she would need to be highly motivated to get off them. The moaning did not bode well for that.

To our pleasant surprise, her skin started showing improvement with each dose increase. By the time she reached full doses of acetretin she was fifty per cent improved. Over a year I managed to wean her completely off narcotics. She lost weight. She started walking again. She continued to moan, but now it was "Ohhh, Dr. Shaaaw. I'm sooo grateful for what you have done!" I guess moaning was the way she expressed positive emotion as well as negative.

At the end of a year, she suffered a setback when she developed seizures and her skin got much worse, possibly from the anti-seizure drug she was given. But we carried on with higher doses of acetretin and pain medications if she required them.

I continue to treat Cindy. She still has her terrible disease but has remained under control for the last five or six years. She requires the highest doses of acetretin I've ever used. She is off narcotics, has a romantic relationship, and now moans about wanting plastic surgery on her eyelids and a laundry list of lesser complaints. That is a huge improvement over where we started. She is one of the most appreciative patients I've ever had, so much so that she wrote an unsolicited two page hand-written letter to the College of Physicians and Surgeons of Ontario (CPSO), praising my care.

Not all patients were as appreciative as Cindy. Kevin, a patient in his late thirties, also wrote to the College of Physicians and Surgeons.

Instead of praising me, he reported me and requested disciplinary action. Such letters, I had learned, were often the first step in a malpractice suit.

I had asked Kevin to come to Wednesday patient rounds because of an undiagnosed problem he described as a burning sensation on his scalp and forehead, along with loss of hair. I was the fourth dermatologist, which did not portend well for my being successful. I had biopsied his scalp but the microscopic findings were non-diagnostic. Like many of my colleagues throughout my career, I had occasionally found it helpful to bring anxious patients to 'rounds' for the positive group effect, even if the disease was not particularly unusual. At rounds, the group of doctors agreed with my diagnostic thinking and treatment plan. I asked to check Kevin's progress in a month or two.

Four months later, I received a three page letter from Kevin. Rounds apparently had not gone well for him. He had been stewing over what he thought was an unsatisfactory interaction during rounds. He complained of not being permitted to tell his full story to the group, and his observation of body language that suggested to him that the doctors at rounds had doubts about my treatment, and more. He requested a private meeting to discuss his concerns further, in person. I acquiesced, and set up the appointment. At that meeting, his controlled demeanor suggested to me that maybe he was getting over his anger.

I was wrong. After another five months, I received the dreaded letter, a formal complaint from the College of Physicians and Surgeons of Ontario. He had viewed me as "arrogant, defensive, and evasive" in our private meeting, and was requesting a formal review of the whole case, with possible sanctions against me. The mission of the CPSO, I quickly learned, is to protect the public, not doctors. It is part of the Canadian way, one that I actually respected. However, all complaints are investigated fully, irrespective of the mental state of the plaintiff. Several of my colleagues had horror stories to tell of rants made against them by unstable patients that resulted in full investigations. I spent the next two months preparing documents for review; I consulted malpractice advisors. Kevin met with my division head and Human Resource people at my hospital to advance his complaint. All parties submitted reports and letters. It was due process, Canadian style. Ultimately, after a long year, the case closed in my favor. There would be no further action by the CPSO. Kevin could still sue me if he chose to.

While not exactly a nail-biting thriller, Kevin's story illustrated how good intentions could backfire. It came with being a doctor, and we were taught in medical school and beyond, that interactions with difficult patients should not be taken personally. In his case, I had to struggle to get over the resentment I felt. Kevin became the last person with a challenging personality that I brought to rounds.

▄ SARS

IN MARCH OF 2003, SARS (Severe Acute Respiratory Syndrome) came to Toronto. It was the scariest medical phenomenon many of us in medicine had ever witnessed. That included long retired doctors who had lived through the influenza pandemic of 1918 and Polio in the 1950s.

I came upon the first reports of SARS in the *International Herald Tribune* on March 17, 2003 during a trip to Rome. The one paragraph article told of a deadly new disease coming out of China. Instead of warning the rest of the world, the Chinese government, in typical fashion, tried to suppress the news, but by March 26, several cases had shown up in Toronto hospitals. The rapidity with which patients got sick, the severity of the illness—ten or more already dead in Toronto—and the degree of contagiousness of this disease were frightening, much worse than any infectious disease we had ever encountered. Mere hands-on contact in caring for the sickest patients, even with gloves and masks, caused many doctors and nurses to contract the illness they were trying to treat. Public health officials got involved right away. Exposed family members and health care workers were quarantined for up to ten days, usually at home. Within the first forty-eight hours in Toronto, some of the patients who became critically ill were transferred to downtown hospitals, primarily Mt. Sinai Hospital. By seventy-two hours, our Minister of Health shut down all Toronto hospitals. Only emergency surgeries were performed, and all educational activities came to a halt. Yellow police tape blocked all but one entrance to every hospital. It was like a modern day Plague epidemic. Only those with dying relatives were permitted as visitors onto the wards. Body temperature monitors were installed at the airports, albeit too late to do much good. The Minister of Health who closed the hospitals went on record saying, "Two weeks from now I hope I will be accused of having overreacted."

All outpatient activities stopped. Some of us in dermatology, those with hospital-based practices, were forced to take a leave of absence. Mohs surgery and ultraviolet light treatments in Toronto ceased for weeks since they were exclusively hospital based. We caught up on our journals and writing, but that got old after a few days. The head of my division and I, the only full-timers at TWH, decided to make ourselves available, and checked into a hotel suite for three weeks, with two bedrooms as examination rooms and a living room that became reception and waiting room. Examination paper crinkling on the king-size beds became the norm, as did positioning patients in front of the big glass windows to examine them in good light. Overall, the hotel experience was a success. I had personally thought it unnecessary, but patients seemed to appreciate our being available. Our loyal office staff worked way beyond their call of duty. There were a few scares. The front desk panicked one time when a Chinese woman entered the hotel wearing a mask, and one patient collapsed in the hotel lobby, triggering a 9-1-1 call and much excited chatter between the concierge and our suite. But no one died or required an ambulance, thank goodness.

Andreas Lapaucis, a University of Toronto physician, contracted SARS and was quarantined in his home for close to three weeks. He was one of many. He had been a member of a medical team at Sunnybrook Hospital where the majority of Toronto's early SARS patients were hospitalized. He rounded on ward patients with SARS. The team would protect themselves with gowns and masks as they had done for years with other contagious diseases. Patients occasionally had to be transferred from the ward to the ICU, and some succumbed to their illness. After a week of this, Andreas developed fever and body aches on the drive home from a standing room only Stanley Cup playoff game in Ottawa he had attended with his wife Karen and their two kids. When he got home there was a message for him to call one of the internists on the wards at Sunnybrook right away. "Several doctors at Sunnybrook have become ill," the internist said. "We think it's probably SARS. You need to come in for a chest film and blood work." With his new symptoms in mind, Andreas got a little nervous at that point. He discussed it with his family and before being given a quarantine order they made an executive decision to send Karen and the kids back up to their farm property outside of Ottawa. It was clear Andreas would need to be quarantined for ten days or more and the rest of the family might as well be far away. The X-ray and bloods were okay, but for the first week, Andreas maintained a steady fever and systemic symptoms much worse than he had experienced with flu in the past. Public health nurses checked on him multiple times daily by phone, monitoring temperature and breathing status. One of the Sunnybrook doctors periodically left food on his porch steps. He was able to read and do some writing. He even recalled with fondness sitting on his closed-in porch with a winter coat, enjoying the peace of a stretch of sunny April weather. Stanley Cup playoffs were on television in the evenings and he sat alone, accompanied only by his son's miniature souvenir teddy bear of hockey star Marián Hossa on the table, watching the games, waiting to either improve or deteriorate.

While Andreas was at home, he learned of one of his internist colleagues at Sunnybrook who did crash. He became sick enough to be admitted, came very close to needing to be intubated, and took months to recover fully. A nurse who called one night thought that Andreas's breathing sounded more labored than usual. The next evening, the doctor who had been managing his care called him. "I have come down with acute diarrhea and I think it might be SARS related." One of her colleagues also had developed diarrhea. "We are going down to Mr. Sinai to be admitted. I'm turning your care over to Allison McGeer."

Dr. McGeer, the infectious disease expert at Mt. Sinai, called Andreas from her home where she herself had been convalescing from SARS. Andreas said, "This is looking more and more like a house of cards about to collapse," when she recommended that he go to Mt. Sinai to be examined. The resident at Mt. Sinai played it safe and recommended hospital admission, but Andreas managed to negotiate returning home after he agreed to have a chest CT scan (which, fortunately, was normal).

Karen and the kids didn't get sick but were plenty worried. There was talk by the young children and their mother, of losing their dad.

Nurses monitored them by telephone. After discovering that one of the neighbor boys had been playing with Andreas's son, a public nurse ordered the neighbor boy to be quarantined. Everyone, justifiably, had become a little paranoid. SARS was as bad an illness as any of us in medicine had ever seen.

After three weeks, when patients had stabilized and no new cases emerged for one week, we doctors started to return to the hospitals, through screening stations and with mandatory tightly fitting masks on our faces *the entire day* with patients. Then, with our guard down slightly, came SARS 2, the name given to Toronto's second wave of sick patients with SARS in the downtown hospitals. An unsuspected case in a resident exposed a whole new set of patients, doctors and nurses. Everything closed again for two weeks, but because we were all more experienced by then, containment occurred faster, and we again returned cautiously to our offices.

Our SARS experience in dermatology was only one small facet of the international outbreak. Our gratitude went to those who cared for SARS patients directly and put themselves in harms way. New trails had to be blazed in public health policy. My only criticism was that stringent screening of passengers on incoming flights from China might have reduced the initial wave of infected individuals. Hospital screening ended after another month, and SARS appeared to have become contained around the world. When the dust settled, over five hundred had died in China, and forty-three in Toronto. It could have been much worse without the drastic public health measures.

ORGAN TRANSPLANT PATIENTS

TOWARD THE END of my first year in Toronto, I created a specialized dermatology clinic for organ transplant patients. Toronto General Hospital, part of my hospital network, had a huge multi-organ transplant program that managed over four thousand patients with transplants. Their surgeons transplanted hearts, lungs, kidneys livers, pancreases, and even some intestinal transplants. After the surgeons were finished with their work, the internal medicine specialists kept the patients alive.

As usual, the surgeons got the glory, but the hard part came after the surgery, with the years of dedicated care from transplant teams and internists to prevent rejection and all the potential complications of living with a transplanted organ. Skin disease, especially skin cancer, was one of the most common complications.

I submitted the proposal for the clinic and met with the multi-organ transplant executive committee, a group of humorless men with skepticism permanently chiseled into their faces. They liked the idea though, enough to give me some clinic space and personnel to schedule a once-weekly clinic. We started managing and documenting transplant patients' skin problems. We screened for risks of skin cancer and infection, taught them how to prevent disease if possible, especially pertaining to sun exposure and skin cancer. Most people, doctors included, were not aware that Toronto had the same latitude—44° North—as Florence, Italy. Toronto got intense sun many months of the year.

Transplant patients are at extremely high risk for developing skin cancers of all types. The highest risk is for squamous cell carcinoma, a cancer known to be induced almost exclusively by sun damage. That being the case, it is also the cancer that patients can influence merely by avoiding the sun. The sad truth, however, was that after many years of successful organ transplants around the world, a significant number of patients continued to die from skin cancer, and many with the highest risk (i.e. fair skin, blue eyes, blond or red hair), ignored our strong recommendations to stay out of the sun.

With the help of the nurse coordinators who were the first-line contact with patients, my clinic at Toronto General Hospital began to grow. Many patients had been under the care of dermatologists in greater Toronto, but I rapidly noticed that many were in need of much more aggressive treatment than they had been receiving. Some required treatments every two to four weeks to gain control and stay ahead of the rapidly growing skin cancers.

Toronto General Hospital had been the flagship of the University of Toronto for over fifty years. Like hospitals everywhere, new wings had been added in an architecturally mismatched fashion, and soon after my first year there, we transferred from one of the older wings into the brand new wing that was to house all of transplant medicine and surgery. The shiny new wing was clean and bright, but there was something missing that I had always liked about older hospitals. In the new building, there was no dark cafeteria with familiar faces dishing up real food twenty-four hours a day for those on call. Times were changing fast, and both Toronto General and Toronto Western Hospitals had undergone renovations. Now instead of cafeterias that served stuffed cabbage and baked fish filets, there were food courts with fast food, pizza, and deli. Mostly junk food, made off-site, served on plastic plates.

Organ transplant patients were among the most appreciative of all my patients. I often used the term 'miracle of modern medicine' concerning their transplants, and they would heartily agree. They were fully aware that they had been given a second chance, that without the transplant they would be dead.

One heart transplant patient, Jose Cortez, a young man of thirty-five years, came to me on an urgent basis with a new skin problem. I had been seeing him for two years because of warts on his hands and face which, like skin cancer, are much worse in transplant patients because of the immune suppressing drugs. We were able to keep his warts in check with regular visits, but this time he had a more ominous problem. Scattered on his body were about twenty water blisters the size of peas, with a rim of red around each one.

"These came up over the last three days, doctor."

"Do you feel sick in any way?"

"Maybe some fever."

This was worrisome. His picture of 'dew drops on a rose petal' suggested the chickenpox virus. He could be harboring the disseminated form of chickenpox (medical term Varicella) and it could easily damage internal organs if not treated. It could be fatal. Just two months before, we had been called to see another patient in the ICU who for days had been covered with the telltale blisters of disseminated Varicella chickenpox, but the ICU doctors didn't call the dermatologists early enough to save the patient. Despite instituting treatment immediately after we saw him, the patient died within twenty-four hours—the virus had caused irreparable liver and lung damage. He could have been successfully treated if the diagnosis had been made earlier. Throughout my career, I had repeatedly emphasized to residents and colleagues that, in ICU patients, if skin is involved, get a dermatology consultation immediately. Even today that recommendation goes unheeded and fatal diagnoses are missed because of delays.

Jose's chickenpox story turned out to be highly unusual. He was in the process of becoming a hospital volunteer and had received the routine chickenpox vaccination given to all volunteer recruits without a prior known history of childhood chickenpox. Jose's heart transplant medications that suppressed his immune system allowed the live vaccine to multiply and spread. He was one of the first cases of disseminated Varicella caused from the vaccine strain of the virus. We hospitalized Jose for I.V. therapy and, fortunately, he survived. The next step was to educate the hospital policy people about when not to administer routine chickenpox vaccinations to their prospective volunteers. My medical student at the time took the initiative to write up the case of Jose and published it in our best clinical journal.

Transplant patients were also at risk for unexpected and rapid death, usually from infections or malignancies, similar to the way AIDS patients died in the 1980s. One patient, Sean Malley, was a hard drinking, hard smoking man with a heart transplant. He had had so much sun damage to his skin and so many skin cancers that I could barely control them. On one visit, while I was preparing to surgically treat several cancers, he complained of a pain in his back, so severe that he had to sit up. "It began on the drive down here but it's getting really bad. I don't know if I can do this." He looked pale. I immediately thought the worst—a dissecting aortic aneurysm—and transferred him to the emergency room. He died in a matter of hours. Ultrasound tests had confirmed a dissecting aneurysm. The atherosclerosis that had led to his original heart failure had ravaged all the major blood vessels of his body, including his aorta. Mr. Malley typified some of the transplant patients I treated who had lived unhealthy lives but had changed after the transplant to be submissively compliant, if a little angry at life. They recognized their mortality as they hadn't before, and were appropriately frightened, as all transplant patients are. Most transplant patients, of course, had nothing to do with the cause of their organ failures that necessitated having a transplant.

Lung transplant patients were often the most complicated and tenuous. I saw a young woman whose left eyelid was covered with a large cobblestone textured tumor that had been treated for a year by our dermatologists as if it was merely a large wart. Suspecting cancer, I took a biopsy, which showed invasive skin cancer. Despite extensive disfiguring surgery and radiation therapy, she only was given about a year before the tumor returned aggressively and took her life. She was in her early thirties.

One lung transplant patient, Mr. Spoder, taught me an important lesson. He required visits every month to remove rapidly growing skin cancers on his head and neck. His blue eyes and fair skin put him at risk for skin cancer anyway, and his double lung transplant necessitated highest doses of immunosuppressive drugs. He used to go out onto Lake Ontario every day, alone. He would fish for hours out there on his boat.

"Boating is about the most intense sun exposure anyone can get around here in the summer," I said during my usual lecture to him about sun avoidance. I knew him quite well by that time.

"But doc, fishing is the most important thing in my life." he said. "I don't have much else now." He had been a highly successful business man his whole life.

That comment was an eye opener for me. How could I be asking a patient to give up the main activity that gave him meaning in life? "Okay," I said. "We'll keep working on these cancers the best we can. Try to wear sunscreens and a hat out there on the boat." From that point on, I tempered my admonitions to transplant patients about sun exposure other than to make them fully aware of the risks. Mr. Spoder stopped showing up a year and a half later. His lung transplant, after eight years, wasn't able to withstand a bout of pneumonia. He had enjoyed eight good years of fishing.

Many of my lung transplant patients were young when they received their transplants for cystic fibrosis. I viewed them as among the luckiest of all. Before the advent of lung transplantation, most kids with cystic fibrosis died by the age of thirty. Because they were young, they didn't get skin cancers as much as older patients, but could suffer with the worst cases of warts I've ever seen. Conventional treatments simply failed in these patients. I often used the painful electrocautery needle approach on them every two weeks to keep the warts at bay. One patient, though, Mr. Harris, experienced a nearly miraculous disappearance of sheets of warts covering the bottoms of his feet. It was a new treatment. If a patient could tolerate a soak of 115° Fahrenheit for fifteen minutes a day, the warts often improved. I recommended the hot water treatment to Mr. Harris, and after two months, his warts completely vanished. This treatment, I decided, needed to be studied, so I recruited the help of one of our residents to initiate a research project. In the end, the home treatment design failed because it was too difficult for patients to maintain the water temperature, and we stopped the study after a year. I still suspect that wart viruses (Human Papilloma virus, or HPV) are susceptible to heat. The difficulty is delivering enough heat to kill the virus but not burn the patient. If HPV could be grown in a laboratory, we would be able to study whether low levels of heat would kill them, but so far, no one has ever successfully grown HPV in a laboratory.

Another successful treatment discovery came from my transplant patients. Many patients developed enlarged oil glands on their faces because of the drugs they were taking. Their faces would become oily and covered in hundreds of yellowish bumps from the large oil glands. We call it sebaceous hyperplasia. I knew that Accutane (the acne drug) was effective in shrinking sebaceous glands in patients with acne, so I tried it, and to my patient's and my pleasant surprise, the large oil glands nearly vanished within one month. They could be clear for up to a year, at which point I could give them another month of treatment. I have treated dozens of patients similarly with equal success.

▰ TEACHING NEVER PAYS THE BILLS

I RECEIVED A call one day from my Physician in Chief, one of the signers of my paycheck. He told me he was reducing my income by one third, effective immediately, because I was in too much 'underage', a term that referred to inadequate revenue production. No warning, no probation. It was a slap in the face. I had been hired to increase the academic profile of dermatology at University Health Network. We agreed that I had accomplished that goal but it looked as if my academic efforts were preventing the patient volumes necessary to cover the salary expectation in the contract I had signed, and clearly the money meant more to 'management' than the academic pursuits did. Transplant patients took much more time than standard patients and I couldn't easily move them through like cattle, the way many dermatologists did with patients in both the community and at university clinics. Furthermore, I had no nurse to optimize my productivity.

I asked for a higher teaching allowance. I had recently won a prestigious teaching award; maybe I could garner some support from that. No response. I then scrambled to find other revenue streams. The departmental Chair of Medicine granted me a small teaching stipend. My citywide dermatology division director connected me with a drug study center where I was able to boost my earnings somewhat, at the expense of spending less time with residents. I tried to get more financial support for my transplant clinic. All the full time transplant physicians had received supplemental funding from the Ministry of Health. Perhaps I could too. No luck there either. I eventually chose to move my transplant clinic back to my main hospital.

After I closed the in-house transplant clinic at Toronto General Hospital, it was the nurses I missed most: the nurse coordinators for the transplant patients, who knew all the patients and made their appointments, who made contacts with consulting doctors and who asked favors of me to see patients on short notice and appreciated the service. The doctors, mostly aloof and arrogant, I didn't miss at all.

Most of what I did with transplant patients was not any more difficult or intellectually challenging than what I did with other dermatology patients. I was merely more aggressive and spent more time with them than others. And it wasn't that my dermatologist colleagues didn't know how to properly care for these patients, they just didn't make the time to do it. They were used to seeing sixty to eighty patients a day, mostly new consultations (which paid more), and chose not to spend extra time or effort to treat the diseases that transplant patients developed. The situation reminded me of when I was taking care of AIDS patients in the 1980s.

My head symptoms were the same in Toronto as they had been in Chicago and Portland. It had been twenty-five years. Every day was a constant battle against the balloon-headed fatigue I experienced throughout the day. I experimented with antihistamines available in Canada that hadn't been over-the-counter in the States. They helped somewhat. I tried nicotine gum for a few weeks after noticing that the symptoms were better after smoking a cigar. No method totally prevented the symptoms, so I would gradually return to living with them because it was the easiest thing to do. At least they had not become incapacitating.

Just as having a daughter allowed me to empathize with the parents of sick children, my illness gave me the privilege of knowing first hand what it is like to be sick. It made me more empathetic with all patients. Whether their pain was physical or psychological, I could put myself, to a small degree, into their shoes. Patients detect empathy from doctors and it usually resonates with them. They are also very good at detecting false demonstrations of empathy.

CHAPTER 14

MY TENNIS GAME IS NO GOOD

"One of the secrets of life is that one must give up caring too much about anything."

-Robertson Davies

■ PATIENTS SHOULD BE TREATED LIKE FAMILY

By 2003, I was reasonably well established in the medical and dermatological community of the University and was thoroughly enjoying living in Toronto. Much of my extended family, however, lived in the Seattle area. My seventy-six year old mother had by then been a widow for two years; I stayed in touch with her through weekly telephone calls and visits twice a year. A music lover herself, she always took a keen interest in the music I was hearing at the Toronto Symphony Orchestra, which, although not the Chicago Symphony Orchestra, was quite accomplished.

During one such weekly phone call, she mentioned a new disturbing symptom. She had started having severe episodes of neck pain. Although I was not her doctor, I put on my physician hat and asked a few questions.

She couldn't pinpoint the pain, but it seemed to begin at the back of her tongue and spread across the back of her neck. The episodes occurred mostly in the middle of the night and kept her awake for an hour or more. On a severity scale of one to ten, the pain rated at least eight or nine.

Given her age and past history of smoking, my concern was clear: "See your own doctor as soon as possible and have your heart checked," I said. "The pain could be angina (the classic symptom of coronary heart disease)."

Her internal medicine physician made space to see her quickly and, to our relief, his examination and electrocardiogram were normal. He made a referral for her to see an orthopedic surgeon because of her long history of spine arthritis. After appropriate X-rays, the orthopedic surgeon reported that, yes, my mother had degenerative arthritis of the cervical spine. He recommended monthly injections into the affected areas of her neck.

Jean followed doctor's orders and started with the injections. She tried to be patient, thinking that several months might be required before any improvement occurred. In the meantime, she continued to have excruciating episodes of neck pain every night. The symptoms were always the same, one to two hours of pain unrelieved by everything she tried.

I stayed in touch, commiserating with her about the pain while trying to be optimistic about the treatments. After six months of injections, she was no better, and the orthopedic surgeon discharged her saying he had little more he could offer. Her internal-medicine doctor, with similar sentiment, continued to see her on an "as needed" basis, essentially not knowing what to do. The painful episodes persisted, and she endured, with characteristic stoicism and ibuprofen.

Eighteen months into this, with no significant letup, my mother dropped the bombshell. For two days she had been having trouble breathing with each episode of neck pain. Just speaking to me over the telephone caused shortness of breath. My heart sank into a deep pit as I thought, *Angina!* It must have been heart disease all along, and now she is having heart muscle failure with each episode! Cervical spine disease had been merely a coincidental finding the doctors uncovered first, a red herring.

"Get yourself to the emergency room immediately," I said. "You need more cardiac evaluation."

The correct diagnosis turned out to be severe coronary artery disease for which surgery would be the only reasonable alternative to a painful, suffocating death. She underwent quintuple bypass of tiny coronary vessels by a superb academic surgeon and his team at the University of Washington.

My mother's neck pain (the angina!) disappeared immediately—an undeniable relief—but she never made a significant recovery. Her heart continued to fail, and she died three months later. Throughout the ordeal, I avoided acting as her doctor and tried not to meddle. I was merely her son. I had viewed my role as supportive and advisory. I still carry some guilt and resentment over the delayed diagnosis, and in my mental replays, I regret not having pushed for more diagnostic evaluations when the treatment attempts were failing.

Angina in women is known to be difficult to diagnose, so I am reluctant to be too critical of the medical profession (although even as a dermatologist, I distinctly recall the back-of-the-tongue symptom, from early medical school days, as being characteristic of angina).

But what I had learned over thirty years in medicine was this: To help every patient requires going beyond our routine bag of tricks. It often necessitates rethinking a case over and over, getting a second or third opinion if answers are not forthcoming and treatments fail. Helping patients often means treating every patient the way we, the doctors, would want our daughters, our spouses, our mothers, to be treated.

I will never know whether diagnosing my mother's angina sooner—when her heart muscle could have been stronger—would have changed her outcome. But in a suffering patient, there is almost always something more that can be done, especially when a diagnosis is not yet established. Too often in medicine, the real cause of a problem is recognized only in retrospect.

I was surprised to discover, months after my mother's death, that, while I thought I had been calling her weekly for her benefit, now that she was gone, I missed our conversations, especially our music discussions. Alone on the telephone, she had been more attentive than when I used to call and speak with both parents at the same time. She researched the contemporary composers I would mention, and usually taught me more about them the next time we spoke. There was no one else in my life with whom I could share my enthusiasms about music in the same way. I had taken it for granted.

I will always be inspired by words my mother spoke on her last day, mere hours before she died. Though mentally intact, she appeared to be deteriorating rapidly, and my brothers decided to call an ambulance to take her to the hospital. The EMT came into the house and knelt beside her, pale and short of breath on the sofa.

"What seems to be the problem?" he said.

My mother looked the EMT and enunciated clearly, "My tennis game is no good."

■ TELEDERMATOLOGY

HOSPITAL CONSULTATIONS, WHETHER in Portland, Chicago, or Toronto, were always the most interesting dermatological cases I saw during my career. The time commitment however, was substantial, anywhere from thirty minutes to two hours initially. My contribution, as the attending, was usually an hour per case. As my Portland colleagues had said years ago, "The reimbursement hardly justifies the time spent." Nevertheless, these were usually excellent learning and teaching cases, and it was part of every faculty physician's job to see hospital consultations, help the patients, and teach about the cases.

One time I was on call and my pager went off while at a movie with my daughter. I went into the foyer to return the call.

"Hi, Dr. Shaw." I recognized the voice of one of our best residents. "I have an interesting consult, it's a woman who has been getting sicker in the hospital with fever and liver failure but no one knows what's causing it. They saw some skin lesions and asked for our help."

"Have you seen her yet?"

"Yes, she has three lesions, two on her abdomen and one on the sole of her foot."

"Only three lesions?"

"Yes, they look raised, red, with possible fluid in them."

"Do you have a digital camera? Could you send a photo to my email and I'll get back to you in an hour or so? I'd come right away but I'm with my daughter and can't easily leave at the moment."

"I'll send pictures in the next few minutes."

I viewed the resident's photos. The solitary 'juicy' red appearance of the lesions suggested a viral infection. I called her.

"I think you need to consider Varicella (Chickenpox). There are only three skin lesions, and the blisters look deeper than usual, but I'm concerned about disseminated disease. The liver and lung disease would fit. I think you should take a biopsy of one of the lesions to confirm, and immediately start I.V. Acyclovir."

"Really? That's interesting. Okay, I'll try."

The patient's medical doctors also showed surprise and some skepticism with my assessment and recommendations, but went ahead with the I.V. drugs. The patient felt better in one day and was improving dramatically in two days. The biopsy came back showing conclusive evidence of infection with herpesvirus, in this case, the Varicella type of herpesvirus.

That case was the first time we had conducted a consult, start to finish, electronically. After that day, we started sharing digital photographs of consultations routinely to get a jump on the diagnostic workup. Residents still saw every patient first, but the potential for streamlining consultations was huge. Nowadays, cell phone cameras and texting allow the crucial parts of a consult to take place during the middle of a busy clinic day. Technology had changed forever how we approached inpatient consults.

▰ THE LURE OF BEAUTY CARE

COSMETIC DERMATOLOGY WAS expanding rapidly across Toronto and the rest of North America and the world. I would get calls to please see a patient in the hospital because they couldn't find a dermatologist to do it. "Have you tried Dr. X?" I once asked the doctor from Mt. Sinai, a hospital we weren't formally covering. Dr. X was the dermatologist contracted to do their consultations. "We called him but he said he had switched his practice to cosmetic dermatology only."

The decline in medical dermatology was creeping into the resident ranks as well. I had recognized applicants whose obvious intention was plastic surgery but who didn't feel like suffering through a residency of four or five years of general surgery followed by several years of training in plastics. Dermatology had become plastic surgery 'light'. You could sleep nights during your residency, and still make a killing once you were out doing cosmetic procedures.

Our dermatology residents were all smart and highly qualified. Most performed their duties diligently throughout the five years of their training. Some excelled more than others of course, but after they finished, many started going directly into cosmetic practices. The sad irony is that nearly all of the training during residency is to diagnose and treat medical diseases of the skin, and here they were using cosmetic surgical skills for which they had received little training and that were easy to acquire on their own after residency. It was a total waste of taxpayer's money, in my view, to train dermatologists who went out and started cosmetic practices. For years I had felt the same way about plastic surgeons. They were throwing away the potential for true surgical or medical expertise for the sake, I suppose, of money and glamour. It pained me to watch. Some new graduates were trying to combine medical dermatology with cosmetic practices, which I could respect to a degree, but I had trouble respecting those who studied hard enough to pass their licensing examinations only to become glorified cosmeticians and purveyors of expensive lotions.

Medical dermatology had already been in decline even before I moved to Toronto. Dermatologists in the U.S. had felt entitled to more and more income for less and less service. In both countries, drug companies 'owned' many dermatologists, as well as most of the specialty organizations. Speakers were supposed to disclose conflicts of interest with drug companies at the beginning of their lectures, but most glossed over them or made jokes about the disclosure. "If there are any pharmaceutical companies in the audience that I don't have a relationship with, please see me after the talk." It got a laugh out of audiences. Lack of an understanding of conflicts of interest got so bad that some doctors agreed to receive honoraria if they permitted drug reps to be in examination rooms *with the patients* during their clinics.

Dermatologists were becoming less willing to actually treat patients, to work with them on an ongoing basis. It didn't pay enough for the effort. One time when I invited a visiting professor up from Johns Hopkins to speak to our residents about blistering diseases, he and I were commiserating about how so few dermatologists were willing to take care of complicated patients or use the more complex systemic drugs. He said, "Let's face it, dermatologists are wimps!" Finally, someone had put into words what I had been thinking for years.

Dermatologists are not just wimpy about drugs. Many do not take biopsies from faces, mouths, tongues, fingers, toes, lower legs and genitals because of fear and timidity. They plead 'scar' or 'bleeding' or 'pain' or 'slow healing' or some other lame excuse. Meanwhile, the patient's problem persists or worsens while they wring their hands and do nothing. We are losing our unique skill, the one we had honed for two hundred years, the ability to make a diagnosis of a perplexing skin eruption.

My disillusionment continued to grow to the point of disgust. Some offices gave their front desk explicit instructions to schedule new cosmetic patients within a few days while giving appointments two or more months in the future to those with actual skin *disease*. Dermatologists often didn't attend conferences unless drug companies provided free airfare and honoraria. Doctors negotiated with drug reps. The most blatant I heard was the doctor who requested tickets to the Maple Leafs hockey games in the winter, and the Blue Jays baseball games during the summer, in exchange for agreeing to prescribe a certain drug. Trade shows at the dermatology meetings were obscene: Acres of glitzy corporate tradeshow booths, convention halls teeming with Armani-clad dermatologists running off with bags bulging with free cosmetic products and swag they had scooped up. I felt unclean in those halls and eventually quit going altogether. My colleagues attended every free drug-funded dinner offered, to hear flimsily disguised talks about the pharmaceutical sponsor's product. Every breakfast, lunch and dinner at U of T functions, some in which I partook, was sponsored by drug companies, every annual meeting, every reunion.

Apart from the pervasive influence of drug companies, I felt let down by my own hospital group. Officially, we shared on-call duties, but I frequently filled in when the secretary (who was handed the job of corralling the doctors into a schedule) couldn't get the doctors to sign up, or when emergency rooms were unable to contact the on-call dermatologist. I had always thought that being on-call meant ensuring that you were available. The group could have used a little more 'hands-on' leadership.

By the summer of 2006, I was probably experiencing major burnout but didn't realize it. Something needed to change, that much I knew. Fortunately, my writing interests had started to pay off during the years of growing disillusionment with my specialty. Toronto publishers McClelland and Stewart published my book *The Quotable Robertson Davies* in 2005. A compendium of over eight hundred quotations from the writings of Canada's renowned novelist, playwright and critic, this book had started me on a path of writing in more literary realms. At the same time, my medical writing took on more editorial tones. I had become weary of science writing, of working for a year on a scientific article that might get published in a reasonably high-impact journal only to sink without a trace. I began to long for a lay readership, where I could expand beyond the limited scope of doctors.

As I wrote more, my piano playing suffered. I had kept up with piano over the first few years in Toronto, but now, weeks went by without touching the keys. I looked upon my piano with affection, though, and because of its height, did much of my writing standing at its curved bow, pencil in hand, filling spiral notebook after spiral notebook.

The more I wrote, the more I realized I needed to learn about writing. I came to the conclusion that English had really been a second language. My first language, music, was sequestered somewhere in the right side of my brain. My memory was better for music than for words. It was music that moved me, not poems, not passages of prose. Who needed words when a 'hip' piano voicing of an E-flat 13 (#11) chord made me cringe with pleasure, or the sound (not the lyrics) of a choral piece made me cry? I had obviously used words enough to get by in school and in medical writing, but real writing was going to be a different story entirely. I had much catching up to do. I started to envy my colleagues who had majored in English in college, and who had studied nothing but James Joyce for four or six months. I fully appreciated what a splendid language English is, however, and looked forward to spending the rest of my life with it, come what may. One thing I knew was that I still had considerable creative drive, and my memory was often flooded with scenes from the past and interpretive ideas, nothing of real importance such as mathematical theorems, but interpretations of life nonetheless. Maybe I could combine that analytical activity with what creative and artistic drive still remained.

It was sometime in the fall of 2006 that I came upon the solution to my dissatisfaction at work: I would take a sabbatical. Transplant patients now consumed about fifty per cent of my practice, but those in charge hadn't been as supportive as I had hoped, so leaving the patients to the others in my clinic seemed acceptable to me. The part-timers were competent enough.

This was not going to be a bona fide sabbatical where one gets paid to go off to Paris and study. The Faculty of Medicine at the University of Toronto had no provisions for that sort of sabbatical. I would be taking an unpaid leave of absence. Using the term sabbatical merely raised fewer eyebrows and commanded more respect than a 'leave of absence', which smacked of twelve-step programs and dissatisfaction.

My real intentions were to escape from the hospital network where I worked, and all the frustrations that went with it: no nurse, low-ball merit scores, little support from my leaders, on-call two or three times as much as the rest of our group, the sense of always being available when others weren't. I might even leave medicine for good.

The goal was to write for my own enjoyment. This could be something I could get serious about as I aged. I'd take courses and workshops like all the other millions of aspiring writers out there. I knew I was starting late in life. Most writers did their best stuff before age thirty; that's what I'd heard. But my literary hero, Robertson Davies, had a quotation I could hang onto for dear life: *"I am a writer, a job in which advancing senility is rarely detectable."*

As January 2007 and the sabbatical start date approached, I began to gear up for the move. At the end of each clinic day in December (I had always been the last one to leave clinic ever since I started in Toronto), I threw out armfuls of files on diseases, drugs, and the science of dermatology that I'd accumulated over twenty-five years. During Christmas break when the office was a tomb, I moved out for the last time, the final task being to transfer my computer hard drive. I left thousands of dollars of grant money on the table, probably never to be used again. I did, however, keep all of my dermatology photographs, the 35mm Kodachrome slides that I hadn't yet converted to digital.

The eight months of sabbatical turned out to be a grand success on a small scale. It was by far the most drastic career move of my life. Others must have thought so too. Many of my colleagues were amazed that I actually did it. They often had imagined a lifestyle change for themselves, but never got around to executing one.

At home, Wendy and I had had concerns about what this 'sabbatical' might mean for our marriage. I had warned Wendy not to expect me to become a househusband. In fact, if I happened to be having a particularly productive day, I warned her that not only would breakfast dishes still be on the counter, I wouldn't necessarily come down at the end of the day to eat dinner with her. Though no one said it directly, some of Wendy's friends thought I was being selfish. And yes, I would agree that, after a lifetime in the service of others, at home and professionally, I was finally attending to myself, I was being gloriously selfish, not irresponsibly so, or at the expense of anyone else, but deliciously, selfishly...selfish.

To our pleasant surprise, however, the sabbatical didn't affect my marriage negatively at all. I usually accomplished enough writing during the day to become more available to Wendy in the evenings instead of coming home from work and wanting only to hide away and write. And, as Wendy put it, "Now, only one of us comes home tired and grumpy." I even renewed my interest in cooking.

▪ THIS WRITING THING

EARLY ON INTO the sabbatical, I experienced the pleasure of my first acceptance. I had written a piece about a patient who died after a long battle with cancer. I submitted it to *The New York Times* and, in the custom of the industry, never heard back from anyone, the pocket rejection. On the recommendation of Dr. David Elpern, my good friend and literary advisor in medicine, I tried *The Los Angeles Times* and to my surprise heard back within a few hours. The editor liked the piece and thought she could use it, but my twelve hundred words needed to be pared down to six hundred and she needed the revision the next day. Elated, I slashed and burned through the original piece, sending back six hundred words two hours later. The piece ran a few weeks later. This writing thing was off to a good start.

Over eight months I was fortunate to publish several pieces in *The LA Times*, mostly about patients I had treated successfully, some about doctor failures and death, some about public beliefs that were sorely in need of being challenged, such as drinking eight glasses of water every day, and the way mothers bounce their infants too much. I made good progress on a novel. There came the time, though, when I needed to decide whether or not to come back to medicine and dermatology.

Women's College Hospital, one block up the street from Toronto General, had been an important part of the citywide division of dermatology. The one hundred year-old hospital had been originally founded to support women doctors who, as a group, were banned by the men of Toronto General Hospital from joining their ranks. Women's College Hospital was once the academic hub of the whole division of dermatology, under the leadership of a woman named Ricky Schachter who had been rejected by Toronto General Hospital early in her dermatology career, explicitly for being a woman and Jewish. I thought it would be a good fit for me and the transplant patients who chose to return to my care. Our new physician in chief at Women's was in need of a division head in dermatology. She approached me. Apparently there had been support voiced for my leadership within the group.

"I'll give it some thought," I said, knowing that it was not likely.

My experience as Section Chief and program director at the University of Chicago certainly had been underutilized in Toronto. But now, I no longer had interest in a leadership position. I was enjoying my new writing career aspirations more than medicine. Besides, I didn't relish the idea of leading certain personalities in the dermatology division at Women's. It would be herding cats all over again, like Chicago or worse. Fortunately the physician in chief expressed interest in having me join the faculty at Women's in any capacity, so I returned to her with a rejection of her offer to be the divisional head, but a request to come back in a limited capacity, one academic day per week, where I would see transplant patients and teach residents and students. She accepted.

The Women's College group turned out to be excellent for me. I felt right at home there. This hospital even had a quaint, old-style cafeteria that served stuffed cabbage rolls and overcooked baked fish like the old days. I had the luxury of one or two lovely nurses to help with procedures in the clinic. I taught the nurses how to inject my patients with local anesthetics, just as I had done with my assistant Bernie in Portland. Not unexpectedly, the dermatology division at Toronto Western, my former hospital, refused to redirect my transplant patients to me at Women's when they asked for me, but many eventually found me and started to trickle back to my care. All the Mohs surgery in Toronto was done just down the hall from my clinic so I could refer my transplant patients who needed large surgeries. One day per week was working well for me.

After a year, the big question still lingered. Would I remain semi-retired or would I decide to reenter the boxing ring to slug it out full-time with a full load of patients, interactions with colleagues around the country, publish papers, teach residents, and embark again on research projects? At the time of this writing, I have yet to answer that question.

CHAPTER 15

We Can Always Do Better

"A doctor's treatment is always a reflection of himself, to some degree."
—Robertson Davies

■ WHITHER DERMATOLOGY?

THE WRITING OF this book has been a bittersweet journey. I suspect that anyone who walks back through his or her own career might dredge up mixed emotions. We all have our successes, our disappointments and failures.

Some of the most bittersweet pangs of my career came from sharing in Wendy's career, which also had its successes and its failures. Wendy always said that in the end, integrity is everything, that ultimately those without integrity get exposed for what they are. Unfortunately, there are plenty of instances in world history to refute that thinking, e.g., cover-ups that are never uncovered, criminals that are acquitted, scapegoats who are sacrificed. Despite her many successes, to recall the interactions she had with hostile colleagues, some who failed, and some who were successful in undermining her leadership, certainly added to my disillusionment.

All eras have their strengths and their weaknesses. I began dermatology on the heels of an era governed by imperious men of great medical skill who were bound by strong ethical mores and adherence to dogmas that had lost the importance they once did. Increasingly throughout my career, women brought fresh new approaches to governance and leadership within the specialty. As I approach the end of my career, dermatology sits perched on the shoulder of a downward slope heading toward irrelevance; of Facebook entries and 'tweets' advertising specials on Botox injections. The decline is driven by an affluent, image-conscious public, and the lure of lucre is hard for dermatologists to resist, so they continue to get on board that ship. To reverse that trend will be difficult, if not impossible.

I sincerely hope that my diagnosis is wrong, that the prognosis for the specialty is rosier than I predict, and that a critical mass of dermatologists whose focus is solving medical puzzles and treating skin diseases, continues to keep dermatology afloat. For that to happen, residency program directors and other leaders in the specialty will need to inspire new graduates to embrace medical and pediatric dermatology, not just beauty care. If I am correct in my prognosis, however, and dermatology continues to slide, the treatment of skin disease is at risk of returning to a more primitive era. Why? Because fewer doctors will be able to make an accurate diagnosis. Patients with serious skin disease will always exist, but if dermatologists spend their time injecting fillers, or see too many patients to spend the time necessary to think deeply about a difficult problem, or refuse to manage the treatment of complex patients that require multiple follow-up visits, patients with real disease will either go untreated, or will have to be bombarded, shotgun fashion, with treatments administered by physicians untrained in dermatology, resulting in unpredictable outcomes. A case in point: I just saw a patient who has suffered eleven years of recurrent skin blisters over much of her body. Her diagnosis was obvious when I met her: recurrent herpes infections followed by eruptions of the disease called erythema multiforme. Every dermatologist should be able to easily make that diagnosis. It is completely treatable. She had worked with at least three dermatologists over the eleven years. According to the patient, not one had made the correct diagnosis or treated her with anything more than a useless cream. Though it wasn't life threatening, it had ruined her life during those years. I was embarrassed to be a member of a specialty that could fail a patient to that degree.

A PROUD WOMAN

I LEAVE YOU with the story of Corina, a patient I saw one afternoon, several months after returning from my sabbatical leave. She epitomized the final take-home message of my career, that no matter how experienced we are as doctors, we can always do better.

My resident saw Corina first. He presented her history to me in the corridor outside the examination room. Corina had been referred by her family doctor after having had disappointing interactions with two other consultants. That usually meant that the doctor didn't 'hear' her—either didn't follow clues she dropped, or blatantly ignored what she had to say.

"This is a fifty year old woman who comes in with itching on her back, chest and abdomen," the resident said. "She's been in reasonable health except for the itching." He reported what he observed on examination and his working diagnosis. It sounded straight-forward.

I said, "If she had been an easy case, she would have been helped by the first dermatologist. After two failures, we're at a distinct disadvantage, but sometimes that gives us an opportunity to help her even more."

We went into the room; I introduced myself and started confirming the resident's findings. Corina appeared to be in normal health. She had numerous scratched-off bumps over her torso and hundreds of tiny rough bumps just as she had mentioned to the resident. I agreed that these were probably benign growths called seborrheic keratoses. I suggested that we perform two biopsies of the scratched-off bumps, in part because, as the third consultant, the buck should stop with me, but also because I also suspected an uncommon disease called Grover's disease, a harmless but annoyingly itchy condition.

Once outside the examination room, I privately discussed the 'explosion' of seborrheic keratoses, explaining that in rare cases it was a sign of internal malignancy. It even had a name: the sign of Leser-Trélat.

237

Corina returned in two weeks. The biopsies were read as non-diagnostic, always disappointing. We were left with a fifty year-old with persistent itching and hundreds of keratoses, without a specific diagnosis. On this visit she also mentioned being fatigued, which she attributed to her relentless itching. I mentioned to her the unlikely relationship to a cancer diagnosis that we might see in older patients.

"I suggest that you update all your age-related cancer screening tests: mammography, colonoscopy, ultrasounds, as well as routine blood tests. We will send your family doctor a note recommending all the tests."

My resident said, "Maybe we could get started with the blood tests here."

"Good idea," I said. "That would speed things up."

We sent her off with lotions and pills for the itching, and told her we would call if any of the blood tests were abnormal. She left, content that we were exploring her problem more comprehensively. That was a Wednesday.

The next morning, deep into my writing, I received an urgent email from my nurse. Corina's white blood cell count had come back CRITICAL. It was fifteen times the normal range, with abnormal looking cells present.

"Oh my god," I thought. "She has leukemia!" The explosion of tiny keratoses must have been the sign of Leser-Trélat after all! She needed immediate treatment.

I tried to reach her. I left messages on her office phone and cell to call me as soon as possible. I left similar messages with her sister Clara, the emergency contact.

Within an hour, her sister Clara called. I told her I needed to reach Corina because of an abnormal test. Clara asked what test. A blood test. "What is abnormal about it, if I may ask," she said. Ordinarily I would not have disclosed more information because of confidentiality issues, but decided to risk it. I told Clara that Corina had a very high white blood cell count and needed to go to an emergency room right away.

While I waited for Corina to call, I spoke with the chief emergency room physician at Toronto General Hospital. The doctor said she would personally see her. Toronto General would be her best access to Princess Margaret Hospital, the regional cancer center.

Corina called within thirty minutes. I didn't use the word leukemia over the phone, but predicted that she would need to be hospitalized for tests and likely needed treatment as soon as possible. She took it calmly. She expressed sincere gratitude for my working with her and trying to reach her. "I can get to Emerge in half an hour."

My heart sank from knowing what was in store for her, but I felt partially relieved that she would be in good hands and receive the best treatment available. That was Thursday.

Monday morning, I received a call.

"Hi Dr. Shaw. This is Clara (the sister). Sorry to bother you. I'm calling to update you about Corina. Have you heard anything more?"

"The last I heard, she was in the emergency room at TGH and I assumed she would be admitted to Princess Margaret."

"Yes, she was admitted Friday but needed to take care of some things at her office and asked for a pass, to return Sunday to start chemo. The doctors thought it was okay and let her go. She ran some personal errands and updated all her business files." Clara paused and took a deep breath. "Early Sunday morning she killed herself."

I was completely stunned. "Oh…my…goodness," I said, my mind racing. This was a fifty year-old woman with a reasonable chance for a remission that I thought could have given her ten years!

Neither of us spoke for a few moments. Then, "She was a proud person." She went on to share Corina's appreciation for my having taken her complaint seriously and having made the effort to reach her directly by telephone. In her words, I had "at least discovered the cause." I was surprised at how much my interactions with Corina had meant to her and her sister in the throes of this tragic outcome. I would never have expected such a response.

I continued to be plagued with questions. "How did this happen? Did we contribute to her suicide in some way? What had gone wrong?" A letter from Clara arrived a week later.

> Dear Dr. Shaw,
>
> I would like to express my gratitude for the interest you took in my sister Corina's case. Notwithstanding the

tragic end to the terrible diagnosis, I know you tried your best to get Corina the help she needed and I can tell you that you were the first doctor that she felt truly listened to her and took her concerns seriously. I am just so sorry that the diagnosis turned out to be so devastating—one, I'm still having difficulty understanding.

Anyhow, it seemed to me (and Corina) that you were 'going above and beyond' the call of duty (at least compared to what we had both experienced to date) and I just wanted to make sure that you know that it was very much appreciated by the both of us.

Sincerely,

Clara

    In reality, I had done nothing heroic, nothing out of the ordinary. It had been a twist of fate (or brilliance) that the resident recommended blood tests at our hospital before she went back to her family doctor. It could have been two weeks before she had the blood tests. She could have died in that time. It had been merely for the sake of completeness that I recommended the cancer screening tests in the first place. The odds of a fifty year-old having the malignancy-associated sign of Leser-Trélat were low. Leukemia can come on quickly. No one was at fault. I could easily have been one of the dermatologists who did not perform any tests.

    I wrote Clara back to thank her for her letter. I invited her to contact me if she wished to discuss what had happened. I still had uncertainty about the details and whether we had done something to contribute to her sister's suicide. Clara wrote back indicating that after a period of time she would contact me again.

    Four months elapsed before we set up a time to speak on the telephone. I asked her to recount the events leading up to her sister's death:

    Clara had joined her sister at the emergency room that first day. There, they had a long wait, so much so that Corina called me again, concerned about the two hour wait. By the time I was able to contact the ER physician, Corina had been brought in and was being seen by a nurse. Both sisters had been searching 'elevated white blood counts' on their internet cell phones and were suspecting the worst. The nurse said they first needed to repeat all the blood work. Apparently they couldn't act on lab results from another hospital, possibly for legal reasons. The doctor saw her, bloods were redrawn, and they returned to the waiting room.

Sometime later, a nurse came out and said to them, "So I guess you know that you have leukemia." It was the first time the word had been mentioned. This was not the way breaking bad news was supposed to take place. Doctors (and, I would have thought, nurses as well) are supposed to learn in their training how to present bad news to patients. It can be done with compassion and support. This was neither compassionate nor supportive. She went on to say that Corina had an appointment the following day at Princess Margaret Hospital, the cancer hospital across the street. She was sent home without the physician returning to speak to her or providing some context to the devastating diagnosis.

Clara accompanied her sister to Princess Margaret. One of the first things they had to do was to take a bone marrow sample, which Corina commented was quite painful. The oncologist reviewed the initial diagnosis. "You have an aggressive type of leukemia". Later that evening, after confirmatory tests came in, the oncologist provided greater detail regarding the diagnosis—acute lymphoblastic leukemia—and the recommended treatment that would definitely include a stem cell transplant. The first step: massive chemotherapy to kill as many leukemia cells as possible; that takes two or three months; then stronger chemo is given to reduce the bone marrow cells to zero; that kills off all the healthy immune cells as well as the leukemia cells. He said she would be susceptible to serious infections. That's another three months. She would feel miserable. She would lose all of her hair.

"We will need to put you on high doses of steroids," the doctor said.

"Will they make me puffy? Will the chemo affect my brain?"

The oncologist didn't answer the second question completely, Clara recalled, but yes, the steroids would make her puff up in the face temporarily. Despite the oncologist's attempts at reassuring them, the prognosis came across as grim, fraught with risk and uncertainty. Both sisters recalled that their mother died a terrible death from breast cancer, with much pain and mental changes towards the end. Corina knew she didn't want that.

Then there would be the stem cell transplant—new stem cells planted in the marrow like seeds in a garden, to multiply and produce new lines of healthy white blood cells. He told her about the risk of having transplanted immune cells try to destroy her normal cells in the disease known as graft-versus-host-disease (GVHD). If that happened, they would need to suppress it with powerful anti-rejection drugs like those used in kidney and heart transplants.

After several months she would start to feel better. The oncologist gave her a positive number, like ninety per cent, as the chances of having a successful chemotherapy to knock out the leukemia cells. He couldn't however, give Corina accurate numbers concerning risks for failure of the transplant or of developing GVHD. They were difficult to predict.

After the bone marrow sample was taken, Corina negotiated for a pass out of the hospital Saturday night to get things in order before her lengthy hospital stay. Chemo couldn't be started until Monday anyway. The oncology team acquiesced to her wishes. Really, Corina wanted some time at home with family before entering Hell for the next two or three months. She would return Sunday morning for the long haul.

Later that day, after Clara had had some time to digest the awful news, she called her sister and said, "I have just one favor to ask. Pretend I am the one with leukemia and do what you would want me to do."

"Don't worry. I'll do what needs to be done," Corina said.

Saturday night was rainy in Toronto which didn't help with the gloom everyone was feeling. Corina, Clara, along with their third sister and two close friends, gathered for dinner at a restaurant, but talk didn't come easily. At the end of the evening, Clara suggested that one of the friends stay overnight with Corina for support. They didn't want her to be alone. Corina surrendered to their wishes.

Clara later learned that Corina had asked the friend to go home, saying that it was the last night she would have to herself for a long time.

"I would like the alone time. I'll be fine. Let's have coffee in the morning before I go to the hospital," the friend reported her saying.

The horrifying telephone call came in Sunday morning from the friend who had returned to her apartment for morning coffee. Corina had jumped from her twenty-second floor window. The police discovered that she had spent hours on the internet during the night, exploring treatments and prognosis of leukemia.

Devastated, Clara tried to piece together some explanations. The best she came up with was "Corina was a strong and proud person." Perhaps she had weighed the misery of treatment with the not-so-great statistics on remission and decided not to put herself and those she loved through it.

When Clara related her version of the story to me, I was trying to find where there might have been failures in Corina's medical care that could have contributed to her suicide. Maybe we could do better with other patients. After hearing Clara's story, though, I couldn't come up with any real failures except the unsatisfactory doctor visits before the diagnosis was made. Clara basically agreed. We both felt that the way the nurse informed Corina that she had leukemia lacked finesse, but I couldn't call it a failure or a mistake, just really bad communication.

A week later I recalled something I had written about end-of-life care and it hit me: There *had* been a failure. The idea of no treatment was never mentioned by the doctors or oncology team.

Corina was a new case so the team didn't think to offer hospice care or palliation as options. Understandable, but if the concepts of hospice care had been presented to Corina, she might not have felt the need to enact such a horribly violent end to her life. She could have been ushered gently, during her remaining weeks, to a peaceful and merciful death. That was the failure. She didn't know palliation was an option. If she had known, perhaps the panic that drove her to suicide might have been lessened somewhat.

I fully appreciate that medical teams place all their emphasis on the fight for survival. To give up and switch to making patients comfortable during their last days, weeks, or months often doesn't enter oncologists' minds until very late in the course, when palliation serves less of a purpose.

Some might say that Corina's reluctance to put up with pain and disfigurement, though possibly temporary, prevented her from receiving treatment that could have cured her. I'm not so sure. Having been involved with leukemia patients throughout my career in dermatology, observing the immediate and delayed problems that they suffer, I can empathize with Corina. I watched a young woman die with GVHD after a stem cell transplant, her skin denuded and excruciatingly painful. I currently see a patient regularly who survived a stem cell transplant, but lives with debilitating GVHD, and who said during a recent office visit, "If I knew it was going to be this bad, I would not have gone ahead with the transplant. Dying would have been better than this."

More than any textbook or article could have, Corina's case confirmed for me that medical teams have a long way to go to achieve a truly patient-centered approach to health care. Doctors, carried aloft by the momentum of science, knowledge, performance and power, rarely reach out to patients for their opinions in a shared decision-making process. In Corina's case, it is entirely possible that neglecting to offer palliation and allowing her to participate in the decision might have contributed to her death. Corina was in the dark. We doctors can be a source of light, but only if we choose to seize the opportunity. Sadly, though, the truth will likely always remain, that despite doing what we think is best, and constantly improving what we do as physicians, it is still possible to fail our patients.

THE END

Afterword

D**R. LOWEY, THE** last I heard, launched a lawsuit against a group of doctors in Chicago because they did not hire him. In California, after a three year stipulated probation for the narcotic-related charges, he managed to have his license reinstated. In the state where Lowey currently resides, the medical board identified fraudulent claims on his license application and issued a notice of contemplated action to revoke his license to practice medicine there. The charges included fraudulent claims of being a Captain in the United States Navy, serving as a naval officer in Afghanistan and Iraq, and receiving a Purple Heart medal for injuries suffered while on duty in Iraq. These and other claims, though imaginative, were complete fabrications. Amazingly, they apparently were supported by at least two letters from long time colleagues (unless they, too, were fabricated), plus a letter from his mother (the one whose death he had invented).

Yolanda, our receptionist who was given the original prescription by Dr. Lowey, never returned to work. The drug company ended up having estimated liabilities of more than fourteen billion dollars to cover the more than fifty thousand claimants in the class action suit. The University of Chicago didn't pay as a result of Yolanda's suit against them, but had to waive any rights to recover their losses from the monies paid to her by the drug company. Eventually, Yolanda was wait-listed for a heart/lung transplant. She died while waiting.

I continue to treat the skin of organ transplant patients. Mostly I try to prevent them from getting life-threatening skin cancers. I am now into my eleventh year at the University of Toronto, fifth year at Women's College Hospital. I do it for the patients, though I very much enjoy teaching residents and students in my clinics. My head symptoms significantly limit my stamina, and I find a full day of patients and teaching difficult. If local dermatologists were to start treating transplant patients aggressively enough to keep their skin cancers under control, and see them frequently in follow-up instead of treating them like all the rest of their patients, I would gladly turn over all my patients to them and retire. So far, that hasn't happened. We recruited one of our superb former residents to perform Mohs surgery and conduct research on transplant patients, but it is not enough. Patients who arrive at my office often feel that they have been undertreated elsewhere, and I often agree with them. Just recently, one of my colleagues missed a diagnosis in a transplant patient because he didn't spend enough time thinking about the case. The patient had arrived late and was seen hastily. The diagnosis was the disease I have presented several times in this book: disseminated Varicella (chickenpox). The patient ultimately required weeks of hospitalization, almost died, and permanently lost vision in one eye, all which could have been prevented with the correct diagnosis and treatment. Organ transplant patients will only continue to increase in number. It is my hope that someone in my community will eventually take up a serious interest in these patients.

In 2003, Wendy became the first woman Chair of the Department of Medicine at the University of Toronto. With more than seven hundred full-time physicians, this one department exceeds the size of most entire medical schools. Herding cats takes on a whole new meaning at that size. She seems to have found the position to be rewarding and has been able to do what she does best, namely, create new direction, collaborate across hospitals and departments city-wide, and help the careers of faculty members. The job has not been without considerable anguish though, because of the resistance, much of it *ad hominem* attacks she has had to suffer, mostly from egomaniacal men who will never recognize women as true leaders and prefer having fiefdoms over which they tightly hold the purse strings. She is starting to ponder what to do when her term is finished.

I still hear about the University of Chicago now and then. They have had their own financial and leadership difficulties over the past decade. The only remaining dermatology faculty members from my time are Keyomars Soltani and Sarah Stein. Allan Lorincz, despite diminishing physical stamina, continued to practice for several years after I left, and after a short retirement, died in September, 2010. Shortly after I left, the onsite dermatopathology processing laboratory was closed. Biopsy specimens are now processed by general pathology. Maria Medenica died at the age of eighty-one in 2006, one year after she retired. Three weeks before her death, she was honored with the Golden Key Award from the University of Chicago for her distinguished and loyal service. The Rothman-Lorincz dermatology library continues to serve the needs of the section.

At the University of Toronto, the dermatology residency training program, a five-year 'entry-level' program out of medical school, currently has over thirty residents, one of the largest in North America. The residents are the best of any I have encountered, and the clinical training they receive is second to none.

February, 2012

Acknowledgments

~

MANY INDIVIDUALS CONTRIBUTED to the making of this book. Some did it knowingly, some had no idea they were providing rich material. Such is the stuff of memoir.

My father John M. Shaw, M.D. and my mother Jean Shaw provided the generous and loving parental support that allowed my entry into medicine and the world of dermatology. My wife Wendy Levinson's career created several opportunities for me that I would not otherwise have had. The sharing of our careers, while stressful at times, was an undeniable source of pleasure for us both. Wendy was one of the early readers of the manuscript and made important suggestions. My New York writing coach Gay Walley kept me on track throughout the entire story. Her editing and input from the beginning were invaluable. I feel fortunate to have found her. My Toronto writing coach, Mari Silverstein, thanks to her early insight and direction, stimulated essential formative thinking about the work. David Elpern, Myra Slutsky, and Douglas Gubitz read early versions of the manuscript and gave me valuable feedback. At the risk of being redundant, I thank some of the doctors who most influenced my career in positive ways: Greg Raugi, Jon Hanifin,

Fred Rabiner, Herb Kloss, Arthur Zbinden, Tony Montanaro, Larry Peterson, Clifton White, Frances Storrs, Kirk Wuepper, Frank Parker, Walter Shelly, Walter and Betty Lobitz, Bernie Ackerman, Philip Andrews, Bert Tavelli, and Neil Swanson. Finally, a special acknowledgement goes to Bernie Severson, my medical assistant during the Portland years.

Made in the USA
Charleston, SC
26 July 2013